The

The Lineup

Ten Books
That Changed Baseball

PAUL ARON

McFarland & Company, Inc., Publishers
Jefferson, North Carolina

ISBN (print) 978-1-4766-8830-5
ISBN (ebook) 978-1-4766-4692-3

LIBRARY OF CONGRESS AND BRITISH LIBRARY
CATALOGUING DATA ARE AVAILABLE

Library of Congress Control Number 2022029745

Front cover images © 2022 Shutterstock

Printed in the United States of America

*McFarland & Company, Inc., Publishers
Box 611, Jefferson, North Carolina 28640
www.mcfarlandpub.com*

Acknowledgments

I am grateful for the advice and information provided by Kevin Beatty, Joseph Flaherty, Jody Macenka, Dave Mannheim, Daniel Okrent, Christopher Richards, Adam Watson, Lewis Wirshba, and Rick Wolff. Thanks also to my agent, John Thornton, and at McFarland to Lisa Camp, Susan Kilby and Gary Mitchem. Special thanks to Stephen Aron and James Mote for their careful reading of the manuscript and their many valuable suggestions.

Table of Contents

Preface

Here are ten books that changed America.

That's a pretty grandiose claim, I realize. After all, they're just books. And no matter how many times one might cite the influence of *Uncle Tom's Cabin* or works by Darwin or Marx or Freud, a strong case can be made that there have never been enough serious readers in America for any book to have changed the course of our history. Moreover, these are *baseball* books, and no matter how many times one might quote Jacques Barzun about baseball being the way to know the heart and mind of America, it's still just a game. To some extent, these books changed baseball, not America, or sometimes just reflected changes in baseball.

But enough backtracking. To some considerable extent, I hope the chapters that follow will convince you that these books really did change both baseball and America; that, for example, Hemingway's dialogue would not have been the same had it not been for Ring Lardner's *You Know Me Al*; or that general managers (and even some managers in businesses other than baseball) analyzed numbers differently because of Bill James's *Baseball Abstract*; or that suburbanites changed the way they thought of cities because of Roger Kahn's *Boys of Summer*; or that Americans thought differently about the sex lives of celebrities because of Jim Bouton's *Ball Four*; or that Pete Rose's *Pete Rose: My Story* and *My Prison Without Bars* exposed and deepened a divide that opened the way for Donald Trump.

One final caveat: I make no claim that these are the *best* baseball books ever written. Some of them certainly deserve to be considered among the best. But this is a book about the influence rather than the quality of these books.

1

1

America's National Game

by A.G. SPALDING

New York: American Sports Publishing Co., 1911

A.G. Spalding's book not only established baseball as America's national pastime but also went a long way toward defining what it meant to be American—or at least what Americans thought it meant—in the late nineteenth and early twentieth century.

"Baseball," Spalding proclaimed in 1911 in *America's National Game*, "is the exponent of American Courage, Confidence, Combativeness; American Dash, Discipline, Determination; American Energy, Eagerness, Enthusiasm; American Pluck, Persistency, Performance; American Spirit, Sagacity, Success; American Vim Vigor, Virility."[1]

Sure, cricket was a fine game—for the British. "Our British Cricketer," Spalding explained, "having finished his day's labor at noon, may don his negligee shirt, his white trousers, his gorgeous hosiery and his canvas shoes, and sally forth to the field of sport, with his sweetheart on one arm and his Cricket bat under the other, knowing that he may engage in his national pastime without soiling his linen or neglecting his lady."[2]

But an American, Spalding continued, "when he dons his Base Ball Suit, he says good-bye to society, doffs his gentility, and becomes—just a Ball Player!" If a slide is called for, "forgetting his beautiful new flannel uniform, he cares not if the mud is four inches deep at the base he intends to reach." If his sweetheart is in the grandstand, "she is not for him while the game lasts."[3]

Considering that football players hit each other a lot harder and more often than baseball players, it's a bit surprising to find Spalding describe baseball as the epitome of American virility. But so it was for Spalding, and not just for players but for the fan, whose "sole object in life for two mortal hours is to gain victory for the home team, and ... is not overscrupulous as to the amount of racket emanating from his immediate vicinity."[4]

Baseball, as Spalding chronicled its history, was embraced by colleges, by the army and the navy (including both Northerners and Southerners during the Civil War), and by the people of Alaska and Hawaii (neither of which would become a state until almost fifty years after *America's National Game* was published). And by presidents: Spalding included an oft-told but dubious story about how Abraham Lincoln was in the middle of a game when he was told a committee had arrived to inform him that he had been nominated by the Republican Party. "Tell the gentlemen, that I am glad to know of their coming," Lincoln said (according to Spalding), "but they'll have to wait a few minutes till I make another base hit."[5]

Above all, Spalding boasted, baseball was democratic. Any boy who played baseball could become president, even if he was born in a log cabin. "The son of a President of the United States would as soon play ball with Patsy Flanigan as with Lawrence Lionel Livingston," Spalding wrote. "Whether Patsy's dad was a banker or a boiler-maker would never enter the mind of the White House lad."[6]

Alexis De Tocqueville couldn't have said it better.

But the world De Tocqueville had visited in 1831 and described in *Democracy in America* was by 1911 more nostalgia than reality. More and more Americans were working in factories instead of farms. More and more were living in cities rather than small towns. A great gap separated the wealthy from the poor, making it highly unlikely that Patsy and Lionel would play together or that Patsy would end up in the White House. This was a world in which Horatio Alger's rags-to-riches stories were increasingly popular and increasingly unrealistic.

And Spalding had done his part to create this new world.

◊ ◊ ◊

1. America's National Game *(Spalding)*

Spalding's own story did not take him from rags to riches but he did rise from middle class to magnate. More specifically, he started as a player and ended up as an owner. He first garnered attention playing for the unheralded Forest City club of Rockford, Illinois. In 1867, the very heralded National Baseball Club of Washington, D.C., took a tour to the west and defeated almost every team it faced by scores such as 113 to 26 and 53 to 26. (The rules and customs of the time most definitely favored hitters; for example, pitchers had to throw underhand and fielders didn't wear gloves.) The Washington team's only defeat came at the hands of Rockford, whose pitcher was the seventeen-year-old Spalding.

At this point in history, wrote the political and baseball commentator George Will, "it is almost fair to say that Chicago was, in baseball terms, a suburb of Rockford."[7] But the big city's pride was at stake and soon after Forest City's big upset, Spalding received an offer from Chicago's Excelsior club. Baseball was still ostensibly an amateur sport; the first openly professional team, the Cincinnati Red Stockings, did not organize themselves as such until 1869. So, rather than paying him directly, the Excelsiors arranged a job for Spalding as a clerk at a Chicago wholesale grocery. He happily accepted, but the grocery soon went out of business and Spalding returned to Rockford.

Writing in *America's National Game*, Spalding conceded the hypocrisy of pretending to pay players for something other than playing. He realized that the future lay with professionals who could focus on their craft and be paid for it. In 1871, the newly-organized National Association of Professional Base Ball Players openly paid players, and Spalding joined its Boston Red Stockings. He led them to four consecutive championships starting in 1872. In 1875, he won 54 games. This was an extraordinary performance even in an era when pitchers might pitch every day. Spalding won twenty in a row and finished the season with only five losses.

In 1876, Spalding returned to Chicago as not just a pitcher but also as manager and secretary of the White Stockings in the new National League. (The White Stockings ultimately became not the White Sox but the Cubs.) Spalding went 47 and 12, leading Chicago to the pennant.

5

At the end of the 1877 season, though only twenty-six, he retired as a player so he could focus on the business side of the game, and here's where he exerted his greatest influence. Having helped players make money, he wanted to make sure that owners did, too. Those two goals were often in conflict, for as Spalding wrote, "the irrepressible conflict between Labor and Capital [was] asserting itself."[8] And there was no doubt that Spalding's sympathies lay with the latter. Only by taking control of the game away from its players, Spalding argued, could the game be rid of such sins as gambling and drinking and playing on Sundays.

Without a touch of irony, Spalding bemoaned the plight of owners. "Ownership of a great ball club in a populous and prosperous city involves man-killing experiences,"[9] he wrote. An owner's "trials" included dealing with the "relentless demands"[10] of the public, the press, and the players. As if that wasn't stressful enough, "he must be present at as many games as possible."[11]

Spalding's sympathies also manifested themselves in his book's focus. What's most striking to today's readers of *America's National Game*, considering it's supposed to be a history of baseball, is how little there is about players or games. What interested Spalding instead were the various associations and leagues around which the sport was organized, and the men who organized them.

Like most histories of baseball, Spalding's credited Alexander Cartwright of New York's Knickerbocker Base Ball Club with being the first to write down rules similar to today's game and to create an organization governing the games. Despite his professed enthusiasm for democracy, Spalding admired the Knickerbockers because they were "gentlemen." Early baseball games were as much a social as a sporting occasion, and these were very much an upper-class affair. The Knickerbockers, Spalding conceded, were not very good at playing the game; they "shone more resplendently in the banquet hall than on the diamond field."[12] Indeed, they sounded a lot like the cricket players Spalding had mocked. But they were deserved to be honored for having imparted to baseball "the stamp of respectability."[13]

Other teams and organizations soon superseded the Knickerbockers, and *America's National Game* applauded the formation of the National Association of Base Ball Players in 1871. But he was much more pleased when it was replaced, in 1876, by the National League. Spalding himself was instrumental in creating the new league, which included his Chicago White Stockings. The league's official name—the National League of Base Ball Clubs—was telling. This was no longer an association of players; this league was to be run by and for clubs and their owners.

The National League's prohibitions on drinking and gambling and Sunday games appealed to the Victorian middle class Spalding hoped to attract. The competing American Base Ball Association, formed in 1882, was happy to take the blue collar fans the National League held in disdain. The American Association charged just twenty-five cents for admission, while the National League charged fifty cents. The American Association also allowed alcohol to be sold in ballparks, which was not surprising since four American Association owners owned breweries.

Lest Spalding be seen as priggish about all this, it's worth noting that prior to the formation of the National League baseball parks did not have a stamp of respectability. Fans were rowdy and players often misbehaved, on and off the field. In an era when there was only one umpire at a game who could not therefore always keep his eye on all base runners, outfielder Mike "King" Kelly, who played for Spalding's White Stockings, was known to go directly from first to third via the pitcher's mound rather than second base. John McGraw, a Baltimore Oriole shortstop and later New York Giant manager, routinely used his spikes to stomp on an umpire's feet. Ed Delahanty, a Washington Senator outfielder, was allegedly so drunk and disorderly that he was kicked off a train near the Niagara River. His body was later found floating below Niagara Falls.

When Chicago owner William Hulbert died in 1882, Spalding bought out his stake in the White Stockings and took over as president of the team. The team continued to be successful on and off the field. The roster included Kelly, whose base-running prowess was celebrated in the song "Slide, Kelly, Slide" but who was also famous for his drinking. An exasperated Spalding hired a detective to document Kelly's late-night visits to the city's saloons. In 1887, Spalding sold Kelly to Boston, having decided he was a bad influence on younger players.

The "respectability" Spalding imposed on his team and league meant banning not only alcohol and gambling but also Blacks. The White Stockings were led by Adrian "Cap" Anson, a first baseman and the first player to get 3,000 hits. Anson was also openly racist. During the 1884 season, the White Stockings were scheduled to play an exhibition game against the Toledo Blue Stockings of the American Association. Toledo's catcher was Moses "Fleet" Walker, an African American who played in this major league more than sixty years before Jackie Robinson joined the Dodgers. Anson threatened to pull his team off the field if Walker played. Walker took the field and Anson backed down, but three years later the White Stockings played another team with Walker on its roster, and this time Anson prevailed. By the 1890s, Blacks had been pushed into separate leagues.

It would be unfair to place the entire blame for segregating baseball on Spalding, or for that matter Anson. Jim Crow laws and practices were too widespread to depend on any individual. But Spalding certainly did not stand in their way. In his life and in his book, he did not hesitate to express his opinions on all sorts of issues, but he remained silent on this one.

◊ ◊ ◊

Of all the rules Spalding enforced, the most important to him was the "reserve rule," which the league adopted in 1879 and which prevented players from jumping from one club to another in pursuit of better pay. That Spalding himself had done so when he left Boston for Chicago did not deter him from decrying the dangers this practice presented to the game's stability.

In 1885, frustrated by the reserve rule and other schemes for holding down salaries, players led by Giant shortstop John Montgomery Ward formed a union. In 1890, the players went further and formed their own league. In this they were following a path tread by The Knights of Labor, an organization of unions in different industries that pushed for worker ownership of companies. The Players' League threatened to overturn the "professional" management of baseball of which Spalding was so proud.

With attendance stretched between the National League, American Association, and Players' League, it plummeted in all three. One of Spalding's public relations hires stooped to some creative counting. Asked by a reporter for a game's attendance, he answered twenty-four eighteen. Later he explained to Spalding: "There were twenty-four on one side of the grounds and eighteen on the other. If he reports twenty-four *hundred* and eighteen, that's a matter for his conscience, not mine."[14]

All three leagues struggled financially, but the Players' League had fewer resources and folded after one season. The players' rebellion did not turn bloody, as did for example a strike by steel workers in 1892 or railroad workers in 1894, but like both of those it ended with a defeat for labor. Thus, Spalding triumphantly proclaimed, "was settled forever the theory that professional ball players can at the same time direct both the business and the playing ends of the game."[15]

The issue was of course not settled forever. But it would take another eighty-six years for players to establish a degree of free agency and change the balance between baseball's labor and capital. Just as Spalding alone was not singlehandedly responsible for establishing baseball's color line, he alone did not establish the owners' firm control over the business of baseball. But he was undeniably management's leader in the crucial showdown with the Players' League and American Association, and he was management's leading propagandist in *America's National Game.*

As for the American Association, its legacy continued through its teams from Cincinnati, Pittsburgh, St. Louis, and Brooklyn, which were absorbed into the National League and exist today as the Reds, Pirates, Cardinals, and Dodgers. The National League also agreed to allow Sunday games and to allow teams to sell alcohol. On these matters Spalding was willing to put aside his misgivings, especially since it increased his team's revenues. So in some sense he did make baseball more democratic, at least if democracy was defined by a nation and a ballpark opening its gates to all fans. Wrote Paul Goldberger, an architecture critic who authored a history of baseball parks: "Baseball may have been reflective of the American character, as Albert Spalding and the National League liked to claim. But that character was far messier and more difficult to define than they were inclined to admit."[16]

Spalding was undoubtedly pleased to see the National League establish a monopoly on professional baseball. Even Spalding, however, thought that there ought to be some limits on the extent of this monopoly. In 1901 Giant owner Andrew Freedman proposed creating a trust whereby the individual owners would give up control over their own teams in return for shares in a jointly-owned league. Spalding balked, denouncing the "monstrous evil" of "Freedmanism."[17]

Fortunately for Spalding and his allies, Freedman alienated the other owners who might have supported his plan. Freedman tended to be verbally and sometimes physically abusive toward anyone who tried to thwart him. He changed managers thirteen times during his seven years running the Giants; baseball writer Bill James later described him as "George Steinbrenner on Quaaludes."[18] In 1902, Freedman gave up and sold the Giants.

Here, too, baseball mirrored changes in America. The abuses of businesses, not just toward workers but also toward consumers, triggered the Progressive movement, which in the last decade of the nineteenth and first decade of the twentieth century placed limits on the power of monopolies. Theodore Roosevelt brought Progressivism to the presidency, just as the anti–Freedman owners did to the National League.

None of this is to imply Spalding was a progressive in the current sense of the word. He opposed Freedman not to protect players but to protect the system he had put in place—and the wealth he had accumulated. And Spalding's book, the literary critic Richard Peterson wrote, reads "like a how-to book on building a baseball monopoly while romanticizing one's actions as patriotic, heroic, and moral."[19] Spalding's system, as described in his book, ensured the success of the business of baseball, and for that matter, other professional sports.

◊ ◊ ◊

Spalding's own early forays into the business world did not indicate he had found a sure path to wealth. The Chicago wholesaler that hired him supposedly as a clerk but really to play for the Excelsiors closed after he received his first and only paycheck. An insurance company that next hired him also went broke. So did an insurance company back in Rockford and a newspaper that hired him while he was playing in Boston.

As a team owner and league official, however, Spalding had superb business acumen. He bought and sold players with a clear understanding of their values on and off the field. In his book, he described how, while negotiating with the Players' League on behalf of the National League, he bluffed representatives of the Players' League into believing he would accept nothing less than their "unconditional surrender," and these terms were "greedily accepted."[20]

Spalding was a master of public relations. "If the man fell into a puddle," wrote Ward's biographer Bryan Di Salvatore, "he would try to convince the world his socks had needed a washing."[21] Spalding would have readily agreed that he knew how to spin a story and to promote himself and his business. Starting in 1877, Spalding published an annual baseball guide with rules and records—and his name in the title. Like Steinbrenner, Spalding reveled in publicity, good or bad. After he sold Kelly to Boston, Chicago newspapers attacked him, and one demanded the team lower ticket prices as a result. One reporter refrained from criticizing him, and when Spalding asked him why, the reporter explained he had nothing to add. Spalding then furnished him with more "ammunition."

"Roasts in newspapers of wide circulation are much more effective than fulsome praise," Spalding explained, "for the latter carries with it the idea that it is paid advertising, and is therefore only read as such, whereas under the roast program the matter is relieved from that suspicion and read by everybody with more or less of sympathy for the poor fellow who has no newspaper in which to defend himself."[22]

Valuable as publicity was for Spalding as team owner and league official, it was even more so when he put on his other hat. In 1876, the same year he returned to play in Chicago, he and his brother opened a sporting goods store there. Taking advantage of his reputation as a player and owner, Spalding turned the store into a national chain and added a wholesale and licensing operation that put his name on an array of goods, including bats, gloves, uniforms, protective equipment for catchers, and balls. Spalding agreed to supply all of the National League's balls for free, establishing them in the public's mind as the official balls and the best balls.

One of his few missteps was a deal to supply all teams with uniforms where the color of a player's stockings was determined by his team but the color of his cap and shirt was determined by his position. Players had to check each other's socks to know what team someone was on. Complained Boston outfielder Jim O'Rourke: "If we are unfortunate enough to play near a lunatic asylum, we are likely to wind up inside looking out."[23]

Soon Spalding branched out to selling equipment for other sports. He published guides and books on other sports as well, which not only sold well but also promoted Spalding goods. The 1909 baseball guide reprinted this from the *Boston Herald*: "Next to Abraham Lincoln and George Washington, the name of A.G. Spalding is the most famous in American literature. It has been blazing forth on the covers of guides to all sorts of sports, upon bats and gloves and all the various accoutrements of the same sports for many years."[24]

The company tapped into a market that was rapidly growing among Americans whose lives were increasingly urban and who yearned for outdoor, physical activities. Spalding shrewdly took over competitors, though he often continued to stamp their names on products associated with them. None of this put him in the same class as John D. Rockefeller or Andrew Carnegie or J.P. Morgan or other Gilded Age monopolists, but it made him a millionaire. However happily he might have played with baseball with Patsy Flanigan, Spalding was intent on joining the ranks of Lawrence Lionel

Livingston. However apt was the title of *America's National Game*, Spalding's middle name—Goodwill—was, as writer Daniel Okrent put it, "ludicrously inapt."[25]

To be fair to Spalding, his company did provide good quality bats and balls and gloves to replace equipment that was often shoddy or, as with protective gear for catchers, hard to find. Spalding's own explanation of his business success was that it came from having played baseball. "A young man playing Base Ball gets into the habit of quick thinking in most adverse circumstances and under the most merciless criticism in the world—the criticism from the bleachers," he said in a 1910 article in the *New York Times* that he reprinted in *America's National Game*. "If that doesn't train him, nothing can."[26]

Similar ideas found their way into popular psychology. In 1913, two years after the book's publication, H. Addington Bruce, who would go on to write *Psychology and Parenthood*, asserted that baseball provided boys with "exercise for the muscles, the healthy expenditure of surplus nervous energy, and practice and preparation for life's work."[27]

Would Bruce have thought the same had it not been for *America's National Game*? Perhaps. But it's worth noting that in his article he quotes Spalding.

◊ ◊ ◊

Eager to make America's national game an international one, Spalding organized a world tour in the winter of 1888–1889. Spalding and baseball were again part of a larger trend; in the late nineteenth and early twentieth century, the United States sent missionaries, products, and troops around the world. Spalding took ten players from his own Chicago team, including Anson, his captain and star. They would play an All Star squad from other National League teams led by Ward, who would soon lead players from the National League to the Players' League.

The teams arrived in Honolulu a day behind schedule and on a Sunday, a day on which Hawaiian law prohibited the playing of games. So it was not until they reached Auckland, New Zealand, that they played their first international game. They then moved on to

Australia, where the tour was originally scheduled to end, but Spalding convinced the players to continue around the world. They sailed on, ultimately playing on five continents.

In Egypt, Spalding proudly reported, they played in front of the Great Pyramids. Spalding did not mention that the players' first reaction to seeing the largest of the pyramids was to try to throw a ball over it. They failed. One player was more successful at a contest to see if any could hit the eye of the Sphinx, the giant statue located near the pyramids.

In Rome, Spalding wanted to play at the Coliseum. City officials reacted as if the Americans were barbarians storming the gates, and Spalding settled for a game at the Villa Borghese, an estate whose gardens were famous.

In Paris, they played in the shadow of the Eiffel Tower, then under construction. Parisians, Spalding conceded, "did not seem to catch on to any appreciable extent."[28]

In England, he watched the game sitting next to the Prince of Wales, who would later become King Edward VII. The prince, Spalding reported, was much impressed by Anson's hitting. Criticized for tapping Edward on the shoulder to point out a player's slide, Spalding defended himself in his book: "If British Royalty honored us by its presence, which I am willing to concede, we repaid it by a splendid exhibition of our National Game."[29]

On their return to America, Spalding and the players were honored at a banquet at New York's Delmonico's restaurant. The centerpiece at each table was a sculpture of a player in action, made of sugar, egg yolks, and gelatin. Guests included Theodore Roosevelt and Mark Twain. Spalding told those assembled he was proud to have established America's national game throughout the world. Twain agreed Spalding and his players had "carried the American name to the outermost parts of the earth, and covered it with glory every time." He toasted them for having "plowed a new equator round the globe stealing bases on their bellies."[30]

Spalding was again spinning a tale. In actuality, he lost money on the tour. Baseball was still an American game, despite the Demonico's toasts and the celebratory account in *America's National Game*.

1. America's National Game *(Spalding)*

Later, of course, baseball would take off elsewhere, especially in Japan and Latin America. "Spalding was right," baseball historian John Thorn remarked. "He was just ahead of his time."[31]

More immediately, Spalding had used the opportunity to establish retail outlets in Australia. Also, whether by design or luck, he had kept Ward, the head of a fledgling players union, out of the country while the owners put together a plan to limit player salaries.

◊ ◊ ◊

For all of Spalding's efforts to spread baseball throughout the world, he was adamant that no one lose sight of its origins in America. It was Spalding who firmly placed those origins in the town of Cooperstown, New York, in 1839, and in the mind of the future Civil War general Abner Doubleday.

In 1905 Spalding suggested forming a commission to investigate the game's origins and then chose its members. Later that year Spalding passed on to the commission a letter he'd received from a mining engineer named Abner Graves in which Graves recalled how Doubleday laid out the rules of the game for him and other boys in Cooperstown. Graves's description of the game differed from the modern game in a number of respects—there were, for example, eleven players on a side—but it was recognizably baseball. Graves even provided Spalding with a diagram like one he remembered Doubleday had drawn for the boys in the dirt.

Spalding was delighted to get Graves's letter. He had spent years squabbling with Henry Chadwick, the British-born editor of Spalding's annual baseball guides. Chadwick believed baseball had evolved from the British game of rounders. Graves's letter arrived in time to convince the commission otherwise.

Doubleday himself had nothing to say on the matter; he had been buried in Arlington National Cemetery in 1892. But for the commission, as for Spalding, Graves's word was enough. Its report concluded: "First—That Base Ball had its origin in the United States; Second—That the first scheme for playing it ... was devised by Abner Doubleday, at Cooperstown, New York, in 1839."[32]

For those, like Spalding, who wanted an American origin for

baseball, Doubleday and Cooperstown were ideal choices. Doubleday was a military hero: He aimed the cannon for the Union's first shot of the Civil War at Fort Sumter and distinguished himself at Gettysburg. Cooperstown was the boyhood home of the great American novelist James Fenimore Cooper and the picturesque embodiment of small-town America.

The Doubleday story has been debunked many times over. Graves was five years old in 1839, making him an unlikely playmate for the twenty-year-old Doubleday. Doubleday was at West Point, not Cooperstown, from 1838 to 1842. And on other matters Graves's memory was at best unreliable. Among his questionable claims was that he was a Pony Express rider in 1852, but the service didn't start until 1860. Moreover, in 1924, the then-ninety-year-old Graves accused his wife of poisoning him, shot her, and was committed to the Colorado State Insane Asylum. There is no evidence that Graves was insane in 1905 when he wrote his letter to Spalding about Doubleday, but these later events sure don't enhance his credibility.

Debunkers also noted how strange it was that A.G. Mills, the former National League president who chaired the commission, was so quick to accept Graves's word. Mills and Doubleday had been longtime friends and Mills had commanded the veteran military escort at Doubleday's funeral. One might reasonably assume that Doubleday would at least have mentioned to Mills that he'd invented baseball. But Mills gave no indication he had any idea of his friend's role until he received Graves's letter.

As for Cooperstown, it was in reality a very inhospitable setting for baseball. As historian Alan Taylor recounted in his book *William Cooper's Town*, in 1816 the village trustees, intent on imposing order on their streets, passed an ordinance banning ballplaying of any sorts in the town center. "Cooperstown," Taylor quipped, "can better claim to have tried to prevent the invention of baseball."[33]

Nonetheless, Cooperstown's boosters were eager to solidify their place in the American imagination. In 1934, Alexander Cleland came up with the idea of collecting baseball artifacts and displaying them in a museum in Cooperstown. Cleland worked for Stephen Clark, a wealthy native of the town. Cleland persuaded Clark to finance the project. Cleland also persuaded baseball executives, including Commissioner Kenesaw Mountain Landis and National League president Ford Frick, that baseball's centennial—with 1839 set as the year Doubleday invented the game—would be a great opportunity to celebrate the game's history. It was Frick who came up with the idea that the museum could include a hall of fame honoring the game's greatest players.

Cooperstown's plan ran into trouble in 1935 in the person of Bruce Cartwright, the grandson of the Knickerbockers' Alexander Cartwright. Bruce Cartwright claimed his grandfather was the true inventor of baseball. Cartwright's claim, though based on more than Doubleday's, was much exaggerated; Thorn has proved that many of the innovations for which Cartwright has been credited (including writing down the rules) predated the Knickerbockers.

But the organizers of the Hall of Fame didn't know that, and they needed to find a way to quiet Bruce Cartwright. In 1938, they came up with one: A special committee was created to consider nineteenth-century players and pioneers, and Alexander Cartwright was elected to the Hall of Fame. His grandson was satisfied. A year later Spalding joined Cartwright in the Hall.

Why was Spalding so intent on establishing Doubleday as baseball's father? Mark Lamster, who wrote a book about the 1888–1889 world tour, suggested that Spalding, who had been brought up without a father, was looking for a father figure. Lamster believed Spalding had found a father figure in White Sox owner William Hulbert and now, in another way, in Abner Doubleday.

But one needn't turn to psychology to explain the appeal of Doubleday and Cooperstown. Like Spalding, many Americans just wanted to believe their national game originated in America. Spalding didn't mind giving some credit to Cartwright for having "proposed to others the formal association of themselves together as a Base Ball club."[34] After all, Cartwright was an American.

For some Americans, there may have been more than national pride at stake. Evolution, whether of humanity or baseball, is a more difficult story to grasp than one about Adam and Eve, or about Abner Doubleday, and many may have longed for a single moment of creation. "Creation myths," wrote paleontologist (and baseball fan) Stephen Jay Gould, "identify heroes and sacred places, while evolutionary stories provide no palpable, particular thing as a symbol for reverence, worship, or patriotism."[35]

In fairness to Spalding, he did not deny that baseball evolved from earlier games. Though he was adamant that baseball did not come from the British game of rounders and that it owed its modern and all-American form to Doubleday, Spalding conceded that that the ancient Egyptians and Greeks had played with balls and so had many others. Indeed, he devoted a chapter in *America's National Game* to imagining how two boys named Tom and Dick might have been playing catch and then, bored for a moment, might have decided to hit the ball with an old axe-handle. This could have evolved into a game called Old Cat, Spalding explained, which involved bases as well as bats and balls. Readers of *America's National Game* would certainly have understood, however, that the ingenious Tom and Dick were *American* boys.

So: How much credit—or blame—does Spalding deserve for the Doubleday myth?

Spalding did not, of course, manage it all on his own, any more than he alone brought about the rise of the National League or the fall of the Players' League. Had it not been for Cleland and Clark and Cooperstown's boosters, it's unlikely the story would have been so firmly implanted in the American imagination. But without Spalding, there would have been no commission to proclaim Doubleday the game's inventor.

Spalding's book, too, can't take full credit or blame. But well before Cleland or Clark or baseball officials got behind the story, *America's National Game* was telling the Doubleday story and Spalding's marketing machine was promoting the book. The book was published by the American Sports Publishing Company, the publishing arm of Spalding's company. Autographed copies went to seventy-five prominent individuals, including President William Howard Taft and Pope Pius X. Neither the president nor the pope sent a personal response but others did, and these testimonials were then sent to newspapers and libraries across the country. Copies also went to baseball managers and players. Spalding's guides pushed the book and ads for the book were placed in every package mailed from one of Spalding's stores.

The marketing campaign paid off. There are no official sales figures, but the Los Angeles *Times* reported that 90,000 copies had been sold during the first six months after publication. Spalding must also have been pleased by the testimonials, many of which he collected in his scrapbooks. One came from Luther Gulick, Yale's football coach, who wrote that baseball expressed "the national spirit more perfectly than ... any other institutions." Gulick added that Spalding "deserved to rank with other great men of the country."[36]

Here's one other way to measure the influence of Spalding's book on how baseball history was to be seen: Compare its fame to the relative obscurity of its competition. In 1910, the year before Spalding published *America's National Game*, Alfred H. Spink published *The National Game*, which was also a history of early baseball. Like Spalding, Spink had at his disposal means to promote his book. He had founded *The Sporting News* in 1886, and the weekly became an immediate success. Yet unlike Spalding's book, which continued to be reprinted, Spink's largely disappeared. So did Spink's perspective: He sympathized with the American Association as much as the National League, in part because prior to founding *The Sporting News* he had worked for the Association's St. Louis Browns. He even sympathized with the Players' League, "brave fellows who believed in standing by one another and who lost out in the battle not because their hearts were not in the right place."[37] As for Spalding's story about Doubleday, Spink bluntly called it a "fake."[38]

In the foreword to his book, Spalding described it as "the simple story of America's national game as I have come to know it," adding that "I hear and now disclaim any desire to exploit my name, my views or my achievements."[39] Historian Peter Levine could not resist writing that if these were Spalding's two goals in writing the book, he "batted .500."[40] The book is about baseball but it is also very much about Spalding.

One aspect of Spalding's life that he definitely did *not* include in *America's National Game* was his affair with and then marriage to Elizabeth Mayer. Mayer was a member of the Theosophical Society, a quasi-religion founded in 1875 by Helena Blavatsky. Blavatsky attracted attention (as well as accusations she was a fraud) by claiming to be a medium between the living and the dead. Most Americans, to the extent they thought about Theosophists at all, thought of them as eccentric spiritualists who dabbled in the occult. After Spalding married Mayer, the couple moved to a suburb of San Diego where Theosophists had established a compound.

Why would a hard-headed businessman like Spalding become involved with such a group? Some attributed it to senility. But what has raised many eyebrows, at least among baseball historians, is that in 1878, after Blavatsky moved to India, the man who became president of the Theosophical Society was none other than Abner Doubleday.

Intriguing as this is, it proves nothing about Doubleday or Spalding. Spalding had plenty of other reasons besides a Theosophical connection to turn Doubleday into baseball's inventor. Indeed, Spalding may not even have taken Theosophy all that seriously; he may just have been humoring his wife. When Anson learned that Spalding had moved to San Diego to live among Theosophists, he commented: "Well, I don't know what in thunder a theosophist is, but if it's something you can make money out of you can bet Al Spalding will be one.... When I knew Al he didn't care a tinker's malediction for the spiritual."[41]

Anson was certainly right to say Spalding cared about money, but he was wrong to imply that was all he cared about. Spalding cared deeply about baseball. Indeed, if he had a religion, it was baseball, not Theosophy. And, thanks to some considerable extent to Spalding, baseball was America's religion as well.

2

You Know Me Al:
A Busher's Letters

by RING LARDNER

New York: George H. Doran Co., 1916

Ring Lardner introduced the world to Jack Keefe, a fictional Chicago White Sox pitcher, in a series of stories that first appeared in *The Saturday Evening Post* in 1914 and then in the book *You Know Me Al: A Busher's Letters* in 1916. The stories arrived in the form of letters supposedly written by Keefe to his childhood friend Al in their home town of Bedford, Indiana. The stories would change the way Americans viewed their heroes. They would also change the course of American literature.

Before Keefe, the best known fictional baseball player was Frank Merriwell. Merriwell first appeared in 1896 in inexpensive paperbacks known as dime novels. He was created by Gilbert Patten, who used the pen name of Burt L. Standish and who ended up writing about three hundred novels and about twenty million words about the character. The name said it all: Frank was always honest and Merriwell handled everything thrown his way cheerfully and skillfully. He triumphed at everything from billiards to big-game hunting. He threw a curve that went in one direction and then the other. Consider a typical conclusion of a Patten book, this one from the 1903 *Frank Merriwell at Yale*. Merriwell had allowed just an unearned run, but going into the bottom of the ninth his Yale team trailed Harvard 1–0. Merriwell came to bat with two outs and one on. He drove the ball past the left fielder and sped around the bases. He heard others calling on him to slide. Finally: "Forward he scooted in a cloud of dust. The catcher got the ball and put it onto Frank—an instant too late!"[1]

Patten had rivals. There was Edward L. Stratemeyer who created the Hardy Boys, Nancy Drew, Tom Swift, and under the pen name of Lester Chadwick, Baseball Joe. There was Zane Grey, who was better known for his westerns but who also ventured into baseball, and there was Ralph Henry Barbour, whose books covered many sports including baseball. What they all had in common was that they were writing for boys and to inspire boys; their heroes were very good, athletically and morally. Indeed, they were too good to be believed.

The same was largely true for non-fiction into the early years of the twentieth century. It was not that no writer would criticize players; Spalding, for one, did not hesitate to point out their flaws. But Spalding generally found a player's behavior or misbehavior worth noting only when it had some impact on the business of baseball. A few sports reporters were sometimes critical, most notably Charles Dryden. Dryden wrote for various newspapers in New York, Philadelphia, and Chicago, and did not hesitate to mock players or teams. He described Giant first baseman Fred Merkle as "bonehead" and White Sox pitcher Ed Walsh as "the only man who could strut standing still."[2] But generally the sports pages of newspapers portrayed baseball players as Merriwell-like paragons. Reporters also tended to echo management opinions, in part because teams and not newspapers covered many of their expenses.

Ring Lardner changed all that, spreading irreverence throughout his columns and the country. Lardner's approach emerged gradually. Starting as a reporter in South Bend, Indiana, in 1908 and moving to Boston and Chicago, he would report on games objectively, eschewing any home-team loyalties. Like Dryden, he would poke fun at players but affectionately and in ways that rarely offended them. Many of Lardner's pieces featured Frank Schulte, a Cub outfielder who as Lardner portrayed him was both quick-witted and quick to deflect blame for any errors. In a 1911 story, Lardner had Schulte answer complaints about his fielding by explaining the only way he could have caught a particular ball was "to have left the park and stood on the approach to the elevated station."[3] Schulte could also turn poetic:

> How glad I am the time is nigh
> When reins and whip I'll wield
> 'Tis easier to drive a horse
> Than run around right field.[4]

Though Schulte was an actual player, much of his persona and poetry was Lardner's invention. When Lardner took over the Chicago *Tribune*'s "In the Wake of the News" column in 1913, he was less constrained by daily reporting duties and freer to entertain his readers by inventing not just player quotes or poems but whole stories— including those that would make up *You Know Me Al.*

◊ ◊ ◊

The first story was "A Busher's Letters Home," a busher in this case referring to a player fresh from the bush leagues, or low minor leagues. Lardner first submitted it to his employer, but the editor of the *Tribune*'s Sunday edition turned it down. This was, wrote Jeff Silverman, who edited a collection of Lardner's stories, "the sports editor equivalent to the *Tribune* nabob who was destined to splash 'Dewey Defeats Truman' across the front page."[5] Lardner then submitted the story to *The Saturday Evening Post*, where it became a hit. Lardner quickly produced nine more stories for the *Post* to publish in 1914, including the six that George H. Doran Company would publish as *You Know Me Al.*

Like the fictionalized Schulte, Keefe has an excuse for anything that goes wrong. When Ty Cobb gets on with a bunt, Keefe explains he would have thrown him out had he not stubbed his toe. When Charlie O'Leary gets a hit off of him, Keefe explains the batter was trying to get out of the way of the pitch when "it hit his bat and went over first base."[6] When Keefe walks a batter, he explains it's because his pitch was too fast for the umpire to see it.

Keefe is talented but self-indulgent and self-deceiving. When his manager gives him advice, Keefe dismisses it:

He says And I noticed you taking your wind up when What's His Name was on second base there today. I says Yes I got more stuff when I wind up. He says Of course you have but if you wind up like that with Cobb on base he will steal your watch and chain. I says Maybe Cobb can't get on base when I work against him. He says That's right and maybe San Francisco Bay is made of grapejuice.[7]

In the six stories that make up *You Know Me Al*, Keefe joins the White Sox, is sent down to the minors, and makes it back to the majors. He falls in love with three different women, all more interested in money than baseball, and he ends up married, stormily, to the last of them.

Other writers speculated about the identity of the real Jack Keefe, and they noted characteristics he shared, albeit in exaggerated form, with actual players, including Schulte. Lardner wouldn't say. Pressed, he once joked that he'd based the character on Jane Addams, an activist for women and the poor.

Yet even as Lardner replaced Merriwell with a very flawed figure, he made Keefe recognizably human and somehow likable. Keefe's enthusiasm for his pitching and his women and his friend Al is, despite all his bragging, appealingly innocent. Again and again Keefe has to borrow money from Al to get out of a jam. Again and again he promises to pay him back, just as soon as he gets the chance to explain to White Sox owner Charles Comiskey what he's worth. Readers can see how unlikely it is that Keefe will repay Al, but Keefe has every intention of doing so.

"He is not very much worse than anyone else," wrote Lardner's biographer Donald Elder of Keefe. "He is not quite like yourself but he bears a fatal resemblance to your friends."[8]

Readers of *The Saturday Evening Post* loved Keefe. The magazine's circulation, which was already more than two million, increased by thousands. Lardner's fee per story increased from two hundred fifty to fifteen hundred dollars.

Much of the stories' appeal came from Keefe's language, which was as distinctively and assertively American as Mark Twain's. "The thoroughly American color of it," wrote H.L. Mencken in his influential 1919 book *The American Language*, "cannot fail to escape anyone who actually listens to the tongue spoken around him."[9]

Keefe's malapropisms were funny but also revealing: He routinely referred to the World Series and the city series (between Chicago's White Sox and Cubs) as the "serious," and these were indeed serious series. When he joined the team on a trip across the Pacific on the ocean liner *Empress of Japan*, he called the ship "the Umpires of Japan."[10] And why not? The ship would determine whether its passengers would arrive safe or out. He's glad when his wife quits working so she "can stay home and pay a little tension to the kiddies,"[11] who were indeed a source of tension.

This was language that revealed how people thought as well as how they talked. Wrote Mencken: "Lardner reports the common speech not only with humor, but also with the utmost accuracy."[12]

Mencken was slightly off the mark here. Lardner's language was indeed carefully crafted from common speech, but his satire depended on exaggerations unlikely to appear in actual speech. The humor comes from his characters' pretensions; they often try to imitate what they think is upper-class or literary language but what's actually a cliché, and then they don't get it quite right. Similarly, Elder's comment about Keefe resembling one's friends ought to be amended to say he embodied exaggerated versions of their traits. Keefe was in his own unheroic way no truer to real life than Merriwell.

This was even clearer in Lardner's 1915 story, "Alibi Ike," which also mined baseball as a setting. Here Lardner created a character who became almost as famous as Keefe and who made even more excuses than him. Ike makes excuses even when nothing goes wrong. When he hits .356, he explains his average was so low because he had malaria. When he wants to go to bed, he explains he isn't tired but he has some gravel in his shoes and his feet are killing him. When he gets engaged, he explains it isn't that he is in love, just that sometimes "a fella gets to feelin' sorry for one of 'em."[13] Alas, his fiancé overhears the conversation.

Lardner brought back Keefe for more *Saturday Evening Post* stories, some of which were collected in 1918 in *Treat 'Em Rough: Letters from Jack the Kaiser Killer* and in 1919 in *The Real Dope*. By then Keefe is in the army, in the former training in Illinois and in the latter in France. Lardner was thus able not just to let Keefe again show off his version of the English language but also to let Keefe give his opinion of the French language:

> The Frenchmens ... would like me still better yet if they could understand more English and get my stuff better but it don't seem like they even try to learn and I suppose its because they figure the war is in their country so everybody should ought to talk their language but when you get down to cases they's a big job on both our hands and if one of us has got to talk the others language why and the he-ll should they pick on the one that's hard to learn it and besides its 2 to 1 you might say because the U.S. and the English uses the same language and they's nobody only the French that talks like they do because they couldn't nobody else talk that way so why wouldn't it be the square thing for them to forget theirs and tackle ours and it would prolongate their lifes to do it because most of their words can't be said without straining yourself and no matter what kind of a physic you got its bound to wear you down in time.[14]

Moving beyond baseball, Lardner's books published between 1917 and 1921 included *Gullible's Travels, Etc.*, in which he satirized American suburbia and *The Young Immigrunts*, in which he satirized marriage, specifically his own. In *The Young Immigrunts* Lardner showed he could be just as funny appropriating the voice of a child as that of a baseball player. The story is supposedly told by his son, Ring Lardner, Jr., who describes a family trip from Indiana to Connecticut. Junior's father starts off in a bad mood, having been to the "worst series"[15] and having bet on the losing team. The trip includes a visit to Niagara Falls, where the Lardner family runs into a "bride and glum" and overhears the glum asking his bride if she is cold. Then:

> I wander will he be asking her 8 years from now is she warm enough said my mother with a faint grimace.
> The weather may change before then replid my father.[16]

For all of Lardner's popularity, it was not until 1925 when Scribner's took over as his publisher that critics generally took him seriously. Lardner was introduced to Scribner's editor Maxwell Perkins by F. Scott Fitzgerald, a Long Island neighbor with whom Lardner would spend many a night drinking, often excessively. Perkins edited not only Fitzgerald but also Ernest Hemingway and Thomas Wolfe.

2. You Know Me Al (*Lardner*)

Scribner's began re-publishing Lardner's old works, including *You Know Me Al*, as well as publishing new works.

Now he was no longer thought of as a baseball writer but treated like Perkins's other writers. John Chamberlain in the *New York Times Book Review* compared Lardner to Marcel Proust, Sherwood Anderson, and Hemingway. Edmund Wilson, the nation's preeminent critic, compared him to Anderson and Sinclair Lewis. T.S. Matthews in *The New Republic* compared him to Shakespeare and Chekhov. Dorothy Parker in *The New Yorker* compared Lardner's "spare and beautiful stories"[17] to the Gettysburg address. There were rumors that Lardner and Parker had an affair. There was no evidence for this whatsoever, but there was plenty of evidence that Lardner was much admired by the circle of writers, actors, and critics, including Parker, who frequented New York's Algonquin Hotel.

Lardner's short "nonsense plays," once thought of as merely funny sequences of non-sequiturs in which people talked to each other but barely listened, also came to be taken more seriously. Wilson placed them in the tradition of Dada, an avant-garde art movement that embraced irrationality as a protest against bourgeois society. Whatever the actual meaning of these plays, they again demonstrated Lardner's ear for how people talked and thought.

Even Virginia Woolf, who as an Englishwoman knew little about baseball, appreciated *You Know Me Al*: "Mr. Lardner has talents of a remarkable order. With extraordinary ease and aptitude, with the quickest strokes, the surest touch, the sharpest insight, he lets Jack Keefe the baseball player cut out his own outline, fill in his own depths, until the figure of the foolish, boastful, innocent athlete lives before us."[18] V.S. Pritchett, also writing in England though decades after Woolf, credited Lardner and James Joyce with creating a "talking prose."[19] J.D. Salinger, whose mastery of dialect contributed to making a classic of *The Catcher in the Rye*, has his narrator proclaim that Ring Lardner is his second-favorite writer. (His favorite is his brother.)

Critics have not only compared Lardner to other writers but also traced how he influenced them.

Damon Runyon, another newspaperman who turned to short

27

stories, followed Lardner in his use of an American vernacular. In Runyon's case, the language was that of show-biz people and small-time gangsters, most famously in *Guys and Dolls*, a musical based on two of his short stories.

Hemingway acknowledged his debt to Lardner. In 1932, he sent Lardner a copy of his just-published *Death in the Afternoon*. It was inscribed "To Ring Lardner, from his early imitator and always admirer."[20]

Lardner's influence on Fitzgerald has been much debated. Of Fitzgerald and his wife, Lardner wrote: "Scott is a novelist and Zelda is a novelty."[21] The Fitzgeralds were equally fond of Lardner and his wife Ellis. After Lardner sent the Fitzgeralds a Christmas poem, Fitzgerald replied, with mock indignation, with a poem of his own:

> But not one gift to brighten our home
> So I'm sending you back your god damn poem.[22]

Lardner and Fitzgerald shared a disdain for the decadent lifestyles Fitzgerald famously portrayed in *The Great Gatsby*, though both were also drawn to that world. Critics including Lardner biographer Jonathan Yardley have argued that there was much of both Fitzgerald and Lardner in the character of Gatsby. Yardley and Elder both argued that the character of Abe North, an alcoholic musician in Fitzgerald's unfinished novel *Tender is the Night*, was based on Lardner.

Literary critic Christian Messenger pointed to additional echoes of Lardner in *The Great Gatsby*. These included the scene involving a meeting with a fictionalized version of the man who fixed the World Series in 1919, an event that signaled to readers Gatsby's immorality and that Lardner may very well have discussed with Fitzgerald. Messenger also thought that Tom Buchanan, a character in *Gatsby*, "resembles Lardner's stereotyped 'boob' athletes transferred from dugouts to polo ponies," and that the honesty, wit, and realism of Nick Carraway, the novel's narrator, "evinced all the traits that could be called 'Lardnerian.'"[23]

Whatever Lardner's influence on him, Fitzgerald was devoted to Lardner. When Lardner died in 1933, Fitzgerald wrote a tribute that concluded: "Ring made no enemies, because he was kind, and to millions he gave release and delight."[24]

And yet, as Yardley put it, there has always been an asterisk next to Lardner's name in the literary record books. There have always been those who questioned whether, talented as he was, he deserved to be mentioned in the company of writers like Fitzgerald and Hemingway.

In the same piece in which he praised Lardner for the delight he brought millions, Fitzgerald expressed his reservations: "Whatever Ring's achievement was it fell short of the achievement he was capable of, and this because of a cynical attitude toward his work."

Fitzgerald continued: "During those years, when most men of promise achieve an adult education, if only in the school of war, Ring moved in the company of a few dozen illiterates playing a boy's game. A boy's game, with no more possibilities in it than a boy could master, a game bounded by walls which kept out novelty or danger, change or adventure. ... However deeply Ring might cut into it, his cake had the diameter of [a baseball] diamond."[25]

Wilson, too, tempered his praise for a collection of stories with disappointment about unrealized potential: "Will Ring Lardner then, go on to his *Huckleberry Finn* or has he already told all he knows?" he wrote. "What bell might not Lardner ring if he sets out to give us the works?"[26]

Hemingway was crueler. In 1933, the same year he so kindly inscribed his book for Lardner, he wrote that, though he had imitated him in his youth, "all he has is a good false ear and has been around."[27]

Even Perkins, Lardner's champion at Scribner's, was frustrated by Lardner. Perkins urged him to write a novel, or at least a long story, "the longer the better."[28] Lardner was happy to let Perkins collect his short stories and columns and plays, but he never agreed to take on a longer work. Indeed, he wouldn't even treat the stories seriously. When Perkins asked him to write a preface to the first Scribner's collection, Lardner delivered one that jokingly described his writing technique: "The first thing I generally always do is try and get hold of a catchy title, like for instance, 'Basil Hargrave's Vermifuge,' or 'Fun at the Incinerating Plant.'"[29] In the same vein, he added a brief self-deprecatory introduction to each story that also served to ward off any literary pretensions, whether of others or his own. For the opening story, he explained that it had been "written on top of a Fifth Avenue bus, and some of the sheets blew away, which may account for the apparent scarcity of interesting situations."[30]

After Lardner died, Perkins wrote Hemingway: "If he had written more, he would have been a great writer perhaps, but whatever it was that prevented him from writing more was the thing that prevented him from being a great writer." Perkins attributed Lardner's failure to be a great writer to his having been a "newspaperman" with "a sort of provincial scorn of literary people."[31]

Other factors also came into play. One was money: Despite Perkins's enthusiasm, it's by no means clear that a novel would have resulted in big sales and royalties. Despite the reviews and prestige of publishing with Scribner's, Lardner made a lot more from magazines than from books. Scribner's paid Doran only five hundred dollars for the rights to *You Know Me Al*; by then Lardner could make nearly ten times that for a single short story. When Perkins pled with Lardner to write something longer, the editor suggested that if it were just twenty or twenty-five thousand words, then "we might be able to even get a financial return that would warrant the sacrifice of magazine publication."[32] But both Perkins and Lardner knew very well that millions read Lardner's stories in magazines like *The Saturday Evening Post* and *Redbook* and *Cosmopolitan*, while thousands bought his books.

Of course, sales alone are not the measure of a book's influence; if that were the case, the thesis of the book in your hands would be immediately discredited. Writers like Fitzgerald and Hemingway were certainly influenced by Lardner the book author more than by Lardner the magazine writer. But Lardner can be forgiven, when considering what to write, for considering money.

Drinking, too, may have played a role in his not writing a novel. Lardner's nights out with Fitzgerald and others at some point crossed over from Jazz Age exuberance to alcoholism. Often his nights out turned into mornings; according to one story, he once drank steadily for sixty hours.

But among all the possible reasons for his not having written a novel, one stands out: He just didn't want to. He had been most successful with his first-person stories written in another's voice, like that of Jack Keefe, and that approach might have been difficult to sustain in a longer work (though *You Know Me Al* is almost long enough and cohesive enough to be considered a novel). Maybe Lardner did not write a true novel because he recognized what he was good at—extraordinarily good—and he decided to stick with it.

Lardner's son Ring Jr. argued that just because his father's work was fun and easy to read, critics ought not to assume it was fun and easy to write. "Dad was reprimanded for not taking his work seriously enough by several reviewers who had no idea how much effort he actually put into it," he wrote in his 1976 memoir. "What he avoided at all costs was taking himself seriously in public."[33]

Lardner Jr. believed that his father's self-deprecatory comments about his work stemmed both from a dislike of pomp and from a personal modesty. He recalled that when a reporter asked how his father had written some lyrics, he answered "Someone gave me a rhyming dictionary for Christmas once and I couldn't exchange it for a tie."[34] (Lardner's sons must also be counted as important parts of his literary legacy. Ring Lardner, Jr., was a successful screenwriter who was jailed and blacklisted during the Red Scare of the late 1940s and 1950s. His Academy Award-winning scripts included *Woman of the Year* and *M*A*S*H*. John Lardner was a sportswriter and war correspondent. James Lardner and David Lardner were also writers; James's career was cut short when he was killed fighting in the Spanish Civil War and David's when he was killed as a World War II correspondent.)

Yardley, like Fitzgerald, blamed Lardner's limitations on his subject matter, writing that "the asterisk was baseball itself."[35] It would be decades before intellectuals and literary figures fully embraced baseball. But baseball then (and now) was as rich a topic as any.

Virginia Woolf understood that through baseball Lardner had

captured a society as well as a language. To be sure, Lardner's base-ball players were not the gentlemen of British society or the would-be gentlemen of the original Knickerbockers. But they were just as interesting.

"Mr. Lardner's interest in games has solved one of the most diffi-cult problems of the American writer," Woolf wrote. She continued:

> It has given him a clue, a centre, a meeting place for the divers activities of people whom a vast continent isolates, whom no tradition controls. Games give him what society gives his English brother. Whatever the precise rea-son, Mr. Lardner at any rate provides something unique in its kind, some-thing indigenous to the soil, which the traveler may carry off as a trophy to prove to the incredulous that he has actually been to America.[36]

Given how much Lardner had done to undercut the Merriwell-like image of baseball players, one might assume he could shrug off any real-life revelations of their corruption. He couldn't. When it became clear that members of the White Sox—Keefe's team—had thrown the 1919 World Series, Lardner was devastated. He was especially unhappy that Eddie Cicotte, a pitcher whom he liked personally and admired professionally, was one of the "Black Sox." Whatever Keefe's flaws, he had too much pride in his pitching to con-sider taking a bribe.

Fitzgerald responded to the scandal by making the fixed games a symbol of a broader corruption in the society portrayed in *The Great Gatsby*. Lardner responded by never again writing a story about Jack Keefe.

It was not just the scandal that turned Lardner away from base-ball. Around the same time as the scandal, home run totals surged. In 1918, Babe Ruth tied for the league's lead with 11. The next year he set a major league record with 29. In 1920, he hit 54. Lardner thought this was the doing of team owners, who he believed had introduced a livelier ball. Conspiracy-minded historians have tended to agree, noting that A.G. Spalding's company, which manufactured National League balls, had secretly taken over the A.J. Reach Company, which made American League balls. The Reach Company denied tam-pering with the ball, and it's by no means clear they did so. But it's very clear that the power surge meant the decline of stolen bases, hit-and-run-plays, and other strategies Lardner admired.

In a 1921 column, Lardner admitted he had "kind of lost interest" in the game:

> A couple yrs. ago a ballplayer named Baby Ruth that was a pitcher by birth was made into an outfielder on acct. of how he could bust them and he begins breaking records for long distant hits and etc. and he become a big drawing card and the master minds that control baseball says to themselves that if it is home runs that the public wants to see, why leave us give them home runs, so they fixed up a ball that if you don't miss it entirely it will clear the fence, and the result is that ball players which used to specialize in hump back liners to the pitcher is now amongst our leading sluggers when by rights they couldn't take a ball in their hands and knock it past the base umpire.
>
> Another result is that I stay home and read a book.[37]

Lardner's language made the column, as usual, entertaining, but that didn't mean his complaints weren't serious. He was completely serious in a letter he wrote after Giants manager John McGraw resigned because of illness. "Baseball hasn't meant much to me," Lardner wrote McGraw, "since the introduction of the TNT ball that robbed the game of the features I used to like—features that gave you and Bill Carrigan and Fielder Jones and other really intelligent managers a deserved advantage, and smart ball players like Cobb ... a chance to *do* things."[38]

Instead of baseball, Lardner focused some of his creative energies on writing plays. The most successful was *June Moon*, which was based on his short story "Some Like Them Cold." Lardner wrote the lyrics for songs in the play and co-wrote the play with George S. Kaufman, who also wrote several musicals for the Marx Brothers and who won a Tony Award for directing *Guys and Dolls. June Moon* opened in New York in 1929 and ran for two hundred seventy-three performances in New York and was made into movies in 1931 and 1937.

But Lardner did not entirely abandon baseball. He continued to cover the World Series. He sometimes wrote short stories about baseball, albeit not Keefe. One of these, the 1927 "Hurry Kane," was turned into a Broadway play and then into two movies, *Fast Company* in 1929 and *Elmer, the Great* in 1933. In none of its various incarnations was it memorable.

In 1932, Lardner returned to epistolary short stories, this time in the form of letters between a rookie Brooklyn Dodger outfielder named Danny Warner and his girlfriend Jessie Graham back home in Illinois. Scribner's published the stories as *Lose with a Smile*. Casey Stengel, at the time a coach for the Dodgers, is Danny's roommate. Stengel later became famous not only for his managing but also for his language—a mix of gibberish and some wisdom that was known as Stengelese and which seemed like something Lardner could have invented. But there's little of that in the stories, since Stengel's words all come via Danny's writing.

The stories in *Lose with a Smile* are entertaining, but they didn't generate anything near the enthusiasm of those in *You Know Me Al.* Perhaps Lardner was tired of the approach. Perhaps, too, he was tired of baseball. But Ring Lardner, Jr., argued convincingly that his father's disillusionment with the game has been exaggerated. In his memoir, Lardner Jr. recalled that his father continued to take him and his brothers to games and to teach them the finer points of baseball. Lardner Jr. repeated a story that others had told about how his father, when he first suspected the 1919 World Series had been fixed, changed the lyrics to a hit tune from "I'm forever blowing bubbles" to "I'm forever throwing ball games."[39] For many, the story showed Ring Lardner turning away from baseball. Lardner Jr. interpreted the story differently.

"I was only four at the time," he wrote, "and can't testify directly to my father's reaction, but I don't think a deeply disillusioned man could toss off that lyric, and the way he spoke about the event later gave me the feeling he was at least as concerned about losing a substantial bet as he was about the moral turpitude of the ballplayers."[40]

3

Pitchin' Man:
Satchel Paige's Own Story

by SATCHEL PAIGE
as told to HAL LEBOVITZ
Cleveland: Cleveland News, 1948

Why a book by Satchel Paige and not Jackie Robinson? It was Robinson, of course, who broke the color bar in 1947; Paige did not play in the major leagues until 1948. And it is Robinson, of course, who is almost universally recognized for having not only integrated baseball but for having paved the way for integrating America. Both Paige and Robinson authored books that were published in 1948, soon enough after baseball's integration to capture the moment and to advance the cause.

Yet it was Paige's 1948 book, *Pitchin' Man*, that better captured this moment. Unlike Robinson, Paige had a long history in the Negro leagues before entering the majors, and his book captured more of the flavor of an era when Blacks celebrated a culture that, though separate, was very much the equal of white America's and would fundamentally change the latter. Moreover, it was Paige who, through his much-publicized exploits in the Negro leagues and his barnstorming against major leaguers, forced white sportswriters, fans, and ultimately officials to recognize that Blacks belonged in the majors.

"Jackie opened the door," said Minnie Minoso, a Negro leaguer who joined Paige on the Cleveland Indians in 1949, but "it was Satchel who inserted the key."[1]

◊ ◊ ◊

The Lineup

The Negro leagues did not keep meticulous statistics, so it's difficult to gauge the reliability of some of Paige's claims. He estimated he had won about 2000 games and pitched between 50 and 100 no-hitters. These were astounding numbers, though not impossible considering that many of those games were against semipro teams and not teams in the Negro leagues, and that Paige often just pitched a few innings. He estimated he had pitched for about 250 teams, which was also not impossible considering he would often pitch one game for a team and then move on. Estimates of his earnings were usually in the range of $40,000 a year, well above what most major leaguers made, though again not impossible, given how Black and white fans flocked to his games.

But it was not numbers but stories that turned Paige into a legend. "Some of them," wrote his sometime Negro league teammate Buck O'Neil, "are even true."[2]

Paige would sometimes promise to strike out the next nine batters, and then would call in his outfielders and sometimes his infielders to show how confident he was that no one would connect with the ball. Against semipro opponents this confidence was usually justified. Paige would also sometimes set up a target, always much smaller than home plate, sometimes a gun wrapper; after putting the gum in his mouth he would put the wrapper on a stick and the stick on home plate. Returning to the mound, he would then knock the wrapper off the stick, usually with his first pitch.

In *Pitchin' Man*, Paige and coauthor Hal Lebovitz captured the mix of cockiness, folksiness, humor, and genuinely awesome achievement that comprised Paige's image. Lebovitz sometimes used dialect that sounded like a mid-century Negro stereotype, but so too did Paige.

Here was Paige bragging about his array of pitches: "I got bloopers, loopers and droopers. I got a jump ball, a be ball, a screwball, a wobbly ball, a whipsy-dipsy-do, a hurry-up ball, a nothin' ball and a bat dodger."[3]

Among the most famous of the stories Paige told in *Pitchin' Man* was his confrontation with Josh Gibson in the 1942 Negro Leagues' World Series. Paige was pitching for the Kansas City Monarchs of the Negro American League. Gibson, who was considered the Negro

3. Pitchin' Man *(Paige)*

leagues' greatest slugger and who was often compared to Babe Ruth, was playing for the Negro National League's Homestead Grays. The Monarchs were ahead by three runs in the eighth inning. Paige retired the first two batters, then gave up a single. At that point he told his catcher he was going to intentionally walk the next two batters to face Gibson with the bases loaded. Despite the protests of his teammates, he did just that.

Paige described what came next:

> I yelled to Josh ... "Now you're too smart to fool, so I'm goin' to tell you what's comin.' I'm goin' to throw you two sidearm fast balls down around the knees." The umpire was John Craig....
> Josh let the first pitch go.
> Craig called, "Strike one."
> Josh let the second pitch go.
> Craig called, "Strike two."
> "Now," I said, "Josh you're too good for me to waste any pitches so I'm goin' to finish you with a sidearm curve."
> I threw it and Josh stepped back. It broke over and he swung a slow motion strike three.[4]

Others' versions of the story added even more drama. O'Neil threw in some more trash talk. "Josh, I got you oh-and-two, and in this league I'm supposed to knock you down," Paige said, according to O'Neil. "But I'm not gonna throw smoke at yo' yolk—I'm gonna throw a pea at yo' knee."[5]

Even Paige told multiple versions. In a story that appeared in the *Pittsburgh Courier* in 1943, he walked just one batter to get to Gibson. In Paige's second memoir, published in 1962, he walked three batters and the lead was only one run.

Since this was a World Series game, a reporter for the Baltimore *Afro-American* was on hand, and his version was probably the most accurate. Paige *did* strike out Gibson with the bases loaded, but it was in the seventh inning and the story said nothing about intentional walks. The later recollections also left out the anticlimactic information that Paige gave up four runs in the eighth and ninth innings, though the Monarchs scored six to win 8–4.

Another oft-told Paige story took place in the Dominican Republic. Paige was notorious for ignoring his contracts and jumping from one team to another if someone offered enough money. The Caribbean was especially appealing to Negro league players, since there were plenty of baseball fans and less prejudice against Blacks. In 1937 the Dominican dictator, Rafael Trujillo, was determined that the team from his capital city—the Dragones de Ciudad Trujillo—would win the league championship. Trujillo's representatives offered Paige $30,000 to split between himself and eight other Negro Leaguers. Paige then recruited Gibson and seven others.

Trujillo's rule was ruthless and bloody, and as Paige told the story in *Pitchin' Man*, the dictator's followers warned the pitcher that he'd better win the championship series. Soldiers chaperoned them everywhere, and Paige's jittery teammates had split the series with their opponents entering the seventh and final game.

"Seven thousand people was in the stands and they all have knives and guns," Paige wrote in *Pitchin' Man*. "I tried to play sick. 'Cause I was sick, believe me. But they stuck a gun at my head and I got well."

The Dragones took a 6–5 lead in the seventh. "I said to myself, 'L-l-l-listen S-s-s-atch,' ... 'pull your self together before they air-condition you." The team held on to win, and "the American consul heard what a worrysome situation we was in and they flew us out in a bird that same night."[6]

Again, there were various versions of this story, including from Paige himself. In *Maybe I'll Pitch Forever*, Paige's 1962 memoir, he added that when the Dragones were down by a run, "you could see Trujillo lining up his army," which "began to look like a firing squad."[7] But according to a 1937 story in the Baltimore *Afro-American*, which appeared under Paige's byline, Paige remained in the Dominican Republic for three days after the series. O'Neil, whose version of the Paige-Gibson face-off was as dramatic as Paige's own, was more skeptical about the Dominican story in *Pitchin' Man*. "I could understand Satchel being afraid, with all those guns around," he wrote, "but I couldn't believe they would have been given thousands of dollars and then shot. And the tip-off was that Satchel didn't even come back right away."[8]

◊ ◊ ◊

3. Pitchin' Man *(Paige)*

Of all Paige's remarkable statistics, the most famously disputed was his age.

The question generated more and more attention as the seemingly ageless pitcher continued to retire batters. After Cleveland Indian owner Bill Veeck signed Paige in July 1948, these were major league batters.

The *Sporting News* was indignant. A week after the signing, with reports circulating that Paige was somewhere between thirty-nine and fifty, editor J.G. Taylor Spink accused Veeck of signing him only for the publicity: "To sign a hurler at Paige's age is to demean the standards of baseball in the big circuits," Spink wrote. "If Satch were white, he would not have drawn a second thought from Veeck."[9]

In his 1962 autobiography, Veeck offered a completely accurate answer: "If Satch were white, he would have been in the majors twenty-five years earlier."[10] More immediately, Paige answered Spink's accusation by finishing the year 6–1 with an ERA of 2.47, helping the Indians win the pennant.

Spink's indignation stemmed less from a desire to uphold the standards of baseball than from a desire to keep Blacks out of baseball. But he was not wrong about the publicity value of signing Paige. The Indians' yearbook listed his date of birth as "somewhere between 1900 and 1908."[11] In *Newsweek*, John Lardner, Ring Lardner's son, wrote that Paige "saved the day at Waterloo, when the dangerous pull-hitter, Bonaparte, came to bat."[12]

Paige himself fully participated in the game. When writers asked his age, he wrote in *Pitchin' Man*, "I tell 'em I'm 45 or 50 or 60—whatever they want me to tell 'em.... Seems they get a bigger kick out of an old man throwing strikeouts."[13] Another time he joked: "Methuselah was my first bat boy."[14]

Paige's actual age, he said in *Pitchin' Man*, was forty, meaning he'd been born in 1908. Paige added: "I'll have to tell my arm."[15]

A 1908 date matched his social security, draft, and passport records, though the exact day varied. No one could find a birth certificate for a Leroy Paige in his hometown of Mobile, Alabama, but there was one for a Leroy Page, which was how Satchel's father spelled his name. The date on that certificate was July 7, 1906, and in Paige's 1962 memoir he settled on 1906 instead of 1908.

Both Veeck and Paige milked the uncertainty for its publicity value and both may have intentionally obfuscated the truth, which was most likely 1906. For Paige, the uncertainty may have been more than a good joke. The Mobile records for impoverished African American families were even more unreliable than Negro League records, and Paige understood this was because to the white world of Alabama, Black lives didn't matter.

◊ ◊ ◊

Paige's jokes about his age were typical of how he dealt with Jim Crow. His storytelling and showboating entertained fans, but they also deflected what must have sometimes been anger and sometimes hurt. They also guaranteed that in a world which rarely saw Blacks as worthy of notice, he would be noticed.

Paige would often arrive late to a game, sometimes with a police escort, and would then slowly amble toward the mound. "Why rush," he would ask, "when they can't start the game without me?"[16]

Sometimes he didn't show up at all, if he was offered more money to pitch elsewhere. Often his excuses for being late had to do with stopping on the way to fish or for a game of craps, or being stopped on the way for speeding. His fellow Monarch pitcher Frank Duncan told of how he and Paige were en route to a game in Wyoming when they were pulled over. The officer told Paige the fine was $25 and Paige handed him $50, telling him to keep the change. "I'm comin' back through here the same way next week,"[17] he explained.

Paige could tell outrageous stories with a straight face, and these also ensured he would be remembered. One involved his coming into a game with runners on first and third and nobody out and a count of 3 and 2 on the batter. He slipped a ball into his pocket before he left the dugout and then took the game ball from the pitcher he was relieving. And then: "I just threw those two balls at the same time, one to first and one to third. I picked off both runners and my motion was so good the batter fanned. That was three outs."[18]

Veeck was awed by Satch's storytelling abilities. "When Satch got on the train—the times he made the train—he would always sit down alone," Veeck wrote. "Pretty soon the whole team would be gathered around.... Satch doesn't hold conversations, he holds court."[19]

Paige was often compared to Stepin Fetchit, the stage name for Lincoln Perry, a comedian and actor who often took on the stereotypical role of a lazy Negro. Paige's long limbs and lazy walks to the mound conjured up the Stepin Fetchit persona for many spectators. Like Perry, to some extent Paige took on the only roles available to an African American man. But he (and some scholars have argued Perry too) also used the roles to challenge, albeit indirectly, white supremacy. Ignoring speed limits, let alone joking with a cop about it, was a dangerous game for a Black man to play, and stories about that were both disarming and subversive.

Paige always stressed that, however much he joked around, he was very serious about his pitching. His slow-motion walk to the mound may even have made his fastball seem even faster by contrast. He was especially serious when he barnstormed against white major leaguers. In 1934 and 1935 Paige faced off against St. Louis Cardinal ace Dizzy Dean six times and won four of them. Dean, certainly no civil rights activist, said in 1938 that Paige was the best pitcher he'd ever seen, adding: "Say, old Diz is pretty fast back in 1933 and 1934, and you know my fast ball looks like a change of pace alongside that little pistol bullet old Satchel shoots up to the plate."[20] Joe DiMaggio, who as a minor leaguer in 1936 barnstormed against Paige and managed one hit in four at bats, said: "I know I can make the majors now."[21]

In *Pitchin' Man*, Paige made clear many times that his pitching was no joke. Speaking of how he sometimes stopped in the middle of a wind-up, he wrote: "The hesitation pitch is the one folks call 'Stepin Pitchit.' I don't care what name they do give it long as the batters don't Stepin Hitit. And they don't."[22]

Paige didn't mind being compared to Stepin Fetchit, but he preferred being compared to another Satch—Louis "Satchmo" Armstrong. "Now I don't look like Louie and I don't act like Louie and can't blow like Louie—except maybe with my fast ball," he wrote in *Pitchin' Man*, but "if 'Satchmo' is good enough for him I won't decline it."[23]

The nickname actually had nothing to do with Armstrong. Rather, it came from his childhood in Mobile. With every cent mattering to his family, Paige would earn change at the railroad station carrying passengers' bags. So that he could carry three or four satchels at once, he rigged together a pole and some ropes. As he explained in *Pitchin' Man*: "When I was full up, the kids couldn't see me 'cause I was camouflaged like a moving satchel tree. After that they called me 'Satchel.'"[24]

Unlike so much else, Paige didn't joke about his nickname and he objected when he was sometimes called "Satchelfoot," which suggested his feet were big or clumsy and which he thought sounded like a clown. "I ain't no clown," he wrote in *Pitchin' Man*. "I'm a baseball pitcher and winning baseball games is serious business."[25]

To many civil rights activists, pitching seriously wasn't enough. Many thought that Paige's joking around, even if it masked more serious anger or hurt, smacked of not just Stepin Fetchit or Amos 'n' Andy but of Uncle Tom.

This was unfair.

For one thing, openly taking on Jim Crow might easily have gotten a Black man lynched. "The way he walked, the way he carried himself, Satchel did not want anyone to know how bright he was," said George "Meadowlark" Lemon, whose Harlem Globetrotters also parodied racist stereotypes. "He'd tell me, 'If they don't know how smart you are, you've got an upper hand on them.'"[26]

For another, Paige's pitching did force whites, including the baseball establishment, to pay attention to Negro League players. In May 1942, an integrated crowd of 30,000 streamed into Chicago's Wrigley Field to watch the Kansas City Monarchs play a team billed as "Dizzy Dean's All-Stars." The Monarchs won 3–1, and the *Chicago Defender*, an African American newspaper, noted that "white and black fans were out to see Satchel Paige."[27] In June Paige joined the Homestead Grays for a game against Dean's All-Stars and the

Grays won 8–1. The headline in the *Pittsburgh Courier,* another African American newspaper, was "'The Great Satchel' Proves He's a Big Leaguer Before 22,000 Witnesses."[28]

By the 1940s, the white press, too, was paying attention to Paige. There were profiles in *Time,* the *Saturday Evening Post,* and *Life,* as well as editorials and columns in many newspapers calling for major league teams to give him a shot in the majors.

Paige sometimes seemed to care more about money than the majors, and critics took that to mean he didn't care about civil rights. In a 1942 interview with the Associated Press he seemed to set back the cause of integration by suggesting that he wouldn't take a pay cut to play in the majors. He also said that whites and Blacks playing together would be "unharmonious."[29]

Paige *did* care a lot about money, often jumping from one team to another in search of a bigger payday. But wherever he played, fans came to see him, and that paid a lot of other players' salaries as well. In a sense, he offered players a preview of what free agency would bring them decades later.

Nor did his interest in money mean that he was oblivious to civil rights. Jack Marshall of the Chicago American Giants recalled: "When Satchel Paige had his all-stars they wouldn't play in a town if they couldn't lodge there.... He'd just tell the Chamber of Commerce, no soap. They were warned beforehand, so they didn't have any trouble."[30] Paige may have done all this in private to avoid any trouble and he may have ended up eating and staying at Black establishments. Still, he was making a stand.

In 1937, a decade before Robinson's debut with the Brooklyn Dodgers, Paige wrote a story for the *Daily Worker,* a communist newspaper, in which he offered to pitch for any team in the majors without being paid unless he proved his worth. Just writing for a communist paper was itself a considerable risk.

And two weeks after the 1942 story that critics considered so damaging to the cause Paige clarified his position. At the Negro Leagues' All-Star game he grabbed a microphone before going to the mound and told the crowd that he meant to say whites and Blacks should play together, but that if they wouldn't then maybe the majors should just add an all-Black team. This may not have advanced the cause of integration but, in Paige's not-unreasonable opinion, it recognized the reality of prejudice. It also recognized that segregation had allowed at least some Blacks in the Negro leagues (and not just Paige) to prosper. They had created a game that, unlike the majors after Babe Ruth, featured speed as much as power, and some white fans as well as Black fans had come to appreciate that.

Other Negro leaguers also recognized that segregation, in baseball as elsewhere, while blatantly unfair, had resulted in a vibrant African American culture. "Baseball and jazz, two of the best inventions known to man, walked hand in hand along Vine Street (in Kansas City)," wrote O'Neil. "We had Satchel Paige and Satchmo Armstrong; Blues Stadium, where we played our ball, and the Blue Room at the Streets, where we had a ball."[31] Asked if he had any regrets that he played before integration, O'Neil said: "Waste no tears for me. I didn't come along too early—I was right on time."[32]

O'Neil also made clear there was more to Paige than generally imagined. He recalled that when he and Paige were on the road with the Monarchs in Charleston, South Carolina, Paige took him to a place near the harbor where slaves had been auctioned. "Satchel and I stood there, silent as could be, for about ten minutes, not saying anything, but thinking a whole bunch of things." Then Paige said to O'Neil: "Seems like I been here before."

Added O'Neil: "*That* was Robert Leroy Paige. A little bit deeper than most people thought."[33]

◊ ◊ ◊

Paige's first year in Cleveland surpassed Veeck's hopes not just for his pitching but for his drawing power. In three consecutive starts, total attendance topped 200,000.

"The signing of Satchel Paige to a Cleveland contract is far more interesting than was the news when Branch Rickey broke baseball's color line by signing Jackie Robinson to a Montreal contract," wrote Tom Meany in the July 21, 1948, *New York Star*. "It was inevitable that the bigotry which kept Negroes out of Organized Ball would be beaten back, but I'd never heard of Robinson at that time. With Paige, it's different. The Satchmo has been a baseball legend for a long time, a Paul Bunyan in Technicolor."[34]

There was talk about making a movie of his life starring Lincoln Perry. The movie didn't happen but *Pitchin' Man* did. There was also talk that his book would be ghost-written by Lester Rodney, the sports editor of the Communist *Daily Worker*, but that also didn't happen. Instead, Paige turned to Lebovitz, who had written a series of articles about him in the *Cleveland News*. It's not clear the extent to which Lebovitz edited the work, but the words were mostly Paige's. In fact, Paige carried around a typewriter which he used to provide Lebovitz with drafts.

In keeping with his image as an entertainer and not an activist, *Pitchin' Man* ducked any serious discussion of racism in the majors. "I heard there was goin' to be discrimination on the ball field," Paige wrote. "There ain't.... I been treated like I been on the Indians for 20 years. I'm just one of the boys."[35]

As was his wont, Paige used humor (in ways that later critics would find demeaning) to defuse racial tensions on the Indians. He got himself invited into some teammates' poker game not by demanding they let him play but by standing nearby and asking, "Did sumbudy ring fo' da portah?"[36]

In 1949 Paige's record was 4–7 with a 3.04 earned run average, a definite drop-off from his first season but still respectable. But Veeck sold the team after the season and when the Indians' new owners tried to cut his pay Paige refused to sign the contract. His major league career appeared over, but when Veeck bought the St. Louis Browns he signed Paige again. In 1952 Paige went 12–10, a remarkable record for a team whose record was 64–90. Paige made the All-Star team. But he slid to 3–9 in 1953 and it seemed the end of the line. Still, he continued to barnstorm and play for various minor league teams. And in 1965, Kansas City Athletics owner Charlie Finley brought Paige back to the majors one last time. By then this clearly was a publicity gimmick, and the nearly-sixty-year-old Paige appeared in the bullpen with a rocking chair and a nurse. But he surprised everyone by pitching three shutout innings against the Red Sox.

Even before then, Paige's image as ageless had been firmly

established. In 1953, an article in *Collier's* magazine included his tips for staying young. These included what became his most famous aphorism: "Don't look back. Something might be gaining on you."[37] In 1962, Paige's second memoir was published, this one co-authored by David Lipman, a writer for the *St. Louis Post-Dispatch*. The title, appropriately, was *Maybe I'll Pitch Forever*.

In this second memoir, Paige explained that the *Collier's* writer had taken some liberties in turning various comments into a list of rules, but "don't look back" was his real rule. "When you look back," Paige wrote, "you know how long you've been going and that just might stop you from going any farther. And with me, there was an awful lot to look back on."[38]

Maybe I'll Pitch Forever presented, in somewhat different versions, many of the same stories as *Pitchin' Man*. The second book was much blunter than the first about racism Paige had encountered. While he reiterated that he was treated "pretty good"[39] with the Indians, he recounted an incident when the Browns stopped in Charleston, West Virginia, for an exhibition game. At the hotel where the team was staying, the clerk refused to give him a room key.

"We don't serve niggers here," he kind of sniffed at me, holding his head back like he was trying to look down his nose.[40]

Paige tried, quietly, to explain that he'd been told he could stay with the rest of the team, but the clerk ignored him.

"I grabbed the edge of the desk and squeezed," Paige recalled. "I had to squeeze like that to keep my hands down, to keep from hitting that man. I didn't hit him. I just turned around and walked out of that hotel. I went to the airport. They had a plane leaving for Washington. I bought me a ticket."

Later, he calmed down and took a cab to the game, explaining: "I didn't have enough meanness in me to disappoint those fans just to get even with the meanness in somebody else."[41]

◊ ◊ ◊

Though this chapter has, I hope, made a case for the importance of Paige and *Pitchin' Man*, that is in no way to suggest that Jackie Robinson was not an important figure. In fact, no baseball player transformed the game and the nation more than Robinson. What I will argue, however, is that Robinson's 1948 book was not as important as Paige's.

Like *Pitchin' Man, Jackie Robinson: My Own Story* downplayed racism, but it did so to an extent that undermined its credibility. There were occasional incidents, Robinson wrote, but he explained them as the result of "the excitement and heat of a hard-fought-game." Under that kind of pressure, "a good-natured guy suddenly goes beserk for a few seconds" and "prejudices and racial epithets subconsciously leap to the surface."

"I believe most of us are sorry and ashamed after such outbursts," Robinson added, "and I'm certain they will happen less and less frequently in America—both in the ball park and outside."[42]

Even when he heard rumors that the St. Louis Cardinals were planning to strike rather than play against a Black man, Robinson stressed "the challenge was short-lived, thanks to the League officials and the press," and "after it was over, I was more firmly entrenched than ever."[43]

My Own Story, though co-written by African American sportswriter Wendell Smith, read as if it were issued by the Dodgers' publicity office. Robinson told the oft-repeated story of his first meeting with Dodger president Branch Rickey—how Rickey tested him to make sure he wouldn't lose his temper if faced with racist taunts, how he promised Rickey he would "stay out of rhubarbs on the field and trouble of any sort away from it";[44] how Rickey became "like the father I never knew,"[45] how Dodger manager Burt Shotten "was always kind and helpful,"[46] how playing for the Dodgers was "the best job I have ever had and I am going to try to keep it for a long time."[47]

The book's almost-obsequious tone toward Rickey—he was always "Mr. Rickey"—led some civil rights activists to see Robinson, as some had seen Paige, as an Uncle Tom. Shortly before he was assassinated in 1965, Malcolm X commented that "sooner or later Jackie will start calling Rickey 'Massa.'"[48] Robinson's reputation among activists also took a hit in 1949 when he testified before the House Un-American Activities Committee. Black actor Paul

Robeson had stated publicly that American Blacks would not fight against the Soviet Union, and the Committee called on Robinson to assure the public otherwise. Robinson denounced racism but ultimately told the Committee what it wanted to hear: that he and other Blacks were loyal Americans. Robinson's connections to the Republican Party further alienated activists; he supported Richard Nixon during the 1960 presidential campaign and later became an advisor to New York Governor Nelson Rockefeller.

Much of this criticism was unfair. Robinson, like Paige, would have lost his shot at the majors if he'd taken a more militant stance. He was not afraid of confrontations, and if he'd been free to follow his own and not Rickey's wishes, he would not have so consistently turned the other cheek. Certainly he had not done so prior to agreeing to Rickey's terms. In July 1944, when he was a second lieutenant in the army and stationed at Fort Hood, Texas, Robinson boarded a military bus and refused an order from the driver to move to the back. He was charged with insubordination and found not guilty. Later that year, while Robinson was playing for the Kansas City Monarchs, the team's bus stopped at a gas station in Oklahoma and the attendant told them they could buy the gas but not use the rest room. Robinson told the attendant that if they couldn't use the restroom, they'd buy their gas elsewhere. The attendant backed down. And after Robinson felt he'd fulfilled his promised to Rickey, Robinson stopped ignoring racist insults and acts and became more aggressive on and off the field.

Robinson's 1972 book, *I Never Had It Made*, reflected this change and—much more than *My Own Story*—represented Robinson's real thoughts and feelings. Like Paige's second book, *I Never Had It Made* was much more honest about the racism he'd faced. In his 1948 book, Robinson had described getting to the majors as a fairy tale. "Cinderella woke up one morning married to a handsome prince," he wrote. "Of course it hadn't been that easy. But when it happens, it seems that way. You say to yourself: 'It wasn't necessary to do all that worrying now was it?'"[49]

The title of his second book signaled a very different—and deeply disillusioned—attitude. "I cannot stand and sing the anthem," he now wrote. "I cannot salute the flag; I know that I am a black man in a white world. In 1972, in 1947, at my birth in 1919, I know that I never had it made."[50]

By 1964, Robinson regretted having supported Nixon. "I have always felt that blacks must be represented in both parties," he explained in *I Never Had It Made.* "I was fighting a last-ditch battle to keep the Republicans from becoming completely white."[51] It was a battle, he now conceded, that had been lost.

Robinson well understood the quandary he faced as he became more aggressive on and off the field.

"As long as I appeared to ignore insult and injury, I was a martyred hero to a lot of people who seemed to have sympathy for the underdog," he wrote in *I Never Had It Made.* "But the minute I began to answer, to argue, to protest—the minute I began to sound off—I became a swell-head, a wise guy, an 'uppity' nigger."[52]

Among those who criticized Robinson for pushing too hard and too fast was Dick Young, a sportswriter for the *New York Daily News.* Young compared Robinson to the less confrontational Roy Campanella, the Dodgers' African American catcher.

"The trouble between you and me, Jackie, is that I can go to Campy and all we discuss is baseball," Young told Robinson, as the latter recounted it in *I Never Had It Made.* "I talk to you and sooner or later we get around to social issues."

"I'm telling as a friend," Young continued, "that a lot of newspapermen are saying that Campy's the kind of guy they can like but that your aggressiveness, your wearing your race on your sleeve, makes enemies."[53]

The *Sporting News* was among the newspapers that repeatedly told Robinson to back off with editorials with headlines like "A Problem Grows in Brooklyn" in November 1949 and "Robinson Should Be a Player, Not a Crusader"[54] in January 1950.

Among those who argued Robinson had the right to speak out about politics was Martin Luther King, Jr. "He has the right," King said in 1962, "because back in the days when integration wasn't fashionable, he underwent the trauma and the humiliation and the loneliness which comes from being a pilgrim walking the lonesome byways toward the high road of Freedom. He was a sit-inner before sit-ins, a freedom rider before freedom rides."[55]

◊ ◊ ◊

Did Robinson and Paige actually change the course of history? Wouldn't integration have come to baseball—and America—even if there had been no Robinson and Paige?

Some baseball historians, most notably Jules Tygiel, have made a convincing case that the particular—and in retrospect, peculiar—partnership between Rickey and Robinson was not necessary. Rickey argued that finding the right Black man, one who like Robinson was able and willing to withstand pressures and provocations without striking back, was the only way to show baseball and America that integration could work. But had Rickey instead brought a few Blacks up to the majors all at the same time, there would have been less pressure on Robinson and more evidence of the benefits of integration. Indeed, Tygiel argued, by presenting Robinson as an experiment to test whether integration could work, Rickey actually gave other owners an excuse to wait and see how the experiment played out before signing other Blacks.

Moreover, had Rickey not signed Robinson, there were plenty of other factors that would have pressured owners to integrate. During World War II numerous commentators noted that the United States was fighting fascism abroad while accepting Jim Crow at home. In 1941, Franklin Roosevelt issued an executive order forbidding discrimination by defense contractors, and in 1946 Harry Truman appointed a commission on civil rights. The press and the public, Black and white, was increasingly paying attention to the talent in the Negro leagues, especially that of Paige. Politicians in New York, in particular Mayor Fiorello LaGuardia and Congressman Adam Clayton Powell, were pushing for laws that would have forced the majors to integrate. Bill Veeck was waiting to buy a team and then sign Black players like Paige. And Rickey himself, baseball historian John Thorn discovered after reviewing Rickey's papers, had once considered signing more than one Negro leaguer.

3. Pitchin' Man (Paige)

Baseball historian Mitchell Nathanson went further than Tygiel. Nathanson argued that by signing Robinson, Rickey derailed the momentum of a broader integration and kept the process under the control of baseball owners, who—except for Veeck—were slow to sign other Blacks. Rickey's stress on finding the right player, Nathanson wrote, implied that integration was not a right that any Black could claim but a privilege owners could bestow on selected players. As a result, when Paige's Indians played an exhibition game against Robinson's Dodgers in 1948, they were still the only two teams with Black players. (The Dodgers had Robinson and Campanella, the Indians Paige and outfielder Larry Doby.)

But these revisionist takes on baseball's integration ought not to detract from what Robinson and Paige accomplished. Even if Rickey's way was not the only or best way to expedite integration, Robinson *did* prove to skeptics that Blacks belonged in the majors. However slow and incomplete was baseball's integration, Robinson did play in the majors seven years before the Supreme Court, in *Brown v. Board of Education*, ruled that school segregation was illegal, and seventeen years before Lyndon Johnson signed the Civil Rights Act that banned job discrimination on the basis of race.

In Robinson's rookie year the Dodgers drew 1.8 million fans and led the league in attendance. Robinson was so popular among whites as well as Blacks that one poll taken after his rookie season ranked him the second most popular man in America (after Bing Crosby). In a 1951 poll, boys ranked Robinson and DiMaggio as their favorite athletes. So it seems reasonable to assume that some of these fans who might once have been skeptical about integrating baseball might now have become more open to the idea that Blacks should be treated equally in other realms as well.

One public convert was Red Barber, the Dodger announcer. Barber was born and bred in the South and readily admitted he was shaken to learn Robinson would play for the Dodgers. But Robinson forced him to reconsider his prejudices. "If I have achieved any understanding or tolerance in my life," Barber wrote, "if I have been able to follow a little better the second great commandment, which is to love thy neighbor, it all stems from this."[56]

Tygiel, despite his skepticism about the way Rickey and Robinson integrated baseball, noted that Black athletes "captured the imagination of millions of Americans who had previously ignored the nation's racial dilemma," and that "for civil rights advocates the baseball experience offered a model of peaceful transition."[57]

For Thorn, too, a revisionist take on Rickey did not detract from Rickey's or Robinson's accomplishments. "I'm most proud to be an American, most proud to be a baseball fan when baseball has led America rather than followed it," said Thorn. "This is the most transforming incident."[58]

And here's Roger Kahn's take on Robinson's influence, as expressed in *The Boys of Summer*, his classic look back at the Brooklyn and the Dodgers:

> By applauding Robinson, a man did not feel that he was taking a stand on school integration, or on open housing. But for an instant he had accepted Robinson simply as a hometown ball player. To disregard color, even for an instant, is to step away from the old prejudices, the old hatred. That is not a path on which many double back.[59]

One could go on and on with the testimony of sportswriters and historians. But perhaps it's fitting to close with the words of Campanella, one of Robinson's and Paige's fellow pioneers: "We were the first ones on the trains, we were the first ones down South not to go around the back of the restaurant, first ones in the hotels. We were like the teachers of the whole integration thing."[60]

4.

The Natural

by BERNARD MALAMUD

New York: Harcourt, Brace, 1952

Ring Lardner, for all his influence on American literature, refused to take himself or his work too seriously. Bernard Malamud took his work very seriously and with the 1952 publication of *The Natural* established baseball as an appropriate subject for literary fiction.

Malamud did so by writing a novel that was about baseball, yes, but also an allegory that drew on literary traditions ranging from Homer to the tales of King Arthur. A.G. Spalding may have created a mythic past for the game but Malamud took myths from humanity's past and grafted them onto a baseball story. From then on, F. Scott Fitzgerald's criticism of Lardner—that "however deeply Ring might cut into it, his cake had the diameter of [a baseball] diamond"[1]— would no longer apply to much of baseball fiction. Baseball novels by writers such as Robert Coover and Philip Roth and W.P. Kinsella were no longer bound by the dimensions of a diamond or, for that matter, the laws of nature. For readers of these books, baseball took on magical and mystical properties that less secular readers found in religion.

Malamud was explicit about his intentions. "Baseball flat is baseball flat," he said in a 1975 interview. "I had to do something else to enrich the subject.... This guy gets up with his baseball bat and all at once he is, through the ages, a knight—somewhat battered—with a lance.... The mythological and symbolic excite my imagination."[2]

◊ ◊ ◊

The Lineup

Putting aside for the moment the mythological and symbolic, the action in *The Natural* takes place in two parts. In the first part, a young pitcher named Roy Hobbs is en route to Chicago to try out for the Cubs. On the train with him are Sam Simpson, the scout who discovered Roy, and Walter Wambold, baseball's greatest hitter, also known as the Whammer. The train stops, giving Roy and the Whammer the opportunity for a quick contest. With Sam catching, Roy strikes out the Whammer on three pitches. His confidence destroyed, the Whammer slinks off, his career over. So hard does Roy throw the third pitch that it knocks down Sam, who dies soon after. Roy flirts with a young woman named Harriet Bird, who invites him to her hotel room in Chicago. There she shoots him.

The second part takes place fifteen years later. It's unclear what Roy has been up to in the interim, but he has now joined the New York Knights as a no-longer-young rookie outfielder. The Knights have set the record for the most consecutive losses in league history. Their manager, Pop Fisher, is in danger of losing his share of the team to Judge Goodwill Banner, whose name belies his conniving nature and who will be able to push Pops out if the Knights continue to lose. The Knights' only star is left fielder Bump Bailey, who, fearing Roy will take his job, attempts a great catch, crashes into the outfield wall, and dies. Roy takes over for Bump and his superhuman hitting propels the Knights into the pennant race.

In the midst of the race, Roy is also involved in a love triangle. He lusts after Memo Paris, a femme fatale who is Bump's girlfriend and Pop's niece but who is involved with the bookie Gus Sands, and he sleeps with the motherly Iris Lemon, who amidst a slump Roy has fallen into literally stands up for him in the stands and restores his confidence. With the pennant down to the final game, the bookie and the judge offer Roy a bribe to throw it. Realizing it's the only way he can make enough money to get Memo to marry him, Roy accepts. With two outs in the bottom of the ninth and the tying run on third, Roy changes his mind. But he swings at a bad pitch and strikes out.

Readers familiar with baseball history would have recognized that Malamud drew on many actual events and people. The

4. The Natural (*Malamud*)

Whammer resembled Babe Ruth. The hotel shooting conjured up memories of Eddie Waitkus, the Phillies first baseman who was shot by a crazed fan in 1949, and Bump's wall-crashing evoked Pete Reiser, the Dodger outfielder who was carted off the field eleven times after hitting the wall. Roy hits a home run for a kid in a hospital, just as Ruth did, and Roy's gargantuan appetite leads to a colossal bellyache, just as Ruth might have suffered. Roy is driven to accept a bribe in part because the judge cheated him out of some of his pay, just as the 1919 Black Sox took bribes because White Sox owner Charles Comiskey was so miserly. After the Knights lose their final game, a young fan approaches Roy and says, "Say it ain't true,"[3] just as one supposedly approached Shoeless Joe Jackson after the Sox lost the Series and begged him to "say it ain't so."

It's not clear that a young fan ever approached Jackson with those words; Jackson, for one, denied it ever happened. But it had become part of baseball mythology and Malamud could therefore use it to evoke images of corruption.

◊ ◊ ◊

The non-baseball mythology that Malamud drew on included a mix of sources, most prominently legends surrounding King Arthur. Roy plays for the "Knights." His name comes from the Norman word for king. His bat, which he calls "Wonderboy," came from a tree split by lightning and seems to have magical powers like those of Excalibur, Arthur's sword. His quest for the pennant is like that of Percival, the knight whose quest was for the Holy Grail, which in some accounts was Jesus's cup at the Last Supper and was endowed with magical powers. Pop Fisher is the Fisher King, who was the keeper of the Grail but whose power is ebbing and whose kingdom has become a wasteland. Memo is Morgan le Fay, a sometimes-evil enchantress who in some versions of the legend seduces knights. Iris, who takes a swim with Roy in Lake Michigan, is like the Lady in the Lake, who in some versions comes to Arthur's aid.

Pop Fisher's baseball field is as barren as the Fisher King's wasteland. "It's been a blasted dry season," he remarks. "The grass is worn scabby in the outfield and the infield is cracking."[4] But as soon as Roy gets his first hit, it starts raining and doesn't stop for three days. Roy ultimately fails but, Malamud hints, this is part of a cycle of death and renewal. Just as Roy replaced the Whammer and Bump, he is struck out by a young pitcher named Herman Youngberry.

Even readers unfamiliar with Arthurian legends will recognize some of Malamud's allusions to knights. Just a few examples: Harriet refers to Roy's confrontation with the Whammer as a "tourney."[5] A pitcher looks at Roy at bat and imagines him "in full armor, mounted on a black charger ... coming at him with a long lance as thick as a young tree."[6] At other times Roy is described as an "undeniable man of destiny"[7] and a "throwback to a time of true heroes."[8] In twentieth-century America, Malamud seems to be saying at the novel's end, a hero is destined to fail. (This is not the case in the 1984 movie version of *The Natural* in which Robert Redford, down to his last strike and bleeding from his old wound, hits a home run and wins the pennant.)

Looking beyond Arthur and his knights, critics have found in *The Natural* shards of plenty of other mythic traditions. Sitting on the bench after Memo has sapped him of his strength, Roy is like Homer's Achilles, the great warrior sulking in his tent. Memo's last name, Paris, was the name of the prince who eloped with Helen of Sparta and thus started the Trojan War in which Achilles was for the moment refusing to fight.

Also from the Greek (and Freudian) traditions, there are echoes of Oedipus. Roy unwittingly kills the scout Sam Simpson, who is like a father to him, and Whammer and Bump, though hardly father figures, are replaced by him. Watching Roy face the Whammer, Harriet compared him to "the first son ... ranged against the primitive papa."[9]

Some critics have argued Malamud also drew on Jewish mythology, which is not so surprising considering many of Malamud's later novels featured explicitly Jewish characters and themes. Harriet compared Roy facing the Whammer not only to a son facing his father but also to "David jawboning the Goliath-Whammer."[10]

Roy understands none of this. When Harriet asks him if he has read Homer, "he could only think of four bases and not a book....

4. The Natural *(Malamud)*

He found her lingo strange with all the college stuff and hoped she would stop it because he wanted to talk about baseball."[11]

What do all these allusions add up to? Despite Malamud's place in the canon, critics then and now have split on whether *The Natural* works. Norman Podhoretz, writing in *Commentary* the year after the book was published, argued that turning everything from baseball bats to men and women into symbols didn't make for a good story. "The habit of … multiplying allusions to the point where they begin to crowd out reality altogether," Podhoretz wrote, "is one of the more unfortunate legacies bequeathed by Joyce and Eliot to contemporary writers."[12] Jonathan Baumbach, writing in *The Kenyon Review* in 1963, agreed that "at his worst, Malamud has a predilection for manipulating his characters in order to accommodate the anti-novelistic demands of his moral allegory."[13] Alan Warren Friedman, writing in *Southern Review* in 1968, concluded that "the baseball formula is too frail to bear the weight of imposed meaning."[14]

But if Malamud's multiple allusions and symbols are sometimes confusing, they also provoke questions that some critics and readers found worth pondering: Does Roy's final strikeout make him a complete failure, or is it part of some cycle whereby he is replaced by a new and younger hero, just as he replaced the Whammer? Is Roy a hero in the classical sense? What does it mean to be a hero in twentieth-century America?

Earl R. Wasserman, whose 1965 essay in *Centennial Review* was one of the most thorough explications of the novel's mythic undertones, denied that Malamud's allegory was contrived; rather, Wasserman wrote, "he has rendered the lived events of the American game so as to compel it to reveal what it essentially is, the ritual whereby we express the psychological nature of American life and its moral predicament."[15] Peter Carino, writing in *NINE* in 2005, agreed with Wasserman: "Though critics have argued that baseball cannot carry the weight of Malamud's examination of myth in the modern world, the novel demonstrates that baseball—with its rich and magical history—is one of the few cultural institutions in America that most certainly can."[16]

Roger Angell, who along with Roger Kahn is generally

recognized as baseball's greatest writer of literary non-fiction, provided a balanced view. Writing in *The New Yorker* in 1989, Angell conceded the novel's "invisibly footnoted references ... felt scholar-strained or showoffy," but added that you nevertheless "hurried along to the next page."[17] (Angell was less forgiving of the movie version.)

◊ ◊ ◊

After *The Natural*, serious novelists did not hesitate to write about baseball.

In 1953, just months after *The Natural* was published, Mark Harris weighed in with *The Southpaw*. Harris took baseball and fiction very seriously, as he explained in a 1996 essay. "We were insisting we were creating literature," he wrote, referring to himself and Malamud, "just as earnestly as Ring Lardner, forty years earlier, was insisting he was NOT creating literature."[18] But Harris strenuously objected to Malamud's myth-laden approach, choosing instead to found what he called a "tradition of realism."[19]

The narrator of *The Southpaw* is Henry Wiggen, a rookie pitcher writing a book. "Why does not somebody write 1 decent book about baseball?" he asks a sportswriter, who tells him there have been dozens of good books. Answers Henry: "There has been only fairy tales."[20]

In reality, Harris was not so much setting a new course for baseball fiction as he was following in Lardner's footsteps. Like Lardner, Harris captured the language of a naïve and boastful rube and used it to great comic effect. Unlike Lardner's Keefe, though, Harris's Wiggen matures over the course of *The Southpaw* and three subsequent novels—*Bang the Drum Slowly* (1956), *A Ticket for a Seamstitch* (1957), and *It Looked Like For Ever* (1979).

While Harris rejected the mythological in baseball, others surely did not. In the 1968 novel, *The Universal Baseball Association, Inc. J. Henry Waugh, Prop.*, Robert Coover goes beyond imposing classic myths onto a baseball setting. Instead, he turns the entire history of the game into a mythology. The novel's first six chapters feature J. Henry Waugh, an accountant whose love of statistics had led him to create a Strat-O-Matic–like baseball game in which outcomes are determined by rolling dice. Unlike in Strat-O-Matic, where real players' records determine the probability of any given result, Henry creates his own players—along with their names and personalities as well as those of the game's managers, commissioners, reporters, and historians. Henry becomes obsessed with the game, gradually losing touch with the real world. He is especially excited by a rookie pitcher, Damon Rutherford, who has thrown a perfect game and fourteen consecutive perfect innings when he comes up to bat against Jock Casey. Henry rolls three die three times and all come up ones, sending him to his "Extraordinary Occurrences Chart"[21] (the game is infinitely more complicated than Strat-O-Matic). The result: Casey's pitch hits Rutherford, killing him. Bereft, Henry takes the unprecedented step of, rather than throwing the dice, carefully placing them down to arrange another extraordinary occurrence and his revenge: Casey is struck fatally by a line drive.

The final chapter takes place one hundred and one years after the deaths of Rutherford and Casey—or, more accurately, one hundred and one Universal Baseball Association seasons later. J. Henry Waugh does not appear anywhere in the chapter. The current players are the only reality, and the memory of the fatal beaning is kept alive by the annual rituals of "Damonsday."[22] By now the players can only speculate about the meaning of Rutherford's and Casey's deaths, and some even wonder whether they really happened. "Can't even be sure about the simple *facts*," says one. "Some ... argue that Rutherford and Casey never existed—nothing more than another of the ancient myths of the sun."[23]

Many critics have noted Coover's allusions to biblical stories. J.H. Waugh sound much like Jahweh, as the God of the Old Testament was known. Jock Casey's initials are the same as those of Jesus Christ. Indeed, the novel can be seen a joke based on Albert Einstein's famous words that "God does not play dice with the universe."[24] Coover's God did indeed play dice before apparently disappearing from the scene, but *The Universal Baseball Association*, though often quite funny, is a lot more than a joke. It raises serious questions about the nature of reality and religion, about whether there is a God, and if so whether he died or went crazy.

Philip Roth's baseball novel made a joke of pretty much all mythology, ancient and modern. *The Great American Novel*, published in 1973, wanders far and wide but has at its core the story of the Patriot League. Roth's conceit is that this was a third major league wiped from the pages of American history because it was infiltrated by communist agents. Most of the players have the names of heroes or gods of ancient civilizations. There's the sensational rookie pitcher Gil Gamesh; Gilgamesh was a hero of a Babylonian epic. There's the big first baseman John Baal; Baal was a god worshipped by the Canaanites. Baal's father was the infamous Spit Baal, who after the spitball was made illegal chose instead to urinate on the ball. There's the catcher Hot Ptah; Ptah was an Egyptian god. There's the one-eyed pitcher Seymour Clops, nicknamed, of course, Sy. There's left fielder Mike Rama; Rama's exploits are recounted in a Sanskrit epic. Mike Rama competed with Pete Reiser and Bump Bailey by being removed on a stretcher five times during his rookie season after crashing into the outfield wall. "Nothing anyone could say," Roth wrote, "was able to implant in Mike Rama a healthy respect for the immovable and the unyielding."[25]

Unlike Malamud's mythological allusions, Roth's didn't add up to a clear allegory. Rather his goal seemed to be to poke fun at anything Americans held sacred. Among his targets, as the book's title suggested, were canonical writers. The book's narrator is named Word Smith and the book's opening line is "Call me Smitty,"[26] clearly playing on the opening line of *Moby-Dick*. Roth describes Melville's novel as "a book about blubber."[27] *Huckleberry Finn* is "Kid stuff."[28]

The Great American Novel sometimes seems like nothing but a collection of jokes, sometimes very funny and sometimes, especially those about women and Blacks, offensive, at least to today's readers. But Roth had a serious purpose. Having grown up as a patriotic child during World War II and having been disillusioned by the Vietnam War, he was out to demythologize America's institutions and beliefs. Baseball, he later explained, provided "a means to dramatize the *struggle* between the benign national myth of itself that a great power prefers to perpetuate, and the relentlessly insidious, very nearly demonic reality ... that will not give an inch in behalf of that idealized mythology."[29]

Abner Doubleday, Roth's Word Smith asserts, did not invent the game of baseball. But the Cooperstown myth is "inconsequential" compared to "a rewriting of our history as heinous as any ordered by a tyrant dictator abroad." The Patriot League was "not merely wiped out of business, *but willfully erased from the national memory.*"[30] The Patriot League was, of course, Roth's invention, but the point he is making is that patriotic mythmakers have erased much of America's actual history from the record books.

Unlike Roth, W.P. Kinsella treated baseball—and the mythology surrounding it—as sacred. In the 1982 novel *Shoeless Joe*, Kinsella's narrator, a failing farmer named Ray Kinsella, hears a voice telling him, "If you build it, he will come."[31] He somehow understands this means that he should build a baseball field on his Iowa farm and that the person who will come is Joe Jackson, who had been exiled from baseball because of his role in the 1919 World Series. A youthful Jackson does indeed show up to play on the field along with the other members of the Black Sox, also restored to their primes. Ray Kinsella's quest takes him to New Hampshire where he kidnaps the reclusive writer J.D. Salinger. The two then head to Minnesota where they find the ghost of Moonlight Graham, a player who appeared in only one major league game but never got to bat. Back in Iowa, the now-youthful Graham gets to realize his dream by playing with the Sox. Ray Kinsella also gets to realize his dream when he gets to talk to his estranged and dead father, who joins the Sox on the field as a catcher. Other believers, too, are drawn to the magical field, and the price of admission saves the farm from foreclosure.

Like Roth, Kinsella can't be tied down to a specific allegory or mythology. Kinsella is certainly not an orthodox Christian; the voice that tells him to build his ballpark sounds not like God or Jesus but like a "ballpark announcer."[32] What he believes in is baseball. "We're not just ordinary people, we're a congregation," Ray Kinsella tells Salinger while they're watching a game at Fenway Park. "Baseball is a ceremony, a ritual, as surely as sacrificing a goat beneath a full moon is a ritual."[33] Later he tells Salinger and Graham: "A ballpark at night is more like a church than a church."[34]

Shoeless Joe is unabashedly sentimental and nostalgic, not just about baseball but about the American past. "America has been erased like a blackboard, only to be rebuilt and then erased again," says the novel's Salinger, who is no longer Ray's hostage and whose faith in America, or at least baseball, has been restored. "But baseball has marked time while America has rolled by like a procession of steamrollers.... It is a living part of history, like calico dresses, stone crockery, and threshing crews eating at outdoor tables. It continually reminds us of what once was."[35]

Field of Dreams, the 1989 movie based on *Shoeless Joe*, was even more sentimental. "It's been likened to a Capra movie or a Disney-world attraction," wrote Angell, "but for me it was a Sara Lee chocolate layer cake, with icing so thick I could feel it dripping onto my shoes." Angell also objected to the way the movie versions of *Shoeless Joe* and *The Natural* insisted on making baseball more than a game: "I like baseball, the game and the games, but I can't always understand why it's so hard to look at the pastime with a clear gaze. We seem to want to go on sweetening it up, frosting the flakes, because we want it to say things about ourselves that probably aren't true."[36] Fair enough. But Angell ought also to have realized that both *Shoeless Joe* and *Field of Dreams* captured a true fan's love of the game.

Whatever the merits of *Shoeless Joe*, Kinsella's brand of baseball magic can be found in plenty of later novels. To mention just a few: Darryl Brock's 1989 *If I Never Get Back,* whose protagonist gets off an Amtrak train and ends up riding the rails with the 1869 Cincinnati Red Stockings; Michael Chabon's 2002 *Summerland*, where small beings known as ferishers ensure perfect weather on the local Little League field; and George Plimpton's 2004 *The Curious Case of Sidd Finch* about a Buddhist pitcher with a 168-mph fastball. Kinsella himself followed up *Shoeless Joe* with the 1986 *The Iowa Baseball Confederacy*, a mix of Indian folklore, biblical allusions, and time travel.

More fundamentally, whatever the merits of *The Natural*, its influence was undeniable. After Malamud, no one could ever be surprised by the suggestion that baseball was about more than baseball. No one could be surprised by a comparison between Odysseus and a base runner heading home, or between a green field and the Garden of Eden. When sportswriter Thomas Boswell titled his 1982 book *How Life Imitates the World Series* and his 1984 book *Why Time Begins on Opening Day*, fans nodded in agreement.

"I am a ... creature ... tied to more primitive patterns and cycles," wrote A. Bartlett Giamatti in 1977, when he was still a scholar of comparative literature and not yet the commissioner of baseball. "I need to think that something lasts forever, and it might as well be that state of being that is a game; it might as well be that, in a green field, in the sun."[37]

5

Ball Four:
My Life and Hard Times
Throwing the Knuckleball
in the Big Leagues

by JIM BOUTON,
edited by LEONARD SHECTER

New York: World Publishing Co., 1970

"There was a time, not too long ago," Jim Bouton wrote in 1980, ten years after the publication of his book about his season pitching for the Seattle Pilots and Houston Astros, "when school kids read *Ball Four* at night under the covers with a flashlight because their parents wouldn't allow it in the house."[1]

I turned fourteen in 1970, just about the right age to hide a book under the covers, and *Ball Four* did indeed have a lot of talk about sex. The editor's foreword warned that the book should be rated X. So I—and millions of others—turned the pages to learn about, for example, beaver-shooting.

"A beaver-shooter," Bouton explained, "is at bottom a Peeping Tom. It can be anything from peering over the top of the dugout to look up dresses to hanging from the fire escape on the twentieth floor of some hotel to look into a window."[2]

We also learned how players covered more than bases for each other. Pitcher Gary Bell's wife once called him on the road at 4:30 a.m. His roommate answered the phone and, without hesitation or shame, said that Gary was out playing golf.

5. Ball Four *(Bouton)*

In our post-me-too era, much of Bouton's talk about sex makes one cringe. At the time, however, the baseball establishment was outraged not by the way players treated women but by the way Bouton violated what many referred to as the sanctity of the locker room. Commissioner Bowie Kuhn said Bouton had done the game "a grave disservice."[3]

Yet *Ball Four* wasn't really titillating. For a book worth hiding under the covers, I would have been better off opening either of two books that were at that moment outselling Bouton's: David Reuben's *Everything You Always Wanted to Know About Sex* (*But Were Afraid to Ask)* or Terry Garrity's *The Sensuous Woman*. As Bouton put it: "I spent seventeen weeks under *The Sensuous Woman* on the *Times* best-seller list."[4]

What made *Ball Four* irresistible was not the sex but the unflinching honesty about life in the big leagues. Bouton talked about sex, yes, but also about how general managers negotiated salaries and how players took "greenies" (amphetamines). He portrayed general managers as stingy and manipulative, coaches as officious and petty, and players as often immature, insecure, narrow-minded, and generally unheroic. *Ball Four* was a countercultural strike against the baseball establishment. It was, the Boston *Globe* review proclaimed, "a document for these days of dedication to the changing of the old order [and] an authentic revolutionary manifesto."[5]

It was baseball's Woodstock.

◊ ◊ ◊

It was not unprecedented. Ring Lardner, as we have seen, took baseball icons down many a peg. But *You Know Me Al* was fiction and satire. Lawrence Ritter captured the actual words of players in his 1966 oral history classic, *The Glory of Their Times*. But Ritter and his subjects were more interested in telling good stories about the good old days than in revealing secrets of the locker room.

More similar to Bouton than Lardner or Ritter was Jim Brosnan. Like Bouton, Brosnan was a pitcher who kept notes in the bullpen and elsewhere and turned them into diaries of a season. Like Bouton, Brosnan chronicled unhelpful managers, bullpen banter, and players drinking. Brosnan's *The Long Season* was published in 1960 and his *Pennant Race* in 1962. Leonard Shecter, who would later edit *Ball Four*, called *The Long Season* "probably the best look ever at baseball through a mature mind."[6]

The Long Season was promoted as baseball's first tell-all but it was really, as baseball historian and Bouton biographer Mitchell Nathanson put it, a "tell-some."[7] Brosnan implied players had sex on the road, but he didn't raise the topic often, and when he did, he preserved some level of deniability. Of the St. Louis Cardinals' trip to Japan in 1959, he wrote: "Early morning sight-seeing—like one a.m. early morning—was not an uncommon venture. Invariably the young Japanese guides that worked at night were able to find a secluded and peaceful—almost discreet, you would say—hotel to visit."[8]

Like Brosnan's books, Jerry Kramer's 1968 *Instant Relay* was an insider's account of a team's season, in Kramer's case that of the Green Bay Packers for whom he was an offensive lineman. Kramer was more open than most athletes about contracts and drugs, but his book was ultimately a celebration of his team and especially his coach, Vince Lombardi. *Instant Replay* most directly influenced *Ball Four* in that both were published by the Cleveland-based World Publishing Company. The football book sold more than two million copies, prompting the company to look for a baseball equivalent.

In addition to Brosnan and Kramer, Bouton was following in the footsteps of a number of young sportswriters who in the 1960s offered candid portraits of players and managers. These writers saw themselves as in the vanguard of the "New Journalism," whose practitioners immersed themselves in their subjects and pushed the traditional boundaries of nonfiction. The New Journalists included Gay Talese, Joan Didion, Tom Wolfe, and sportswriters Robert Lipsyte, Larry Merchant, George Vecsey, and Shecter. One way these sportswriters found their stories was by skipping the predictably bland interviews with stars like Mickey Mantle and Whitey Ford and instead talking to younger and more outspoken players. On the New York Yankees these included infielder Phil Linz, first baseman Joe Pepitone, and especially Bouton, who had been a Yankee before they shipped him off to Seattle. Bouton was happy to pontificate on anything from pitching to politics.

This did not go over well with everyone. Well before *Ball Four*, more conservative players and coaches—and baseball was very much a bastion of conservatism—considered Bouton a blowhard, a hippie, or even, as Yankee pitching coach Jim Turner suggested, a communist. Conservative writers jumped on the anti–Bouton bandwagon. In August 1965, with Bouton in the midst of a season that would end with a won-loss record of 4–15, Dick Young quoted him in *The Sporting News* as saying that his two loves were pitching and painting, and that when he was doing badly at one, the other would cheer him up. "If that was the case," Young wrote, "he must be painting Mona Lisas this season."[9]

Bouton's prospects, and those of his book, did not appear bright heading into the 1969 season. He was no longer the hard-throwing Yankee who had won twenty-one games in 1963 and two games in the 1964 World Series. His fastball was gone and he was relying on an inconsistent knuckleball. In the three seasons following his dismal 4–15 record in 1965, he had won just five games. The Yankees had given up on him and his only hope of getting back to the major leagues was with the Seattle Pilots, an expansion team. World Publishing had offered a $10,000 advance to be split between Bouton and Shecter, hardly a sign they expected their book to be a bestseller. World had higher expectations for another baseball diary in the works from Bill Freehan, the catcher of the Detroit Tigers, who had just won the World Series.

As it turned out, Bouton's teammates on the Pilots—all, like Bouton, rejects from more promising rosters—turned out to be ideal subjects. Throughout the season, Bouton furiously took notes about what the players and coaches said. In the evenings, he recorded the day's events and thoughts on a tape recorder along with recollections of his days with the Yankees. The transcripts of these recordings, edited by Bouton and Shecter, became *Ball Four*.

The revelations about his Yankee days were as sensational as those about the Pilots and Astros. Mickey Mantle, Bouton recalled, had hit a home run while hung over. Pitcher Whitey Ford used his wedding ring to scuff up a ball, which he could then make dive or jump.

Unlike Brosnan, Bouton did not rely on literary flourishes. Readers felt they were hearing Bouton and his teammates and coaches talking. And what they had to say was stupid and sexist and yet boyishly innocent and often very funny. A typical conversation went like this:

> "Gee, your wife was great last night."
> "Oh, she wasn't all that great."
> "You should have been there earlier. She was terrific."[10]

The cast of characters included first baseman Greg Goosen, who could imitate what Casey Stengel once said about him: "We got a kid here named Goosen, twenty years old, and in ten years he's got a chance to be thirty."[11] There was first baseman Mike Hegan; when the team's publicity department sent out a form that asked what's the most difficult thing about playing major league baseball, his answer was "explaining to your wife why *she* needs a penicillin shot for *your* kidney infection."[12] There was third baseman Mike Pagliarulo who after scoring a run ran from home plate and slid into the dugout. There was pitcher Mike Marshall, an intellectual who was therefore, like Bouton, a misfit. Marshall and Bouton regularly played chess, which alone was enough to rouse suspicions among their teammates.

The Pilots' pitching coach, Sal Maglie, was Bouton's nemesis. Maglie discouraged Bouton from relying on the knuckleball, by this time his only effective pitch. His advice was useless and often contradictory. Pilot first baseman Don Minchner told Bouton he liked sitting next to Maglie in the dugout just so he could listen to the nonsense:

> "If a guy hits a fastball when Marshall is out there," Minch said, "Sal says, 'Son of a bitch, he's throwing that fastball too much.' In the very next inning a guy will get a hit on a curve ball and Sal says, 'Son of a bitch, why doesn't he go to his fastball more?"[13]

The Pilots' manager was Joe Schultz, whose advice to the troops included: "Men, you got to remember to touch all the bases,"[14] "Put your hat on,"[15] "Stomp on 'em."[16] "Okay men, up and at 'em. Get that old Budweiser."[17] Most often, though, Schultz would stick to his favorite word, "shitfuck." His second favorite was "fuckshit."

And then, of course, there was Bouton himself, who loved being part of this team while also setting himself apart from his teammates and feeling lonely as a result. The book, Nathanson wrote, was "about high jinks and pep pills and booze and broads but, lurking underneath all of that ... about the one thing no sports book had ever touched before—the third rail of men's feelings."[18]

At the end of August Bouton was traded from the Pilots to the Astros. He finished the season with two wins, three losses, two saves, and an earned run average of 3.81. This was respectable but by no means spectacular, and Bouton recognized that his best years were behind him. But he intended to hang on as long as possible. As he explained in his book's famous final line: "You see, you spend a good piece of your life gripping a baseball and in the end it turns out that it was the other way around."[19]

◊ ◊ ◊

A few months before the book was published, excerpts appeared in *Look* magazine and critics pounced. The attacks continued after the book came out.

Among those offended by the book was Roger Kahn, whose lyrical and nostalgic ode to baseball, *The Boys of Summer*, would itself soon transform the way we looked at the game. Kahn did not believe baseball players were above criticism, but he thought *Ball Four* was an unseemly attack on their dignity and an unfair invasion of their privacy. Kahn also suggested Shecter and not Bouton was the real author. This was untrue; Shecter had provided invaluable guidance and editing but he was not a ghostwriter.

By far the loudest and most persistent critic was Young, a reporter and columnist for the *New York Daily News* and *The Sporting News*. Week after week, Young denounced Bouton for having betrayed the trust of his teammates. If Mantle drank, Young insisted, it was only to dull the pain of his injuries. Bouton was a "social leper."[20]

The Lineup

The reporters who had embraced Bouton as a source when he was a Yankee rose to his defense. Robert Lipsyte wrote in the *New York Times* that Bouton's anecdotes and insights were "enlightening, hilarious, and most important, unavailable elsewhere," and that "they breathe new life into a game choked by pontificating statisticians, image-conscious officials and scared ballplayers."[21]

Literary figures also rallied round. Writing in the *New York Times'* Sunday book review, Rex Lardner, Ring Lardner's nephew, called *Ball Four* "the funniest, frankest book yet about the species *ballplayer satyriaticus* and his numerous bosses."[22] In *The New Yorker*, Roger Angell wrote that the book offered "a rare view of a highly complex public profession seen from the innermost inside along with an even more rewarding inside view of an ironic and courageous mind."[23]

To a considerable extent, the split over *Ball Four* mirrored the nation's ideological split during the sixties, with conservative writers attacking Bouton and liberals defending him. The generally liberal *Sport* magazine placed *Ball Four* in the context of the changing times in which "there is a new morality in the land—in books, movies and public life."[24]

Conservatives were so angry about the book that many attacked it without reading it, or at least without reading it carefully. In the *Detroit Free Press*, Joe Falls used as an example of Bouton's betrayal of his teammates the story about how Gary Bell's wife, Nan, called his hotel room at 4 a.m. and was told by his roommate that he was out playing golf. Bouton may have embarrassed some players but Bell wasn't one of them. As Bouton told the story in *Ball Four*, he made clear that he had heard it from Nan Bell, and that she had been laughing when she told it to him.

Liberals, too, often had a knee-jerk response to the book. Bouton later reported an encounter with Young in which both revealed, inadvertently, their biases. "You know who's listening to you?" Bouton said to Young. "The hard-hat types, that's who, the dum-dums...."[25] Responded Young: "I happen to know some very nice hard-hats."[26]

Major league players tended to agree with Young. Many had already looked askance at Bouton as some sort of rabble-rousing hippie and the book confirmed their suspicions. The season after the book was published, Bouton was still pitching for the Astros, and when he entered one visiting locker room, he found a burned copy of the book. Pitching against the Cincinnati Reds, Bouton heard Pete Rose yell from the dugout, "Fuck you, Shakespeare."[27] Many of Bouton's teammates from the Pilots, Astros, and Yankees denounced the book, though most admitted they hadn't read it. Mantle's response was perhaps more cutting: Asked repeatedly what he thought about the author, he often responded, "Jim who?"[28]

Owners generally hated the book more than players. They were less disturbed by revelations from the locker room than by revelations about their negotiating techniques. *Ball Four* revealed to players and public alike how stingy owners were, and how the reserve clause that bound players to one team left players no choices other than to accept a team's offer or to walk away from the game. No wonder, then, that in the 1975 arbitration hearing in which Dodger pitcher Andy Messersmith and Expo pitcher Dave McNally challenged the reserve clause, *Ball Four* was introduced as evidence. Messersmith and McNally won their hearing, which ultimately led to players gaining some free agency. Bouton alone was not responsible, of course. Messersmith and McNally deserved some of the credit as did players' union director Marvin Miller and outfielder Curt Flood, who after the 1969 season took his challenge of the reserve clause to the Supreme Court. But *Ball Four* certainly went a long way toward undermining the owners' image as benevolent stewards of the game.

The Astros' management was so irate that they forbade the team's radio announcers from mentioning the name of the book. "One wonders," columnist Stan Isaacs wrote in *Newsday*, "what the announcers will do when Bouton goes 3–2 on a batter and then throws a bad pitch. Will they refuse to say 'Ball Four'?"[29]

The most publicized criticism of *Ball Four* came from Bowie Kuhn, the commissioner of baseball. Kuhn summoned Bouton to his office and told him, Bouton later recalled, that all he had to do was sign a statement saying the book was a bunch of lies and that his editor was to blame. "When I politely told the Commissioner what he could do with his statement" Bouton said, "he turned a color which went very nicely with the wood paneling."[30]

The attacks of the baseball establishment generated tremendous publicity and turned Bouton into an anti-establishment hero. The book went on to sell more than five million copies. "If Bowie Kuhn and his public relations assistant, Joe Reichler, had entered into a conspiracy to sell copies of the book, they would have done nothing different,"[31] Bouton later wrote.

What Kuhn and other critics failed to understand was that *Ball Four* was a service and not a disservice to baseball. At a time when baseball was losing fans to football and basketball, *Ball Four* made baseball cool again. Many fans, especially younger ones, were rejecting traditional idols in everything from the military to music, and they weren't buying into the belief that all baseball players were all-American icons and that the game they played was sacred. To them, Bouton's more realistic portrayals were much more appealing. Even Mickey Mantle, despite the outrage over Bouton's stories about Mantle's drinking and his brushing off autograph-seeking kids, was if anything more beloved after the book. He may have drunk and he may have sometimes brushed off fans, but Mantle ultimately came across as funny and charming, a hero whose flaws made him all the more interesting.

The Seattle Pilots lasted only for one season. They finished in last place and before the 1970 season began the team left Seattle and became the Milwaukee Brewers. In retrospect, that further cemented the Pilots' reputation as the antithesis of the corporate, pinstriped Yankees. "The way I like to think about the Pilots," reminisced Steve Hovley, an outfielder who spent part of the 1969 season in Seattle, "it's like an upside-down postage stamp. The most important one is the one they screwed up."[32]

"If you publish *Ball Four* in 1950 or 1960," said sportswriter Jeremy Schaap, "it would have been more revolutionary, but it probably couldn't have gotten published, and even if it had, it would have turned people off rather than fascinate them."[33] Or as Nathanson wrote: "It fitted the zeitgeist as satisfyingly as the last piece of a puzzle."[34]

◊ ◊ ◊

5. Ball Four *(Bouton)*

After *Ball Four*, sports books were not the same. As a book editor in the 1980s, I would meet with players and the questions my colleagues and I asked generally came down to this: What do you have to say that's shocking (and likely to make headlines)? As Bouton wrote in 1980, "the books that have come after mine make *Ball Four*, as an expose, read like *The Bobbsey Twins at the Seashore*."[35]

Sensational books were not necessarily good books, and there were many bad ones.

One of the good ones was *The Way It Is* by Curt Flood with Richard Carter, which came out the year after *Ball Four*. Flood's challenge to the reserve clause ultimately changed baseball more than anything Bouton did, but Flood's book made much less of an impact than Bouton's. Why did Bouton's book become a sensation and Flood's not? It wasn't because of sex: Flood was if anything more open about players' sexual behavior. The difference may have come down to race: Bouton noted racism in baseball but Flood focused on it. Indeed, it was clear that Flood's experiences with racism, in and out of baseball, made him more sensitive to the injustice of the reserve clause. Flood described looking through his mail: "A child begging an autographed picture. An old ball player wishing me luck. And the third ... began with 'Dear Nigger.'"[36] Flood could be witty but what most readers felt was his anger, which made his book a lot less fun to read than Bouton's.

In 1973 came Maury Allen's *Bo: Pitching and Wooing*, written with "the uncensored cooperation of Bo Belinsky."[37] If Bouton's talk about sex was sometimes cringe-worthy, Belinsky's was downright creepy. Belinsky won only 28 games in his career, but one of them was a no-hitter for the Los Angeles Angels. He took full advantage of that moment of fame. In the era when *Playboy*'s circulation peaked, Belinsky was baseball's most famous playboy. He proudly provided a "scouting report"[38] for women he'd dated, including actresses Ann-Margret and Tina Louise (who starred in *Gilligan's Island*).

Bouton's one-time Yankee teammate, first baseman Joe Pepitone, weighed in with *Joe, You Coulda Made Us Proud*, written with Barry Stainback, in 1975. Pepitone's talk about sex was even more explicit than Belinsky's, and the book was appropriately published by Playboy Press. Pepitone did sometimes regret his lifestyle, however, for example when his wife found slips of paper with the names and phone numbers of one hundred fifty women he had slept with, including her closest friends.

One of the best of the post–*Ball Four* insider accounts was Yankee pitcher Sparky Lyle's *The Bronx Zoo*, coauthored by Peter Golenbock and published in 1979. Lyle and Golenbock had a lot going for them. The season they chronicled ended with a Yankee championship and included plenty of controversy. There were feuds between manager Billy Martin and outfielder Reggie Jackson, and between owner George Steinbrenner and almost everyone on the team. There was Lyle's resentment over free agent pitcher Goose Gossage taking his job as the team's closer. Like Bouton, Lyle was candid about what went on in the clubhouse. That included not just the anger and pettiness but also the silliness. Lyle took great pride in his practical jokes, which included putting his arm and leg in a cast for no reason other than to freak out his manager. His favorite prank was to sit naked on teammates' birthday cakes. Pitching coach Jim Turner, who loved cake, would grab a knife and try to snag a piece before Lyle got to it. "Poor Jim," Lyle wrote, "he never beat me to the cake."[39]

Even Ford and Mantle, who Bouton had supposedly blasphemed, got into the tell-all game. In their 1977 book, *Whitey and Mickey: An Autobiography of the Yankee Years*, coauthored by Joseph Durso, Ford described how he mixed turpentine, baby oil, and resin into a "magic elixir"[40] that he'd ooze onto his hands and fingers between innings. Ford kept the mixture in an empty deodorant container, which wouldn't have been a problem had catcher Yogi Berra not helped himself to what he thought was Ford's deodorant. Berra ended up with his arms stuck together, and the team's trainer had to apply alcohol to un-stick him. As for Mantle, he described how the night before an All-Star game he and Dodger pitcher Don Drysdale got drunk and decided they were in no state to face each other the next day. So they made a deal: Drysdale would throw everything outside to avoid hitting Mantle, and Mantle wouldn't swing at any of the pitches.

By the end of the seventies, the tell-all had become so common

5. Ball Four *(Bouton)*

that *Saturday Night Live* parodied the genre by having Chico Escuela, a made-up ex-Met played by comedian Garrett Morris, talk about his equally made-up book, *Bad Stuff 'Bout the Mets.* Among the scandals revealed in the book were that pitcher Tom Seaver always took up two parking spaces and that first baseman Ed Kranepool borrowed Chico Escuela's soap and never returned it.

◊ ◊ ◊

It wasn't just sports books that changed. Sports reporting would never be the same.

Bouton himself became a television sportscaster, landing a job at ABC's *Eyewitness News* in New York. Again he pushed back the boundaries of what could be said, this time on air instead of in print.

Bouton refused to stick to the results of games, which was most of what sportscasters, especially ex-jocks, did. Rather than just covering the Yankees or Mets, Bouton instead chose to spend time on offbeat sports like the rodeo or women's roller derby. He made fun of the way coaches always said the same things when their teams lost. When he did go down to Florida to cover the Yankees during spring training, no one would talk to him. So Bouton disguised himself with a wig and mustache and went as a pitching prospect. The plan fell apart when someone asked him what year he was born. Bouton knew he was supposed to be twenty-one, but he hadn't memorized the year of his birth: "Not being able to subtract quickly under pressure I blurted out the first date that came to my mind and seemed reasonable. 1961. This indicated I was twelve years old."[41]

None of this went over well with traditional sportscasters. Sal Marchiano, a fellow WABC sportscaster, thought Bouton didn't take sports seriously enough. "I give him credit for trying to be different," Marchiano said. "But he found reportage of the night's events—scores—to be mundane to him. He was more interested in promoting himself."[42]

If Bouton's timing was just right for *Ball Four*, he was a bit ahead of his time for sportscasting. By the 1990s, ESPN and its imitators embraced an irreverent attitude toward sports. But in 1973 WABC decided not to renew Bouton's contract.

After ABC, Bouton tried sitcoms. CBS bought the rights to *Ball Four*, but they mostly ignored Bouton's suggestions and entirely missed the spirit of the book. Bouton had in mind a locker-room version of *M*A*S*H*. Instead, he wrote, "it turned out more like *Gilligan's Island* in baseball suits.... We were first in the American League and last in the hearts of our countrymen, according to the Nielsen ratings."[43]

CBS aired the show in 1976 and cancelled it after five episodes. Bouton returned to sportscasting, this time for WCBS in New York.

Throughout his television career, however, he remained in baseball's grip. Indeed, he continued to dream that his knuckleball could get him back into the game. In 1977, he joined the Portland Mavericks, finishing with a 5–1 record, albeit in a low minor league. In 1978 Bouton convinced Atlanta Braves owner Ted Turner to give him a shot, and the thirty-nine-year-old pitcher was back in the big leagues. He wound up with a 1–3 record and a 4.97 ERA.

Bouton's stint in Portland turned out to be very lucrative. He and Maverick teammate Rob Nelson went into business together to sell shredded chewing gum manufactured to look like the tobacco that players chewed. Big League Chew, now owned by the Wrigley Company, has sold about eight hundred million pouches. Bouton's entrepreneurial drive also manifested itself when he and baseball historian John Thorn founded the Vintage Base Ball Federation, through which teams played games as they would have been played in the nineteenth century. Tournaments were held in Massachusetts in 2007 and 2008.

In 2016 I was working as an editor and writer for Colonial Williamsburg, which operated the restored eighteenth-century capital of Virginia, and I suggested it might be appropriate to revive the Vintage Base Ball tournaments in Williamsburg. Thus could we combine Colonial Williamsburg's "living history" of the eighteenth century with Bouton's and Thorn's of the nineteenth century. Thorn helped me write a story for Colonial Williamsburg's magazine about early forms of baseball played in and around Williamsburg. The case for Williamsburg as baseball's Eden was, alas, as dubious as the case for

5. Ball Four *(Bouton)*

Cooperstown, and nothing came of my suggestion that vintage baseball be revived in Williamsburg.

While pursuing his various interests, Bouton continued to write. In 1971 came *I'm Glad You Didn't Take It Personally*, in which he told about his final half-season in Houston, the reactions to *Ball Four*, and his introduction to sportscasting. The book's title came from a conversation between Bouton and Dick Young that took place in the visitors' clubhouse at Shea Stadium the day after Young had written that Bouton was a social leper. Here's Bouton's description:

> "Hi Jim," Dick Young said.
> "Hi Dick," I said. "I didn't know you were talking to social lepers these days."....
> "Well," he said, "*I'm glad you didn't take it personally.*" I think the italics are mine.[44]

In 1973 came "*I Managed Good, But Boy Did They Play Bad*," a collection edited by Bouton and sportswriter Neil Offen. In 1994 there was *Strike Zone*, a novel by Bouton and Eliot Asinof, who had gained fame, deservedly, for *Eight Men Out*, his book on the 1919 Black Sox. Asinof and Bouton alternated chapters with Bouton writing in the voice of a career minor leaguer and Asinof in the voice of an umpire forced into retirement. In 2003 there was *Foul Ball*, in which Bouton recounted his efforts to save one of the oldest ballparks in America, Wahconah Park in Pittsfield, Massachusetts. Bouton also wrote updates to *Ball Four*. *Ball Five* appeared ten years after the original, *Ball Six* twenty, and *Ball Seven* thirty. None of Bouton's later work generated the attention or sales of *Ball Four*, but all showcased his iconoclasm, his drive, and his wit. Bouton died in 2019.

Well before then, the passions that had surrounded the publication of *Ball Four* had faded. In 1998, they were far enough in the past for the Yankees to invite Bouton back for Old-Timers' Day. When his turn came, Bouton headed to the mound. The first pitch he threw was a ball. Over the public address system the play-by-play announcer intoned: "Ball Four!"[45]

6

The Boys of Summer

by ROGER KAHN

New York: Harper & Row, 1972

The façade of Citi Field, where the New York Mets have played since 2009, was designed to evoke memories of Ebbets Field, where the Brooklyn Dodgers played until they moved to Los Angeles in 1958. Citi Field further evoked the Dodgers by naming its rotunda after Jackie Robinson. The stadium was clearly a repudiation of the Mets' previous home, Shea Stadium, which was one of what architectural historian Paul Goldberger called the "concrete doughnuts"[1] built in the 1960s and 1970s. Citi Field did not, of course, bring the Dodgers back from Los Angeles, nor did it entangle itself in the streets of Brooklyn as Ebbets Field once had. Citi Field sits amidst parking lots in Queens, right next to the site of Shea Stadium, and the lots are clearly meant to accommodate suburban fans.

But the same nostalgia that led Citi Field's architects to copy elements of Ebbets Field has drawn people back from the suburbs to Brooklyn in search of the kinds of neighborhoods their parents and grandparents abandoned for Long Island and Westchester and New Jersey. That nostalgia was memorably evoked by *The Boys of Summer*, Roger Kahn's 1972 ode to the Dodgers and the Brooklyn of his youth. In the first part of the book, Kahn reminisces about growing up in Brooklyn and then covering the Dodgers as a young reporter for the *New York Herald Tribune*. In the second part, Kahn visits the Dodgers more than a decade after they'd retired. Both parts lament what's been lost, as Kahn makes clear right from the book's epigraph, which begins with the line from a Dylan Thomas poem: "I see the boys of summer in their ruin."[2] As Kahn drives away from New York to visit the former pitcher Clem Labine in Rhode Island, he muses about its decline: "When last Labine snapped curves at Ebbets Field, the city was a cleaner, lighter place."[3]

It would soon be, again, a cleaner place. The gentrification of Brooklyn and other cities in the late twentieth and early twenty-first centuries cannot, of course, be attributed solely to Kahn's nostalgia. There were many reasons for Brooklyn's decline and many reasons for its renaissance. Indeed, there were other books—notably Jane Jacobs' 1961 *The Death and Life of Great American Cities*—that prompted many to reconsider what they had sacrificed for the comforts of suburbia. But no book could match the eloquence and influence of *The Boys of Summer.*

The Brooklyn of Kahn's memory—and of the memory of millions of others who grew up there before and after World War II—was defined to a large extent as being *not* Manhattan. Brooklyn had once been a city in its own right but in 1898 it became a borough of New York City, and to much of the world New York meant Manhattan. From Brooklyn you could look across the East River to the world's most famous skyline; in Brooklyn the closest thing to a skyscraper was the 512-foot Williamsburg Savings Bank building. To much of the world, Brooklynites were a comedian's joke, people whose funny accent revealed their low class. Brooklynites had an inferiority complex; when they talked about going to Manhattan, they described it as going to the city.

The Dodgers' woes added to their sense that Brooklyn wasn't in the same league as Manhattan. In the late 1920s the team was consistently and often embarrassingly bad. They were best known for having once managed to have three men on third base at the same time, thus turning what might have been a triple into a triple play. In the 1940s the team was consistently excellent yet still kept coming up short. With such stars as Jackie Robinson, Duke Snider, Roy Campanella, Pee Wee Reese, Gil Hodges, Don Newcombe, Carl Erskine, and Preacher Roe, the Dodgers won six pennants between 1947 and 1956, but they lost all but one World Series to that symbol of New York's superiority and arrogance, the Yankees. Not to mention the heartbreak of losing the 1941 Series after a third strike got past catcher Mickey Owen, or of blowing a thirteen and a half game lead in 1951 and then losing the resulting playoff when New York Giant outfielder Bobby Thomson hit his "shot heard round the world."

In his 1993 memoir *My Life as a Fan*, novelist and essayist Wilfred Sheed compared his love for the Dodgers with a marriage in which the "'better or worse' clause would be invoked early and often."[4] The borough's residents were left to console themselves by saying, again and again, "Wait til next year."

But if Brooklynites accepted that their team was an also-ran and their borough was a backwater, they were nonetheless proud of both. They were proud of being immigrants striving to make it in America, proud of their neighborhoods where people looked after each other, proud of their team. They may have called the team "da bums" and the stereotypical Dodger fan, as drawn by cartoonist Willard Mullin, was also a bum, but the team and the fans embraced their image as underdogs. These were, as Kahn put it, "people who knew defeat and rose to heroism."[5]

Talk-show host Larry King was typically chauvinistic when he titled his 1992 memoir "When You're from Brooklyn, Everything Else is Tokyo." Dodger pitcher Preacher Roe was equally assertive. "I know one of these days the good Lord is going to come calling," Roe said to Kahn, "and when that happens I certainly hope he sees fit to send me up to heaven. But heaven will really have to be something to be better than what we had long ago in Brooklyn."[6]

Brooklyn's heart was Ebbets Field. It held only 32,000, far fewer than the Yankees' grand stadium, but that meant all fans were closer to the field and their gatherings more intimate. Fans talked to each other, whether they knew each other or not, and they recognized such eccentric stalwarts as Hilda Chester, who would clang her cowbells to annoy Dodger opponents, and the "Sym-Phony," the self-appointed team band whose members, when they disagreed with an umpire's call, would play "Three Blind Mice."

"No one, at least no one sober, ever compared Ebbets Field to the

Acropolis," Kahn wrote in his 2006 memoir *Into My Own*. "Yet to my father and me (and to Pee Wee Reese and Jackie Robinson) gray, sooty, dun-colored, undersized Ebbets Field was a shrine."[7] Fans who could not attend games in person could hear broadcasts through the windows of pretty much any store in Brooklyn they happened to be passing. "You could walk ten blocks," wrote journalist David Krell, "and not miss a pitch."[8]

Some of those Brooklyn blocks included the homes of Dodger players. In an era before players were millionaires, they lived alongside their fans. For his 1984 oral history of the team, *Bums*, Peter Golenbock interviewed many such fans.

"We would be playing stickball," recalled one neighbor of Dodger centerfielder Duke Snider. "It was like he was one of the boys in the neighborhood.... He could poke! Three sewers easy!"[9]

All this is what made the departure of the Dodgers to Los Angeles such a trauma for so many Brooklynites. "It's no laughing matter," sportswriter Dick Young warned in August 1957. "Yank this ballclub out of Brooklyn where the people have been living and dying with it for three generations, and you tamper seriously with the fabric of their lives."[10]

Historians have generally agreed. The team, Neil Sullivan wrote, was "a tangible symbol of the community and its values. In a changing world, they were one of the few means for getting one's bearings."[11] Wrote Carl Prince: "The erosion of community in Brooklyn cannot fully be laid at the door of the Dodgers, for that erosion was part of a larger malaise in most American cities. But the Dodgers' departure contributed."[12]

Decades later, Dodger fans recalled for Golenbock their sense of betrayal. Said one: "Maybe Brooklyn was a minor borough compared to Manhattan, but Brooklyn had the Dodgers.... With the Dodgers you could swagger ... and when the Dodgers left, the feeling died."[13] And another: "That woke me up to the reality of life, waking up to discover there is no Santa Claus in December, no Dodgers come the spring."[14]

◊ ◊ ◊

For many Brooklynites and former Brooklynites, nostalgia for their team and their borough melded with a more general nostalgia for their youth. After the last game at Ebbets Field, Sheed wrote, "no one ... had dared to say 'Wait till next year'—it was too horrible to contemplate. Wait till last year was more like it: the past was our home now and our consolation and would have to do."[15] Golenbock looked back on a more innocent era, only half-jokingly, as "a time when crime was infrequent and rarely violent and when property, traditions, and parents were all respected. Girls were all virgins, the institution of marriage was inviolate, and best of all, a bleacher seat at Ebbets Field was only fifty-five cents."[16]

Kahn's celebration of youth extended into his 1985 *Good Enough to Dream*. Having given up his childhood dreams of playing in the majors, he bought a minor league team—the Class A Utica Blue Sox. Unlike the Dodgers of *The Boys of Summer*, these Blue Sox were still young enough to dream of the future rather than the past. *Good Enough to Dream* chronicles the team's fortunes over a season as well as Kahn's relationship with his teenage daughter, who takes on the not very lucrative job of selling Blue Sox programs.

But the relationship at the heart of *The Boys of Summer* is not that between fathers and daughters but between fathers and sons. Much of the first part of *The Boys of Summer* has to do with the young Roger's difficulties connecting with his somewhat pedantic father, except when the topic was baseball. His father died just as Kahn's tenure covering the Dodgers came to an end, but "the breaking of a team was not like the greater tragedy: incompleteness, unspoken words, unmade music, withheld love, the failure ever to sum up or say good-bye."[17] In some sense, *The Boys of Summer* was Kahn's effort to make that incompleteness complete.

Talks about fathers and sons cropped up throughout his visits to the aging Dodgers: Labine talked to Kahn about how his having been on the road affected his relationship with his son. Pitcher Carl Erskine talked about his love for a son with Down Syndrome. Jackie Robinson mourned his son, who died in a car crash in 1971.

Kahn returned to the theme of fathers and sons in subsequent books. The 1977 *A Season in the Sun* opened with him pitching to his twelve-year-old son while recalling playing catch with his father and then recalling how he and his father had not talked about some serious things. But: "We talked seriously (and joyously) about baseball. That was a serious thing and that was enough."[18] In *Good Enough to Dream,* his relationship with his daughter drew him back, again, to thoughts about his relationship with his father: "When you play catch with your father and perform reasonably well, you are striding away from the gardens of childhood and toward the world of men."[19] In the 1997 *Memories of Summer,* the seven-year-old Kahn's heart leapt when he realized his father was going to talk to him about baseball and not lecture him about botany. Better yet was a game of catch: "The passion to play dominated my spirit, that and the distinct but overlapping passion to win the good opinion of my father.... When I stayed with a nasty grounder—and my father saw me stay with its final, hostile hop—I felt I had achieved something worthy of pride."[20]

Kahn was not the first to write about fathers and sons (and sometimes daughters) and baseball, but his success, both commercial and literary, surely inspired others to pick up on the theme. Donald Hall titled his 1985 collection *Fathers Playing Catch with Sons,* and though the title alone would surely suffice to show Hall's interest in the topic, Hall's poetic prose is worth quoting further: "Baseball is the generations, looping backward forever with a million apparitions of sticks and balls, cricket and rounders, and the games the Iroquois played in Connecticut before the English came. Baseball is fathers and sons playing catch, lazy and murderous, wild and controlled, the profound archaic song of birth, growth, age, and death."[21] Dick Wimmer took along his own sons to talk to players, active and retired, about their relationships with their sons, and wrote about it in the 1988 *Baseball Fathers, Baseball Sons. Field of Dreams,* the 1989 movie based on W.P. Kinsella's 1982 novel, ended with a tear-jerking scene in which the main character fulfilled his dream by asking his father—or rather, his father's ghost—to have a catch. Doris Kearns Goodwin's 1997 memoir, *Wait Till Next Year,* offered a moving portrait of her relationship with her father. After her father taught her how to keep score, she dutifully did so, so she could recount to him the play-by-play (of Dodger games, of course) when he came home from work. As an adult, she took her sons to games (Red Sox games at that point), where she felt "an invisible bond among our three generations, an anchor of loyalty and love linking my sons to the grandfather whose face they have never seen but whose person they have come to know through this most timeless of sports."[22]

◊ ◊ ◊

The reminiscences of ex–Brooklynites often extended beyond their families to their neighbors. Many remembered the borough as a place where people of different ethnicities and races mingled, if not always closely then at least mostly amicably. These memories were partly accurate. By signing Negro Leaguers like Robinson, Campanella, and Newcombe, the Dodgers not only guaranteed a place atop the National League standings but also took the lead in integrating America. Some white writers, notably Dick Young of the *New York Daily News,* criticized Robinson for being too confrontational in the face of the racist insults hurled at him, but Dodger fans were generally on Robinson's side.

Jews, who were generally liberal, took special pride in rooting for Robinson. Joel Oppenheimer, who would later write a book about the Mets, recalled going to a Dodger game and finding himself for the first time in a crowd of Blacks. "During the game Jackie made a good play in the field," he told Golenbock, "at which point everyone was yelling, 'Jackie, Jackie, Jackie,' and I was yelling with them. And suddenly I realized that behind me someone was yelling, 'Yonkel, Yonkel, Yonkel,' which is Yiddish for Jackie."[23]

Kahn, whose father was Jewish but not religious, prided himself on his support for Robinson, which gradually turned into a friendship. He believed—as did many—that since Blacks and Jews both had a history of being oppressed, they were natural allies. He reported on the racism Robinson experienced, and he described his frustration when editors told him to stick to covering the games.

But Brooklyn's embrace of Robinson, however genuine and widespread, masked continuing racism. There may have been uneasy peace between various ethnic groups, but fears of Blacks moving into their neighborhoods was what drove many whites to leave for the suburbs. And during the 1950s Jews, as much as they supported integration in principle, abandoned Brooklyn for the suburbs as quickly as any other ethnic group.

Kahn didn't delve into this quandary. Instead, he focused on the progress Jews had made and the obstacles they still faced. In 1968, three years before *The Boys of Summer* was published, he came out with *The Passionate People*, a book about Jews in America. Some of the stories in the book illustrated how successfully Jews had assimilated and how anti–Semitism had declined. For example, when Ring Lardner wrote "Alibi Ike" in 1915, Ike complained about the nickname because "I ain't no Yid."[24] Ike and his teammates had been dead for decades, Kahn noted, but he then went on to quote an unidentified American League pitcher who recounted how opponents would call a Jewish player "a long-nosed son of a bitch."[25]

Dodger fans certainly rooted for members of the team who were of a different race or ethnicity, but they remained very much aware of both. In *The Boys of Summer*, Kahn described sitting in the stands and hearing an Irishman cheer for outfielder Goody Rosen to "bring home the bacon for Jakey." Added Kahn: "You could see Rosen's shoulders stiffen."[26]

Kahn continued to brood about anti–Semitism in later books. In *Good Enough to Dream*, he bitterly recalled that at school he was nicknamed Izzy, that Cleveland Indian third baseman Al Rosen was often called "Jew bastard," and that Dodger pitcher Sandy Koufax was "Superjew."[27] In his 1993 *The Era*, which covered baseball from 1947 to 1957, he recounted how Dick Young had insisted Dodger owner Walter O'Malley told him he wanted to leave Ebbets Field "because the area is getting full of blacks and spics." When Kahn told Young that O'Malley had denied saying that, Young answered: "Oh, yeah. O'Malley also said the trouble with Brooklyn was that the place had too many blacks and spics *and Jews*."[28] In *Into My Own*, Kahn recalled that he had expected to speak at Jackie Robinson's funeral but had been told only ordained ministers could do so. Wrote Kahn: "All forms of bigotry and, most-particularly anti–Semitism, stirred the white heat of [Robinson's] rage, and I thought, perhaps unfairly, perhaps not, that my Jewish last name, more than any lack of ordination, led the cleric to redline me away from the pulpit."[29]

My own talks with Kahn occasionally gravitated toward the subject of anti–Semitism. As a young editor at Doubleday, I was assigned to work on *Good Enough to Dream* (which was then titled *Diamonds in the Rough*) when the acquiring editor left the company. Kahn seemed to think that my primary role was to put his scotches on Doubleday's expense account. I, on the other hand, saw my primary role as to listen to his stories and, occasionally and timidly, to suggest that in addition to telling them to me over drinks he might also want to put them down on paper and send me his manuscript. Perhaps because I was, like Kahn, ethnically Jewish but not religious, he would sometimes vent about what he perceived as the anti–Semitism he faced. In particular, he resented Roger Angell, who was generally acknowledged to be—along with Kahn—a master of literary baseball non-fiction. Kahn felt Angell's reputation was based on the WASP establishment's embrace of someone who came from Manhattan and wrote for *The New Yorker*. Kahn felt that Angell's books shouldn't be considered real books, because they were collections of his magazine stories.

I later read a story on the website *SB Nation* in which the writer Alex Belth recounted similar conversations with Kahn about Angell. Belth noted even the titles of their books seemed to spark competition: Kahn's *The Boys of Summer* and Angell's *The Summer Game* were both published in 1972. Kahn's *A Season in the Sun* and Angell's *Five Seasons* were both published in 1977. Belth quoted his father—who, as in so many reminiscences that touched on baseball was the real subject of the piece—asking: "Why does one have to be better than the other? Why can't they both be good?"[30]

Belth's father's position was of course quite reasonable. Kahn didn't see it that way. He told Belth that Angell had conspired with others to ensure negative reviews of *The Boys of Summer*. Belth later asked Angell about Kahn's accusations, and Angell laughed: "He thought I'd changed my name to Roger to be confused with him. He was so paranoid."[31]

Angell noted that though his book received rave reviews Kahn's far outsold it. (*The Boys of Summer* was number one on the *New York Times* bestseller list for eight weeks, stayed on the list for twenty-five weeks, and ultimately sold more than three million copies.) At some point Angell said to Kahn, "Look, Roger, here's the deal: You can have my reviews and I'll take your royalties." Continued Angell, still according to Belth: "He did not laugh, he did not smile."[32]

"Who lost the Dodgers?" baseball historian Henry Fetter wrote, "is a question that has aroused emotions perhaps comparable to those stirred by the 'Who lost China' debate—except that they have proven to be far more enduring."[33] Most of Brooklyn blamed O'Malley. Newspapermen Jack Newfield and Pete Hamill once decided to collaborate on an article about the worst human beings who ever lived. Over dinner, the two decided to write their top three on their napkins. Each wrote down the same three names and in the same order: Hitler, Stalin, O'Malley. Kahn described O'Malley as "venal and mendacious."[34]

It was not as if O'Malley moved the Dodgers to Los Angeles because they were going broke. Unlike the Braves, who abandoned Boston for Milwaukee in 1953, or the Philadelphia A's, who moved to Kansas City in 1955, the Dodgers routinely drew more than one million fans. But O'Malley saw two million pack into Milwaukee's new County Stadium, decided he wanted that for himself, and played New York against Los Angeles until he got what he wanted.

Still, a strong case can be made that the Dodgers needed a new stadium, and that O'Malley hoped to build it in Brooklyn rather than Los Angeles. Ebbets Field, though beloved, was aging. It had, wrote historian Jerald Podair, "dirty bathrooms, rusting pillars, and a general down-at-the heels raffishness that charmed only those who did not patronize it regularly."[35] The team was also getting old. The Braves were not only outdrawing the Dodgers but threatening to supplant them as the dominant team in the National League. And Dodger attendance, though still healthy, was trending downward. In 1947, the year Robinson joined the team, it peaked at 1,807,526. By 1957, the team's final year in Brooklyn, it was 1,026,158. This decline wasn't as damaging as O'Malley pretended, since it was due in part to more fans watching games on television, and what O'Malley lost in ticket sales he gained in TV revenues. Still, the trend was worrisome, as was the fact that outside Ebbets Field there were spaces for only about seven hundred cars. "The Dodgers had earned their nickname when the fans dodged trolleys to get to the ballpark," O'Malley complained. "Now the public was on wheels."[36]

For help in building a new stadium in New York, O'Malley turned to Robert Moses, who many consider the villain of the story. Moses headed the Triborough Bridge and Tunnel Authority, the New York Parks Commission, the Construction Commission, and the Slum Clearance Committee. Although he was never elected to any post, he oversaw billions of dollars that went toward building everything from highways to housing projects. O'Malley asked Moses to condemn land near the intersection of Brooklyn's Atlantic and Flatbush Avenues, where he wanted to build a new stadium. By condemning the land, Moses would enable O'Malley to buy it at far less than he could in an open market. O'Malley argued that, like Moses' other projects, this would serve a public purpose: it would keep the team in Brooklyn and also stabilize the neighborhood.

Moses didn't see it that way. A private stadium, he argued, was not a public amenity. Instead, Moses proposed to build a new stadium at Queens' Flushing Meadows, where Shea Stadium would eventually be built. O'Malley's answer was that if the Brooklyn Dodgers played in Queens, they wouldn't be the Brooklyn Dodgers. He headed west.

In doing so, O'Malley was very much a part of a broader trend, and in this sense neither he nor Moses can be blamed for losing the Dodgers. The highways in and around Los Angeles grew beyond anything Moses built in New York, and in 1962 California surpassed New York as the most populous state.

Similarly, the flight to the suburbs in New York (and elsewhere) can't be blamed solely on O'Malley or Moses. Long Island's Levittown, which opened in 1947, was just one of the many developments that beckoned Brooklyn apartment dwellers longing to own their own home. Though many might have denied it, they were also fleeing the Blacks who during the 1950s had moved from the South to cities like New York. Moses' highways made it easier to move away from Brooklyn, but they didn't create the desire to do so.

As for the late twentieth- and early twenty-first-century desire to move back to Brooklyn, it's impossible to know how much to credit Kahn. At the very least, the success of *The Boys of Summer* inspired other writers to reminisce about the Dodgers and Brooklyn. Search amazon for Brooklyn Dodgers and you'll get more than seven hundred hits. Some are at best peripheral to the topic but enough are on the mark to justify Kahn's 2006 comment that "writing about old Brooklyn and the Dodgers has become heady stuff" and that "everybody these days wants to try."[37]

Those who gave it a try included writers of fiction as well as non-fiction. It is probably a stretch to suggest that Brooklyn's sense of loss is reflected in a number of murder mysteries involving the Dodgers, among them Donald Honig's 1992 *The Plot to Kill Jackie Robinson* and Robert B. Parker's 2004 *Double Play*. It is less of a stretch to suggest that the important role the Dodgers played for immigrants assimilating into American society is reflected in serious works of fiction for children and for adults. The former include Barbara Cohen's 1974 *Thank You, Jackie Robinson*, in which a fatherless Jewish boy and a Black man share their love for the Dodgers, and Bette Bao Lord's 1984 *In the Year of the Boar and Jackie Robinson*, in which a girl whose family has moved from China to America is inspired by Robinson's efforts to assimilate into the major leagues. The latter include Robert Mayer's 1984 *The Grace of Shortstops*, featuring a family of Jewish immigrants, and Colm Tóibín's 2009 *Brooklyn*, with an immigrant from Ireland and an Italian-American. And the fantasy of so many ex-Brooklynites was played out most explicitly in David Ritz's 1981 novel *The Man Who Brought the Dodgers Back to Brooklyn*. Here two Dodger fans set out not only to bring the Dodgers back from Los Angeles but also to rebuild Ebbets Field.

In some sense, that fantasy was realized with the building of Citi Field, despite its being located amid parking lots in Queens. Perhaps more fundamentally, it was realized in 2012 when, three years after Citi Field opened, a new arena opened at the downtown Brooklyn site where O'Malley had wanted to build a new stadium. Barclays Center wasn't built for baseball but it did become home to the National Basketball Association's *Brooklyn* Nets, and in a repudiation of Moses' vision the arena was more convenient for people coming by subway or train than by car.

Perhaps most fundamentally, the fantasy of a revitalized Brooklyn was realized when the children and grandchildren of those who fled to the suburbs in the 1950s chose to live in the city. "A curious phenomenon has swept the land," Kahn wrote in 2006, "from Cambridge to San Diego. I call it Brooklyn Chic. Where once old Brooklyn was regarded as the borough of dese, dem and dose, Brooklyn Chic recasts the place in a new roseate light."[38]

7

The Bill James Baseball Abstract

by BILL JAMES

New York: Ballantine, 1982

Bill James has been called "the Sultan of Stats."[1] His *Baseball Abstract* has been called "the most important scientific treatise since Newton's *Principia*,"[2] the full title of which, translated from Latin, is *Mathematical Principles of Natural Philosophy*. Both descriptions are misleading. Despite his reputation, James is not a math whiz. Rather, his genius lay in his willingness to challenge established dogma and to do it so entertainingly that he inspired new ways to think not only about baseball but also about business and politics.

James was certainly not the first to think about baseball's statistics, which have been part of the game since the nineteenth century. The British-born writer Henry Chadwick created a box score as early as 1859, recording runs, hits, putouts, and assists by hitters and fielders and strikeouts by pitchers. As editor of the annual *Beadle's Dime Base Ball Player* and then A.G. Spalding's annual *Official Base Ball Guide*, Chadwick invented and collected statistics for decades. These included runs per game, hits per game, total bases per game, and putouts and assists per game. Chadwick did not invent batting average, but when a fan suggested dividing hits by at bats rather than by games Chadwick happily added the stat to his 1872 and subsequent guides. Chadwick also didn't invent the RBI, but he was again happy to include it when the National League added it as an official stat in 1891. He did invent ERA, which the National League made official in 1912.

James was also not the first to criticize official statistics. In 1916, Ferdinand Cole Lane, the editor of *Baseball Magazine* and just one of many such critics, objected to the way batting average gave equal weight to a single, double, triple, or home run. Asked Lane: "Would a system that placed nickels, dimes, quarters, and 50-cent pieces on the same basis be much of a system whereby to compute a man's financial resources?"[3] Lane also noted that batting averages didn't take into account walks or stolen bases, or the effects of a player's home ballpark.

Nor was James the first to suggest that managers and general managers might benefit from a better understanding of statistics. Again to take just one example of many, Earnshaw Cook argued in his 1964 book, *Percentage Baseball,* that in most situations attempting stolen bases and sacrifice bunts generally didn't pay off, nor did platooning. Cook also proposed using a relief pitcher as a starter and pinch hitting for him before he could bat.

Some teams even acted on the advice of unorthodox statistical analysis. When he was general manager of the Brooklyn Dodgers, Branch Rickey hired statistician Allan Roth. Roth noted that in 1948 Jackie Robinson had batted .350 with men on base. As a result, Robinson was moved to the cleanup spot in 1949, even though he'd hit only twelve homers the year before. Rickey also embraced on-base average as a better gauge than batting average of a hitter's overall value. In the late sixties and early seventies, Earl Weaver managed the Baltimore Orioles to four pennants and one World Series by largely steering clear of stolen bases and sacrifice bunts. Weaver also kept stacks of index cards in the dugout so he could quickly check how each of his hitters had fared against any pitcher.

In short, long before millions pored over the latest reports on their fantasy baseball teams—and long before Bill James's *Abstract*—statistics were an integral part of the game. Kids (and adults) mastered math by playing the board game All-Star Baseball, starting in 1941, and the dice game Strat-O-Matic, starting in 1961. They studied the numbers on the backs of Topps baseball cards, starting in 1952, or the vastly larger number of numbers in *Balldom: The Britannica of Baseball,* first published in 1914, or in the *Official Encyclopedia of Baseball*, first published in 1951, or in *The Baseball Encyclopedia*, first published in 1969 and reasonably called "the national pastime's equivalent of the *Oxford English Dictionary*."[4] As James put it: "To imagine baseball without statistics would be a zen exercise, I would think, akin to contemplating the sound of one hand clapping. If a baseball game is played in a forest and no one keeps stats, does it count in the standings?"[5]

In Robert Coover's 1968 novel, *The Universal Baseball Association Inc., J. Henry Waugh, Prop.*, Henry Waugh invents a dice-based game that bears some resemblance to Strat-O-Matic but is almost infinitely more complex. So immersed is he in the game that the line between his reality and fantasy blurs; his players turn from numbers on a page into real people. And that brings us back to James, who in his annual *Baseball Abstract*s, would make his numbers come alive, in his case through the liveliness of his thinking and his writing.

James's *Abstract*s would create, as Alan Schwarz wrote in his history of baseball statistics, "an earthquake that rocked all of baseball."[6]

◊ ◊ ◊

In 1976, James was working as a night watchman at a bean-canning plant in Lawrence, Kansas. The job was not demanding and he spent much of the night calculating and contemplating baseball statistics. The result was the *1977 Baseball Abstract—Featuring 18 Categories of Statistical Information That You Can't Find Anywhere Else*. The book was mostly numbers. James published it himself and sold just seventy copies, mostly through a small classified ad he took out in *The Sporting News*.

The 1978 *Abstract* was the first to resemble the later ones that would shake the world. There were numbers, of course, but also commentary on each team and on key players, and there were essays proclaiming that traditional ways of looking at the game were just plain wrong.

James continued to put out an *Abstract* a year, each one overflowing with new ways of thinking about baseball. A sampling:

Prime years. Conventional wisdom held that a player's prime came between the ages of 28 and 32. James looked at players' performances over the years and found they peaked between 25 and 29. Conventional wisdom also held that finesse pitchers lasted longer, since there wasn't as much strain on their arms. James found that power pitchers, at least if measured by strikeouts amassed, lasted longer.

Range factor. The standard measure of fielding was fielding percentage: putouts + assists / putouts + assists + errors. James believed this was meaningless at best and misleading at worst, since the best way to avoid an error was to be too slow or too poorly positioned to get near the ball. He advocated instead using "range factor," which was simply the number of successful plays per game.

Runs created. Others, including Earnshaw Cook, had played with formulas that tried to translate batting statistics into the number of runs a batter contributed to his team. James started by finding a formula that correlated with a team's total runs scored, since the team number could be checked. James then assumed that by plugging into that formula an individual batter's stats, he could gauge that player's value more accurately than with any other stat. Though he continued to tinker with the formula, his most often-cited version was remarkably simple: (Hits + Walks) × (Total Bases) / (At Bats + Walks).

Note that sacrifice bunts and steals didn't even figure into the formula; James's values were very much in keeping with Earl Weaver's strategies. To illustrate how confused most people are about the value of a sacrifice bunt, James noted that it's the only play in baseball for which when it works both sides cheer. As for steals, James found that teams that led the league in steals finished lower in the standings than teams that led in any other offensive category, and that teams that finished last in stolen bases finished higher in the standings than those that finished last in any other category except triples. "You cannot win a pennant by stealing bases," James wrote. "Nobody ever had, nobody ever will."[7]

Park effects. Everyone knew Boston's Fenway Park was good for righty power hitters, whose pop flies could sail over the enticingly close left-field wall. Red Sox outfielder Fred Lynn, one of the team's lefty hitters, claimed Fenway helped him not at all. James noted Lynn's batting average was 80 points a year higher at home than it was away. James also noted that general managers tended to develop teams without taking the park effects into account. The Red Sox, for example, during the period James analyzed, were thought to have a strong offense and mediocre pitching. Management and fans agreed on this. But both management and fans failed to appreciate that the park effect warped the team's statistics, and that the Red Sox actually had a mediocre offense and strong pitching.

James called what he did "sabermetrics." SABR came from the Society for American Baseball Research, which had been founded in Cooperstown in 1971. Metrics obviously had to do with measurement. But James's math was usually pretty easy to follow. Others might come up with a better formula for, say, measuring runs created. James was less interested in coming up with definitive answers than in raising and exploring the issues.

James continued to self-publish the annuals through 1981, and the sales gradually increased to about twenty two hundred in 1981. This was still a cult-like following, however, and the *Abstract*s might not have reached a mass market without the help of Daniel Okrent, a reader who was also a freelance writer. Okrent introduced himself to James after the 1978 *Abstract* came out and then wrote a profile of the author for *Sports Illustrated.*

The story almost didn't run, partly because James's analyses were so unorthodox. "There was a fact checker assigned to the story who kept nitpicking it to death,"[8] Okrent recalled. For instance, Bill had singled out Oakland A's catcher Gene Tenace for his on base percentage, which unlike batting average includes walks as well as hits. In 1977, Tenace achieved an astonishing .415.

"Bill had included it in the *Abstract*, and I had cited it in the piece, as .413," Okrent said. "The fact-checker used this as primary evidence that Bill was an inaccurate amateur who didn't deserve a profile in an *SI* piece—without noting that the keepers of the official stats had refused Bill access to them, and he had instead been compelled to compile all of them, by hand, from the box scores of all 1,944 games played each season."[9]

The Lineup

Okrent rewrote the piece and *Sports Illustrated* finally ran it in May 1981. That caught the attention of book editors, who offered to publish James's work. I was working at Doubleday at the time, and I was one of the editors interesting in publishing James. Readers of this book may think I mention this to show off how insightful or foresightful I was. Alas, no. I admired the *Abstracts*, to be sure, but I thought a book could be better organized. Rather than focusing on one year, albeit with all sorts of digressions about baseball history and strategy, why not approach this more systematically? Why not organize the book chronologically or thematically? That would let readers focus on the history and strategy. Or so I thought.

What I didn't grasp was that James's digressions were not a structural flaw but part of his appeal. If he seemed to be meandering away from the topic at hand, it was almost always worth following him. Take, for example his discussion of Milwaukee Brewer third baseman Roy Howell in the 1982 *Abstract*. Howell had been traded from the Toronto Blue Jays to the Milwaukee Brewers. That meant Howell moved from a weak-hitting lineup to a great-hitting lineup, and players generally said they hit better if they had better hitters around them. Yet Howell's average declined by 31 points. So James's entry on Howell turned into a discussion of how much a player's home ballpark affects his stats (Toronto's Exhibition Stadium was a hitter's park and Milwaukee's County Stadium was a pitcher's park), and how little, despite common wisdom to the contrary, a player's offensive stats are affected by those hitting around him. James turned an entry on a generally unremarkable player into something surprising. And the surprising conclusion was more effective for having popped up in a surprising place.

Just two entries down, James moved on to California Angel third baseman Butch Hobson. Hobson's reputation for always playing all-out and often risking injury made him a fan favorite. This led to a discussion about the differences between football, where that approach works, and baseball, where, James argued, the long season rewards those who play the percentages. As for Hobson: "He's slow, scatter-armed and GIDP [grounds into double play]—and strikeout—prone. That's quite a price to pay to get somebody who plays hard in the lineup."[10] Again, what might have been a standard entry on a player became an enlightening essay.

Sometimes James's tangents were worth following just because they were funny. In the midst of a discussion of Kansas City Royal second baseman Frank White, he noted that players named "White" are almost always black and players named "Black" are usually White. As always, he did the numbers. His tangent stretched on to discuss how names, like peacekeeping missiles, can disguise the truth: "Horace Speed stole only four bases in his career. Vic Power was a singles hitter. Bill Goodenough was not good enough, and Joe Blong did not belong for long."[11]

Team entries, too, could head off in all sorts of directions. The analysis of steals mentioned above, for example, came in James's 1983 entry on the New York Yankees, written soon after owner George Steinbrenner declared the Yankees were going to change from a team based on power to one stressing speed. This strategy was particularly inane, James noted, for a team that played in a stadium built for left-handed power hitters. James's analysis of the value of steals may have veered away from the Yankees but it was very relevant to the chance of the Yankees winning by running. The chance of that, James wrote, "was roughly equal to the chance that Ronald Reagan might elope with Joan Baez."[12]

Just one more example of James's digressions: In the 1986 entry on the California Angels, James noted that the team was an outstanding 30–13 in games won by one run. This led to a discussion of how wrong was the frequent assertion that good teams win close games; in fact, the opposite is true: the smaller the margin of victory, the more likely it is that the better team will lose. But a manager who tends to use one-run strategies, as the Angels' Gene Mauch did, is more likely to win more one-run games. And James was open-minded enough to credit Mauch for this, despite James's general disdain for such one-run strategies as the sacrifice bunt and stolen base.

In suggesting that the *Abstract* be organized chronologically or thematically, I underestimated how well his digressions worked.

I also grossly underestimated the value of organizing the book by analyses of current teams and players rather than issues. It was fascinating to read about the differences between football and baseball, but if you were a Red Sox fan you wanted to know what James thought about their past year and their prospects for this year, and despite all the digressions you could find that in the entry on the Sox. You also wanted to be able to quickly find out what he thought about Butch Hobson, and the player entries became even more important as fantasy baseball games exploded in popularity and fantasy team owners considered whether they wanted to draft Hobson.

James rightly ignored me and accepted an offer from Ballantine Books, which turned the *Abstracts* into bestsellers, selling about 150,000 some years. Readers appreciated that James was a master of words as well as numbers. As the critic and novelist Wilfred Sheed wrote, the *Abstracts* were to other stats books "roughly what Dr. Johnson is to the latest Merriam-Webster: eccentric, personal, *written*."[13]

◊ ◊ ◊

Not everyone agreed with Sheed. There were plenty of players and managers and even reporters who criticized James. Some of them didn't like what James had said about them, but it was more than that. A numbers nerd, they explained, couldn't understand what really happened on the field or in the dugout or locker room. Cincinnati Red and Detroit Tiger manager Sparky Anderson called James "a little fat guy with a beard ... who knows nothing about nothing."[14]

Anderson's ire was understandable, given what James had written in his 1983 entry on Tiger first baseman Enos Cabell: "I want to look at a player on the basis of what, specifically, he can and cannot do to help you win a baseball game, but Sparky's so full of 'winners' and 'discipline' and 'we ballplayers' [like Cabell] and self-consciously asinine theories about baseball that he seems to have no concept of how it is, mechanically, that baseball games are won and lost."[15] Anderson must have been *very* annoyed, since he very rarely had anything negative to say about anyone. When I edited his 1990 book, *Sparky*, I encouraged Anderson and his coauthor, Dan Ewald, to include a few negative comments that might generate some controversy and help sell the book. They were both too nice to argue with me, but their niceness nevertheless prevailed; the book includes plenty on Anderson's favorite players and nothing on his least favorite players. Anderson was too nice even to hold a grudge against James, whom he later said "does a great job at what he does."[16]

When managers or players or reporters criticized James for not understanding what it was really like on the field or in the dugout or locker room, he readily agreed. James reveled in his status as an outsider.

"This book is not about the things that I see at baseball games with my own eyes, at least not mostly," he wrote. "This book has a breadth and scope in its vision of the game that requires a perspective that comes only with distance."[17] Rather than look at the trees up close, he chose to look at the forest.

What infuriated James was not criticism from players or managers like Anderson but the work of those who seemed to be on his side of the inside-outside divide. He couldn't stand it when commentators cited statistics that were useless or misleading. Many noted, for example, that the 1981 Yankees had an "incredible"[18] won-lost record of 51–3 in games they led going into the eighth inning. James pointed out that the average record for American League teams leading after seven innings was 49–5. The Yankee bullpen was better than average but not significantly so.

James was especially infuriated by the Elias Sports Bureau, which supplied statistics to the media and to major league teams and which refused to share data (such as Tenace's on base average) with James. Partly this was because James wasn't offering to pay for the stats, and partly it was because Seymour Siwoff, who ran Elias, didn't think fans would be interested in much of what they compiled. But when Siwoff saw the success of the *Abstract*s he decided to create his own book. *The Elias Baseball Analyst* hit the shelves in 1985 and came out annually until 1993. The *Analyst*s included lots of stats— batters' performances against lefty and righty pitchers, with runners on base and bases empty, at home and on the road, and on grass and turf, for example. But, though they looked a lot like the *Abstract*s, the *Analyst*s lacked an analyst as provocative—and fun—as James. They were more a reference book and less a reading book. And, as Schwarz put it, "they put millions of statistics in the hands of people who didn't know how to use them, like handling a chainsaw to a hyperactive teenager."[19]

Eventually, James became so disgusted with the misuse of statistics that, after 1988, he stopped writing the *Abstract*. "I'd be watching a game on TV, and there'd be a graphic on the screen: '83 percent of his RBIs have come in the first seven innings of the game,'" he recalled. "I thought, 'Good lord, am I responsible for this crap?' ... I'm not taking full responsibility for all the statistical trash that comes out of TV sets during ballgames ... but I was contributing to it."[20]

Besides, James later admitted, he himself was in danger of falling prey to what infuriated him in others. Striving always to say something new, he found himself resorting to more that was trivial: "In 1981 the average baseball fan didn't know that 72 percent of Bob Horner's home runs came at home. The average fan didn't know that Bob Horner didn't really have a lot of power if you took him out of Atlanta-Fulton County Stadium. The average fan didn't know that Dave Parker was one of the rare left-handed hitters who had more power against left-handed pitchers than against right-handed pitchers. As the years went by, the public was more and more aware of such things, and I was driven to find smaller and smaller pieces of information to pass on."[21]

◊ ◊ ◊

Annoyed though James was with some of his imitators, others were making substantial contributions to our understanding of baseball.

In 1984, baseball writer John Thorn and American League statistician Pete Palmer teamed up on *The Hidden Game of Baseball*, a book that delivered what I had asked of James; namely, an approach to the game's new statistics that was organized thematically and covered all of the game's history. The book included a history of baseball statistics and systematically took on longstanding debates about history and strategy. Who would have been most helped if, as writers and fans speculated for years, Joe DiMaggio had played in Fenway Park and Ted Williams in Yankee Stadium? Thorn and Palmer offered a convincing case that the Red Sox were smart not to make that trade. Is pitching really 90 percent of the game? Actually, it's 44 percent, Thorn and Palmer explained. And, not surprisingly for readers of James, they argued that the sacrifice bunt is rarely a wise move while, more surprisingly, trying to steal home is often a good play. The book also presented Palmer's linear weights measure, his version of Runs Created.

I edited *The Hidden Game*, but I should quickly add I didn't suggest the idea to Thorn and Palmer. The two along with an editor named David Reuther had originally planned to put together a comprehensive encyclopedia. *The Baseball Encyclopedia,* though updated regularly after its original 1969 publication, included none of the new statistics. It also included numerous errors Thorn and Palmer wanted to correct. They put together a proposal and received a six-figure offer from Simon & Schuster but decided they couldn't meet the publisher's deadline. It was then they came up with the idea for the ambitious but more manageable *Hidden Game.* James generously wrote that "fans will learn more from *The Hidden Game* than from any other baseball book that they will read this year."[22]

In 1989, Thorn and Palmer ultimately did produce their mammoth encyclopedia, the nearly three-thousand page *Total Baseball.* When the fourth edition came out in 1995, Major League Baseball endorsed it as its official encyclopedia.

Also important was the work of analyst Nate Silver, who in 2003 introduced a remarkably accurate method of projecting player and team performances. It was known as PECOTA, which stood for Player Empirical Comparison and Optimization Test Algorithm but also alluded to Bill Pecota, a very average player for the Kansas City Royals, New York Mets, and Atlanta Braves.

Well before then, James-like thinking had begun to infiltrate major league teams. In 1981 the Texas Rangers hired Craig Wright as a sabermetrician, the first to hold that title on a major team. Wright advised the Rangers and later the Los Angeles Dodgers on various personnel decisions; he suggested, for example, that Charlie Hough should be a starter and not a reliever.

In the early eighties a company called STATS, Inc., which stood for Sports Team and Tracking Systems and in which James had a small stake, began selling stats to major league teams, including the Oakland A's and the Chicago White Sox. The Sox contracted with the company in the hope of using its numbers in contract negotiations, but the numbers also convinced them the team's young power hitters would benefit from a field with smaller dimensions. Since the Sox couldn't move their fences in toward the plate, they instead moved the plate out toward the fences. STATS, Inc. would ultimately sell its stats not just to teams but to media outlets like ESPN and *USA Today* and through the newly-emerging Internet. Rupert Murdoch's News Corporation bought the company in 1999 for $45 million.

In the mid-eighties, Mets manager Davey Johnson read the *Abstracts*, as did his coach Bobby Valentine, who later became manager of the Rangers, Mets, and Red Sox. Most famously, Oakland A's general managers Sandy Alderson and then Billy Beane read the *Abstracts*. Beane became a celebrity after the 2003 publication of the bestselling book *Moneyball* by journalist Michael Lewis.

Lewis offered an inside account of the A's front office, as they put together winning teams despite one of the game's lowest payrolls. Beane understood, as did James, that teams were undervaluing certain kinds of players, such as college (as opposed to high-school) pitchers and hitters who walked a lot. Beane persisted in drafting and trading for such players, despite the objections of his more traditional scouting staff.

Beane himself had been exactly the type of player scouts loved. He was a first-round draft pick. He *looked* like a star, and he was played by Brad Pitt in the 2011 movie based on Lewis's book. But he never lived up to his hype and retired after six years with a .219 lifetime batting average. The players Beane liked had the opposite profile: They didn't look like major leaguers but they got results. A scout would say about a player, "I just don't see it." And Beane would respond: "That's all right. We're blending what we see but we aren't allowing ourselves to be victimized by what we see."[23]

7. The Bill James Baseball Abstract *(James)*

After the 2001 season, the A's lost their star first baseman and center fielder to free agency. Jason Giambi, who had 38 homers and 120 RBIs, signed with the Yankees. Johnny Damon, who scored 108 runs and stole 27 bases, signed with the Red Sox. Beane replaced them with players other teams were for various reasons ready to cast off, primarily Scott Hatteberg, David Justice, and Jason's brother Jeremy Giambi. Of the very slow Jeremy, A's manager Art Howe complained that he was the only manager who had to pinch-run for his leadoff man.

But all three of Beane's acquisitions had the ability to get on base, often via walks. Hatteberg tied for the league's lead in one category to which few other than Beane paid attention: pitches not swung at. Despite the loss of Giambi and Damon, the revamped 2003 A's won 96 games and again made the playoffs.

◊ ◊ ◊

Though there were no more *Abstracts*, James continued to write. He continued to publish annuals: *The Bill James Baseball Book* (1990–1992), *The Bill James Player Ratings Book* (1993–1996), *The Bill James Gold Mine* (2008–2010), *The Bill James Handbook* (2003–2022). He played with different structures with varying success. In the *Abstracts* his refusal to accept conventional thinking was reinforced by his refusal to stay within the bounds of any conventional structure. These later efforts, though still filled with interesting pieces, seemed to veer either toward a collection of miscellaneous thoughts or toward traditional stat books, albeit with untraditional stats. Many included pieces written by someone other than James.

More successful were his various *Historical Abstracts*, which appeared in 1985, 1988, and 2001. On the surface these might sound something like what I originally had in mind for James. The structure was very clear: There was a section on the history of the game, decade by decade, and there were essays and statistics on players. But, James being James, the book was filled with surprises. He tracked trends in everything from nicknames to uniforms, and he turned numbers into people. There was a profile of Bill Thomas, for example, who never pitched in the majors but won 383 games in the minor leagues including 35 in 1946 when he was forty-one years old. James not only analyzed the numbers but also investigated a gambling scandal that led to Thomas being banned from baseball, perhaps unfairly.

In 2002, the year after the last of his *Historical Abstracts* was published, James—the consummate outsider—became an insider. Other teams couldn't help but notice the A's successes. In Boston, the new owner of the Red Sox was John Henry, who had made his fortune analyzing numbers in financial markets and saw comparable opportunities in baseball. Henry tried to hire Beane as his general manager, but Beane decided to stay in Oakland. Henry then turned to Theo Epstein, who at twenty-eight became the youngest general manager in the history of the majors. Both Henry and Epstein admired James, and they hired him as an advisor.

In truth, James had never been as fully an outsider as he sometimes portrayed himself. Back when he was self-publishing the *Abstracts* and was largely unknown, some player agents and some teams knew of his work and hired him to help prepare arguments for salary arbitration cases. The agents for pitcher Steve Trout, for example, called on James to explain that Trout's 9–16 record for the White Sox in 1980 was the result of poor offensive and defensive support.

But the Red Sox job was much more public, and his critics exulted when the team's first big sabermetric experiment turned out to be a debacle. James had long questioned the wisdom of saving the team's best reliever for save situations, and the 2003 Sox chose instead to use a number of different pitchers in the role. The 2003 bullpen's combined ERA was an abysmal 4.83. The Sox abandoned the experiment and signed Keith Foulke to be a traditional closer for 2004; Foulke saved 32 games with a 2.17 ERA and the team won the World Series. James and Epstein never conceded they had made a mistake. They maintained, quite reasonably, that the bullpen's improvement was a result not of better strategy but of better pitchers.

By the second decade of the twenty-first century, most other major league teams had joined the Red Sox in hiring sabermetricians, and many teams started looking for an edge elsewhere. Rather than just figuring out how to acquire more valuable players, they also focused on how to develop them. This was not an entirely new idea, of course. In the 1920s when Branch Rickey ran the Cardinals, he invested in minor league teams and other major league teams followed his lead in creating their own farm systems to develop players. In Douglas Wallop's 1954 novel *The Year the Yankees Lost the Pennant* and in *Damn Yankees*, the musical and movie based on the book, a middle-aged fan of the Washington Senators turns himself into a young star by making a deal with the devil. In the 1990s, players built themselves up using steroids. Today's teams are using a variety of technologies that can, for example, provide input on batters' swings and pitchers' spin rates and other measurements invisible to the human eye.

◊ ◊ ◊

To what extent did James revolutionize the world beyond baseball? As with others of the books discussed in this book, it's often difficult to distinguish between trends of which a book is a part and trends of which a book is a cause.

James's influence was most quickly and clearly visible in other sports, where new forms of statistical analysis took hold. This was challenging, since however misleading some baseball stats were, it was at least possible for James and others to try to isolate an individual player's contributions. But if a defensive back had fewer interceptions, numbers alone could not tell you if it was his fault or if quarterbacks weren't throwing to his side of the field. The best of the Jamesian approaches to other sports was *Football by the Numbers* by George Ignatin and Allen Barra. Ignatin and Barra tackled questions like: How could you make sense of a statistic like pass completion percentage, which equates a 75-yard touchdown pass with a pass for a four-yard loss? They did so with a Jamesian irreverence, and James himself called them "the twin gurus of football statistics."[24] (Disclosure: I was the editor of these books.)

Coaches and general managers in other sports also began analyzing the numbers in non-traditional ways. In Boston, the Celtics signed Kevin Garnett after their top statistical analyst noted that twenty-four of the previous NBA champions had on their roster a league MVP or top fifty all-time player. And Patriot coach Bill Belichick was noted (and criticized) for not punting on fourth down after his statistical analysis concluded that other coaches were generally too conservative about going for first downs.

Sabermetrics extended into political analysis as well, most obviously via Nate Silver, the statistician who developed the PECOTA forecasting system. Silver moved on to forecasting elections and by balancing poll data with demographic data he had remarkable success. His blog, FiveThirtyEight, was licensed to the *New York Times* in 2010. Silver sold his company to ESPN in 2013, and then it 2018 it came under the auspices of ABC News.

It's more difficult to gauge James's influence on financial markets, but there's no question that in the early 1980s, as James's *Abstracts* were opening up new ways of thinking about baseball, financial markets were also being revolutionized by quantitative analysis. "If you got an MBA in the early 1980s, one of the mantras you kept hearing was 'if you can't measure it, you can't manage it,'"[25] recalled Lewis Wirshba, who got his MBA from the Wharton School of the University of Pennsylvania and went on to become chief operating officer for Credit Suisse America, a leading financial services company.

Just as James was counting alternative stats like how many runners in scoring position a hitter left on base (as opposed to how many runs he batted in), investment managers started collecting alternative data. Some, for example, used satellite images of parking lots to count cars, which turned out to reliably predict a retailer's corporate profits.

"I'm not sure what came first, Bill James or his way of thinking applied to investing," said David Mannheim, who became a portfolio manager for MFS, an investment management firm. "It's a chicken and egg thing. But the rise of quantitative investing was during the same period. Investors, like Bill James, were trying to look at historical data to find patterns that could predict future results."[26]

This was especially the case for products known as derivatives, such as options and futures, which offered traders and investors a chance to make fortunes. Not all financial analysts were disciples of

James, of course, but some were. At one point Morningstar, a global financial services firm, instructed its analysts to read James's work and apply it when judging mutual funds.

John Henry, before he bought the Red Sox, read the *Abstracts* and *The Hidden Game of Baseball* with more than baseball in mind:

> I probably got into my business because of growing up with batting averages. I think I excelled at knowing which statistics had meaning, and which didn't; what constituted a significant statistic in the financial markets, and what didn't ... Actual data means more than individual perception or belief. It's true of baseball, just as it is in financial markets.[27]

Beyond politics and business, the evidence of James's influence is largely anecdotal, and thus would probably not meet James's own standards. But there's no shortage of readers willing to testify about how they applied lessons from the *Abstracts* to fields other than baseball. A collection of essays titled *How Bill James Changed Our View of Baseball* is filled with the words not just of experts but also of fans, including a doctor on how James changed his approach to medicine, an industrial engineer who chose his field because of James, and a lawyer who after reading James looked at criminal cases differently.

Lewis, who worked at an investment bank and before writing *Moneyball* wrote a bestseller about Wall Street, suggested James's type of thinking could be applied in almost any field:

> If gross miscalculations of a person's value could occur on a baseball field, before a live audience of thirty thousand, and a television audience of millions more, what did that say about the measurement of performance in other lines of work? If professional baseball players could be over- or undervalued, who couldn't? Bad as they may have been, the statistics used to evaluate baseball players were probably far more accurate than anything used to measure the value of people who didn't play baseball for a living.[28]

8

Rotisserie League Baseball

by GLEN WAGGONER

New York: Bantam, 1984

Isn't the book *Rotisserie League Baseball* just a spinoff of *The Bill James Baseball Abstract*? For that matter, aren't the people who play the various games that spun off of Rotisserie baseball just stats-obsessed nerds who, unable to play or even appreciate the real game, took refuge in a fantasy world?

In some senses, yes. The fantasy baseball phenomenon grew alongside the James phenomenon. The two fed on each other and both fed on statistics. Both the *Abstracts* and the *Rotisseries* came out annually, with the first national edition of the former in 1982 and of the latter in 1984. Both James and the editors of *Rotisserie* included analyses of players, and many of the readers of both books were looking for an edge to help them in their fantasy leagues. Both the *Abstracts* and *Rotisseries* also had irreverent tones and both sometimes made fun of the baseball establishment.

But in another sense the game of Rotisserie baseball in its original form and as set forth in *Rotisserie* was a rejection of all James stood for. To play Rotisserie baseball, you got together with other members of your league in the spring for an auction at which you drafted actual players. At the end of the season the league crowned a winner based on the statistics of his (or occasionally her) team's players. The teams were ranked in eight categories: batting average, home runs, RBIs, and stolen bases for hitters; wins, ERA, saves, and WHIP (hits plus walks per innings pitched) for pitchers. With the exception of WHIP, these were the very stats whose value James and other sabermetricians had denigrated. To win at rotisserie baseball, you had to ignore much of what James had taught about real baseball.

More fundamentally, fantasy sports did not grow into a billion dollar industry because of Bill James. Many factors drove the growth of fantasy. Free agency made fans much more aware of player salaries and undercut traditional allegiances to players and teams; fantasy offered fans a new way to connect with—indeed, to own—players and teams. Some fantasy participants who had traditionally been, say, Red Sox fans, found themselves rooting against the Red Sox if one of their players was batting or pitching against the Sox. But fantasy participants were certainly as passionate as other fans, and they were usually better informed. To follow and manage their teams, they watched ESPN and read *USA Today*, studying the box scores in the latter with a focus Henry Chadwick, who invented the box score, could not have imagined. Indeed, the growth of *USA Today* was driven in part by fantasy players tracking their players' statistics, and while it would be a stretch to argue that the growth of the Internet was the result of fantasy players, they certainly were among the early web's most dedicated users.

◊ ◊ ◊

The game and the book took their name from a Manhattan restaurant called La Rotisserie Francaise. It was there that Daniel Okrent, the editor-turned-writer who discovered Bill James, met with friends and explained the rules of a game he'd devised.

"It wasn't enough to watch baseball, or to study it in the box scores and leader lists," Okrent recalled in the first edition of *Rotisserie*. "We all wished, in some way, to possess it, to control it. Lacking twenty million bucks, membership in the right country club, and a pair of plaid pants, I was clearly never going to own a major league club—unless I invented my own major league."[1]

Okrent would readily admit he was not the first to conceive of a stat-based baseball game. Growing up he had played Strat-O-Matic, the dice-based game where the odds were based on a player's past performance. As a student at the University of Michigan, he had learned from his advisor, a film historian named Robert Sklar, of a game Sklar and some colleagues played called the Baseball Seminar. Unlike in Strat-O-Matic, the Seminar's winner was determined not by odds based on a player's past performance but by a player's actual current performance. The rules of the Seminar were simpler than for the game Okrent would invent and involved tracking only two statistical categories. But like the participants in Rotisserie, the academics in the Seminar drafted real players and followed those players' stats throughout the season. Sklar and Okrent became friends, and Sklar became one of the participants in the first Rotisserie league and one of the editors of some editions of *Rotisserie*.

The first Rotisserie League's first draft was held in the spring of 1980. There were ten "owners." To make sure that no one could dominate by outspending others, Okrent instituted a salary cap of $250 (later increased to $260) for each roster of twenty-two (later increased to twenty-three) players. As an admirer of James, Okrent well understood the problems with the stats he chose. He stuck with them nonetheless, since they were easily understood and easy to find in box scores.

Okrent's team finished its first season in eighth place. "On the way to my dismal finish," he wrote, "I contemplated firing myself."[2] The winning team was owned by Peter Gethers, a book editor, and Glen Waggoner, who would become the editor of *Rotisserie* and the author of other sports books. Gethers and Waggoner received their winnings and, at an awards dinner, were doused not with champagne but with Yoo-hoo, the chocolate drink promoted by Yogi Berra in the 1960s.

Many of Okrent's friends who owned teams in that first league had New York media jobs, so news of the game spread quickly. Within just a few months of the draft, the *New York Times* and *CBS Morning News* had run pieces on Rotisserie. *Inside Sports* magazine ran a story by Okrent called "The Year George Foster Wasn't Worth $36."

By the late 1980s millions of Americans were meeting in board rooms and dining rooms to draft their Rotisserie teams. Bill James himself played for one year in a league filled with experts that called itself the League of Alternative Baseball Reality. Billy Beane, general manager of the Oakland A's, joined a league that included several A's staffers.

Fantasy players depended first on *The Sporting News* or local newspapers. *USA Today*, which launched in 1982, bested both by providing box scores from across the country, and fantasy players fueled the paper's growth.

"Back in the day, I used to run down to the local convenience store at 6 a.m. every other Tuesday morning to get the *USA Today*," recalled David Mannheim, the "commissioner" of a Boston-based league. "They published every major league team's stats on Tuesdays. I then went home or to work and closed my door, spending all Tuesday morning inputting every player's stats onto a spreadsheet, calculating the league's stats, putting together the standings, writing an update, and then mailing a package out to all the owners."[3]

Kevin Beatty, who owned a team in Mannheim's league, recalled that a state trooper once pulled him over on the Massachusetts Turnpike because he was reading the box scores in the newspaper while driving. "I tried to appeal to his sense of sports and explain Rotisserie," Beatty said. "He just shrugged."[4]

For some Rotisserie owners, the newspaper wasn't enough. They besieged the offices of major league teams, sometimes demanding to speak directly to the general manager. It seemed like there was no limit to how far some Rotisserie owners would go for their teams, and that included approaching players directly.

"They tell me to steal bases,"[5] Atlanta Braves outfielder Andruw Jones told sportswriter Sam Walker, who was himself scouting players for his own Rotisserie team. Walker asked Seattle Mariners outfielder Randy Winn whether he should draft him. "I *guess* I'd want myself on my team," Winn answered and then added after more thought, "I don't know. I'd have to look at the categories."[6]

The Internet ultimately replaced *USA Today* as the go-to source for team owners, and stat services provided owners with the numbers commissioners had once meticulously calculated. "I love the Internet,"[7] said Mannheim, though he admitted a part of him missed those Tuesday mornings spent behind closed doors.

◊ ◊ ◊

Rotisserie League Baseball, the book, propelled the game by providing the official rules in its first edition and by including player analyses in its later editions. More than that, the book captured the spirit of the original league, whose players could be both grandiose and ironic about their grandiosity. They called themselves the game's "founding fathers," and they presented its rules as a "Constitution," whose preamble played off that of the United States: "We, the People of the Rotisserie League, in order to spin a more perfect Game, drive Justice home, kiss domestic Tranquility good-bye...."[8]

The early 1980s, Walker noted, launched both *Rotisserie* and *Late Night with David Letterman.* "In the context of the times, the tone was pitch-perfect," Walker wrote. "The Rotisserie League was, as Waggoner puts it, 'smartalecky as can be.'"[9]

After Ken Burns came out with his documentary, *Baseball,* *Rotisserie* couldn't resist including as a parody a script for an equally epic documentary about, of course, Rotisserie. Written by Lee Eisenberg, one of the game's founders and the editor of *Esquire,* its narrator began:

> It was the greatest game for baseball fans since baseball ... and the worst game for baseball fans since baseball. It was played in the nation's dining rooms, on cornfields, in church pews, in paneled rec rooms, on kitchen tables, on conference tables, in hotel lobbies, in home offices, in airport club lounges, in barracks, and in backstreet pool halls haunted by the ghost of Edward Hopper.[10]

The books were often very funny, but as with Letterman, sometimes too many inside jokes left outsiders feeling, well, left out. In 1990, a friend of mine named John Rosen and I were asked to join Tony's Italian Kitchen League. The original Rotisserie League involved only National League players, but some of the original owners, including Waggoner, wanted an American League version and ended up in Tony's. I remember how carefully the league's owners vetted something as silly as team names to make sure they captured the spirit of the league. John and I put our heads and names together and came up with the "John Paul Popes," which was deemed acceptable though uninspired.

Not surprisingly, some more traditional sportswriters found

Rotisserie players obnoxious. In 1990, Steve Rosenbloom and Kelly Garrett wrote in *Sport* that Rotisserie combined "the worst of the '70s Me Decade (how can I use this thing to validate myself?) and the 80s Greed Decade (how can I cash in without actually doing anything?)"[11] A year later, Murray Chass wrote in the *New York Times* that Rotisserie warped fans' allegiances, for example when a lifelong Los Angeles Dodger fan whose Rotisserie roster included Atlanta Braves outfielder David Justice would cheer when Justice hit a home run against the Dodgers. Chass called Rotisserie players "baseball boors" and quoted Eugene Orza, a Players Association lawyer who advocated outlawing the game.

"It's unseemly for adults to be preoccupied with what one player on a team did in a game," Orza told Chass. "I believe that when Rotisserie players were younger, they had slide rules in their pockets. I offered to buy a guy dinner on the condition that he not talk about his Rotisserie League. He had to think about it."[12]

The 1991 edition of *Rotisserie* provided an opportunity to respond to Chass. It came in the form of an essay by Steve Wulf, one of Rotisserie's early players and a writer for *Sports Illustrated*.

"We don't mind if people poke fun at us; we do enough of that ourselves," Wulf wrote. But he objected to being called a boor and said it was Chass whose writing was boring. *Rotisserie* could be both funny and nasty, and so was Wulf. He compared Chass's columns to a W-2 form with "a forest full of words and not so much as a pine needle of wit."[13] Wulf also denied that Rotisserie had undermined traditional loyalties: "We can devote ourselves to the team closest to our heart, e.g., the Red Sox, even as we revel in the HR hit against them by the DH for the Brewers, B.J. Surhoff."[14]

Most Rotisserie players conceded that traditional loyalties were weakening. This was a result of more than Rotisserie; it was no coincidence, historian Jules Tygiel asserted, that fantasy baseball took off about the same time that free agency did. Fans resented both the soaring salaries of players and the obnoxious behavior of owners, and Rotisserie offered them the chance to feel more in control of the game, or at least to fantasize about being in control. Okrent routinely compared Rotisserians to general managers, but most saw themselves as team owners. A 1988 article in *Playboy* called fantasy owners "Armchair Steinbrenners."[15]

Unlike Steinbrenner, fantasy owners did not have unlimited money to spend, but that didn't limit their drive to win. "Some Rotisserie League owners have been known to abstain from sex for up to two months before Draft Day," Waggoner wrote in the 1984 *Rotisserie*. "This is nonsense. Three weeks is plenty."[16] More seriously, the game's defenders argued that they were better fans because of their obsession, even if it meant they sometimes rooted for their own players instead of their home team.

What the league did, Waggoner and Sklar wrote in the 1991 edition, "was to liberate men and women of every age to revive their baseball imagination. More than that: to revive their baseball knowledge. And more than that: to expand their baseball knowledge beyond any depth they thought possible in their benighted pre–Rotisserie days of simple fandom."[17]

Peter Golenbock, author of numerous baseball books including one on Rotisserie, defended the way Rotisserie owners followed their teams this way: "You begin to see nuances you never saw before. It makes you a better fan."[18] His wife, Rhonda, put it another way one morning after Golenbock looked up from the box scores and recounted his team's performance: "It's like reading about yourself in the paper every day."[19]

This was not just a new way of reading the newspaper. It was, almost, a new way of reading reality, and Tygiel, semi-seriously, suggested Rotisserie had introduced to baseball postmodernism. Rotisserians did share much with postmodernists in other fields: they were skeptical and ironic about traditional ways of understanding the world, and they embraced their own alternative realities. "The Rotisserie League," Tygiel wrote, "deconstructed baseball, breaking down the game from its normative team emphasis and reconstituting it on an individual statistical basis."[20]

Well before *Rotisserie*, some writers had used baseball to create alternate realities. As previously discussed, in Robert Coover's 1968 novel, *The Universal Baseball Association Inc., J. Henry Waugh, Prop.*, the protagonist becomes so immersed in his fantasy baseball league that the players come alive. The novelist Jack Kerouac invented a fantasy baseball game as a teenager. He charted the stats of his imaginary players, chronicled the games in newsletters and mock press reports, and continued to play the game until a year or two before his death in 1969.

Most Rotisserie players kept one foot in the real world and one in the fantasy world. After Walker's Rotisserie season ended (with his team in eighth place, despite his scouting of Jones and Winn), he looked back on it with words that echoed Jim Bouton's famous conclusion to *Ball Four*. "Ten months ago, I assumed that the game was *the game* and Rotisserie was just a preposterous satellite orbiting in its gravity. Now I know ... it's the other way around."[21]

Or as Wulf put it: "You could say these teams are imaginary, but we prefer to think of them as real and the Chicago Cubs as imaginary."[22]

◊ ◊ ◊

The book was one way Okrent and the other founders tried to keep control of their invention—and also tried to cash in on the fantasy phenomenon. Among their other products and services were a stat service, a clothing line, a video, and a convention they hosted. None were very successful. The founders copyrighted the term "Rotisserie," but savvier entrepreneurs got around that by calling it "fantasy baseball."

Even if the founders had been savvier entrepreneurs, it's unlikely they could have maintained control of their game. Fantasy sports were simply growing too quickly. According to the Fantasy Sports & Gaming Association, which represents the interest of companies in the field, the number of people playing some form of fantasy sports in the United States and Canada was about three million in 1994. Ten years later it was more than thirteen million, and the most recent estimates are about sixty million.

For owners in leagues created by Yahoo and ESPN, the experience is still similar to that in the original Rotisserie league. You may not know your fellow owners, but you generally create your team at the start of the season and follow it throughout the season. Two newer companies, however, have radically changed the way fantasy games are played. If you play fantasy sports through FanDuel, a company founded in 2009, or DraftKings, founded in 2012, you participate in tournaments, some with thousands of contestants. Winners are paid not at the end of the season but hours after creating a team. Long-term allegiances to a player, let alone a team or a city, matter no more than the corporate allegiance of a gig worker who drives for both Uber and Lyft.

DraftKings and FanDuel award millions of dollars in prize money each year. Major League Baseball, despite a history of opposing gambling that dates back to A.G. Spalding, signed a deal in 2015 with DraftKings that gave the company the right to use official baseball data and logos.

Fantasy games have extended well beyond baseball to include sports ranging from football (the most popular) to beach volleyball. There's even a fantasy Iditarod. Indeed, fantasy games have extended well beyond sports. There was a Fantasy Bachelor for fans of ABC's reality television show and a Fantasy Democratic debate featuring Joe Biden and Bernie Sanders. Thousands competed. These games—they can hardly be called sports—are perhaps best described as something taking place over the course of a televised event, or a series of events, where a player owns a set of actions that may occur and receives points when those actions occur.

Okrent watched his creation explode with horror. "I feel the way that J. Robert Oppenheimer felt having invented the atomic bomb,"[23] he said in 2015. Sometimes a note of envy crept in, though still mixed with good humor. "Rotisserie baseball had a lot to do with the success of *USA Today*," he said in 2014. "If you were playing Rotisserie baseball, you had to have *USA Today*. They haven't thanked me either."[24]

Okrent has achieved much beyond Rotisserie. He brought Bill James to the attention of a wide public. He was the co-editor of *The Ultimate Baseball Book*, a coffee-table book so lavish it almost lives up to its title. He was the author of *Nine Innings*, a book that's on one level about a single game between the Milwaukee Brewers and Baltimore Orioles but which uses that game to delve into normally unseen aspects of the sport, from a catcher's signals to a pitcher's physiology. (Okrent proved himself to be as much a master of the digression as James.) He was the first public editor of the *New York Times.* He wrote important history books on prohibition and immigration.

Yet what Okrent said in 2002 probably still holds true: "If between now and the time I die I find a cure for cancer and bring lasting peace to the Middle East, my obituary will still say, 'Okrent Dies, Invented Rotisserie League Baseball.'"[25]

9

Pete Rose: My Story

by PETE ROSE *and* ROGER KAHN

New York: Macmillan, 1989

and

My Prison Without Bars

by PETE ROSE *with* RICK HILL

Emmaus, Penn.: Rodale, 2004

The end of the Trump presidency was just the beginning of the post–Trump analyses. Well into the future historians will surely debate what led America to Donald Trump. So, here's one theory to consider: What led to Trump was Pete Rose.

The ex–baseball player and ex-president have much in common. Both are liars. Rose lied about having bet on baseball games and Trump lied about, well, more than can be covered here. Both appealed to blue collar workers, especially whites, who overlooked the lies because they saw Rose and Trump as fighting against systems rigged against them. That Trump appealed to blue collar whites has been amply documented; the percentage of blue collar whites who described themselves as Republicans jumped from 45 percent to 57 percent between 2010 and 2020. For Rose, the evidence is more anecdotal, but as Red shortstop Barry Larkin put it: "Cincinnati is a blue-collar town. Pete represented that."[1]

The divide between Rose's supporters and detractors offers a preview of the divide between Trump's supporters and detractors.

Indeed, Rose's supporters may have become so fed up with the baseball establishment that they were more likely to support Trump's attacks on the political establishment.

There is, of course, some irony to any attempt to understand Rose or Trump through their books. Both are most certainly not avid readers and both would be quick to dismiss anything that smacked of intellectualism. While they were working together on the 1989 book *Pete Rose: My Story*, Rose told the book's writer, Roger Kahn, that he'd written more books than he'd read. Kahn counted a final score of about 14 to 2, and that didn't count the books that Rose coauthored after the Rose-Kahn collaboration. Trump famously prefers television to books, and Tony Schwartz, who worked with him on their 1987 book *The Art of the Deal*, said that during the eighteen months they worked together he never saw a book in Trump's office or apartment.

Nonetheless, both Rose and Trump saw their books as key to how they presented themselves. They may not have written their books themselves, but they were very aware of their publicity value, and their books reveal much about their changing positions, strategies and ambitions. In the case of Rose, what's particularly revealing is the contrast between two books: *Pete Rose: My Story* from 1989 and *My Prison Without Bars* from 2004.

◊ ◊ ◊

Well before he became an author, Rose was courting writers. Unlike most players, he was happy to provide reporters with good quotes. Journalist Dick Schaap told Michael Sokolove, author of a 1990 biography of Rose, that of all the athletes he'd met the only one with a quicker wit than Rose was Muhammad Ali.

Rose's early works took standard approaches to hero-building. There were autobiographies such as, from 1970, *The Pete Rose Story* with Joe Garagiola and, from 1975, *Charlie Hustle* with Bob Hertzel. There were instructional manuals such as, from 1969, *How to Play Better Baseball*, co-authored by the Detroit Tiger pitcher Denny McLain who, like Rose, would later go to prison, and from 1985, *Pete Rose on Hitting* with Peter Golenbock. There was also a diary, from 1985, *Countdown to Cobb* with Hal Bodley.

The early books talked about Rose's achievements, which would ultimately include more hits and more at bats and more games played than anyone in baseball history, ten seasons with more than two hundred hits, and a forty-four-game hitting streak that set the National League record. But as Rose himself often pointed out, his achievements came not just from his natural ability but from his non-stop drive. Only Rose ran to first after a base on balls. Only Rose, in his day, routinely slid into bases head-first. Only Rose earned the nickname Charlie Hustle.

Rose's drive made him a controversial figure even before his gambling problems became public. He scored the winning run in the 1970 All-Star game by plowing into and injuring Ray Fosse, the American League catcher. Some thought that Rose was too aggressive for what was, after all, an exhibition game. Rose was unapologetic. During the 1973 National League playoffs, Rose slid hard into Met shortstop Bud Harrelson, leading to a fight with the much lighter Harrelson and leading many Met fans to see Rose as a bully. When Rose took the field, they threw so much stuff at him that the Mets almost had to forfeit the game.

Not everyone liked the way Rose flouted playing norms. It was New York Yankee pitcher Whitey Ford who christened Rose "Charlie Hustle" after one of Rose's showy post-walk runs to first, and Ford didn't mean it as a compliment. After another of Rose's unnecessary dashes, Los Angeles Dodger announcer Vin Scully commented, "Pete Rose just beat out a walk."[2]

Despite such cynicism and controversy, most fans, especially those in Cincinnati, loved him. When he first came up to the majors, players, including Rose, couldn't live on their baseball earnings and had to supplement those with off-season jobs. During the 1970s and 1980s, player salaries, including Rose's, escalated into the millions, yet he remained a player with whom fans could identify. He often talked about his humble beginnings, which were not quite as humble as he made them out to be (his father worked as a clerk at a bank) but were decidedly not wealthy. After he became rich, Rose continued to be approachable. He didn't complain when someone asked for his autograph, and he not only signed what was put in front of him but chatted with his fans. He was more likely to show up at a bowling alley than a fancy restaurant.

It helped that he was white. More than that, he was what many saw as the prototypical white athlete: slower than his Black teammates and opponents but able to make up for that with hard work and smarts. To say that whites were more dedicated and intelligent athletes than Blacks was, of course, racist, but such stereotyping was widespread at the time. (Here it should be noted that Rose himself was not racist. As a rookie with the Reds, he was much friendlier with his Black teammates than his white teammates, despite management pressure to stick with his own kind.)

My Story would firmly establish Rose's image as a hero of the working man. For this, Kahn was an unlikely collaborator. *The Boys of Summer* had established Kahn as a master of literary non-fiction about baseball. The title set forth Kahn's literary intentions, or what some of Rose's fans might consider his literary pretensions. Kahn took it from a Dylan Thomas poem, and Kahn made sure no one missed the allusion by using the first lines of the poem as his book's epigraph. Further complicating what was supposed to be a book by and about Rose was the fact that, in both *The Boys of Summer* and his subsequent books, Kahn tended to reminisce as much about his own life as about whatever or whoever was the ostensible subject of his book.

The collaboration got off to a rocky start. Kahn and Rose originally signed with Warner Books, but the manuscript was very late and Warner ultimately cancelled the contract. Macmillan then took on the book, paying an advance of $250,000, less than Warner had paid but still a lot for Macmillan at the time. The Macmillan editor, Rick Wolff, had an unusual background for New York publishing. Wolff had been a minor leaguer in the Detroit Tiger system before becoming a leading sports book editor. He was confident the collaboration could work.

And the book was, finally, coming together. The voice that emerged was unmistakably Kahn's, though he quoted Rose and others at length. Rose's love for the game came across loud and clear. During game six of the 1975 World Series, a game which many consider the most dramatic in Series history and which the Red Sox won on a 12th-inning home run by catcher Carlton Fisk, Rose came to bat with the score tied. He turned to Fisk and said, "Can you believe this game?" "It was almost as if," Kahn wrote, "in the midst of a transcendent *Hamlet,* one actor turned to another and remarked, 'Can you believe this script?'"[3]

Then came the gambling accusations. At the behest of Major League Baseball, Washington attorney John Dowd investigated the accusations. Dowd presented evidence that Rose had not only bet on baseball but, even worse, on the Cincinnati Reds, the team he was managing. Rose cut a deal. He agreed to a lifetime ban from baseball. In return, Major League Baseball agreed there would be no formal finding that Rose had bet on baseball games.

Once the gambling accusations hit the headlines, it became clear *My Story* would have to explain Rose's reasons for accepting the deal and provide his defense against the Dowd report. Kahn and Wolff flew to Cincinnati and met with Rose and his lawyer Reuven Katz.

Kahn, despite having often proudly written about his days as a reporter for the *New York Herald Tribune,* was now reluctant to ask tough questions of Rose. Perhaps this was because he'd become friendly with Rose. Perhaps it was because Kahn now saw himself as a literary figure and not an investigative reporter. Perhaps it was because he suspected Rose wasn't telling the truth and didn't want to stake his reputation on repeating his collaborator's lies. In any case, it fell to Wolff to push Rose and Katz for answers to the gambling accusations.

The meeting went on all day. Wolff left confident they had what they needed to add a solid chapter about Rose's gambling, and at least to raise a real question of doubt about the charges. On the flight back to New York, Wolff told Kahn he needed a draft in 24 hours. Kahn agreed. Wolff headed to the Macmillan offices the next day and, this being a pre-email era, at around 5 p.m. he and Macmillan publisher Bill Rosen waited eagerly by the fax machine.

"The first page comes. The second page comes," Wolff recalled. "We were waiting for the third page. Nothing happens."[4]

9. Pete Rose *(Rose; Kahn) and* My Prison… *(Rose; Hill)*

Wolff frantically called Kahn and told him only two pages had come through. Kahn said that was the best he could do. So Wolff and Rosen sat down, stitched together Wolff's notes from the trip to Cincinnati, and quickly crafted what became Chapter 10 of the book. They then sent it to Kahn for his approval. He made some edits to make sure the chapter had the same voice—Kahn's—as the rest of the book.

The chapter presented a coherent defense of Rose, attacking his accusers and raising lots of questions about Dowd's report. Baseball Commissioner A. Bartlett Giamatti made an ideal target, having spent much of his career as a professor of Renaissance literature and the president of Yale University. No one embodied the elitism and intellectualism so resented by Rose's and Trump's admirers better than Giamatti. After the settlement with Rose was announced and Giamatti was surrounded by reporters, he pleaded with them to let him answer one question at a time. "There are many of you, and only one of me," he said. "I'm just a baseball commissioner, wandering, as the poet said, lonely as a cloud."[5] He was paraphrasing a line from a poem by William Wordsworth. Giamatti understood the "beau ideal"[6] of baseball, Kahn wrote, but he did not get the reality of the game.

Giamatti made matters worse by promptly providing Rose's fans with evidence that he was biased against their hero. Among those who testified to Dowd about Rose's gambling was a bookie named Ron Peters who was awaiting sentencing on a drug charge. In return for his testimony, Dowd wrote and Giamatti signed a letter to the judge in Peters' case saying Peters had been candid, forthright, and truthful. As Rose's lawyers quickly pointed out, if Giamatti had already concluded Peters was telling the truth about Rose's gambling—as his letter to the judge clearly stated—that meant the commissioner had already decided Rose was guilty even before Rose had a chance to present any defense. No wonder Rose felt he had to cut a deal. And if Rose hoped the deal would allow him to stress that there had been no formal finding he'd bet on baseball, Giamatti quickly undermined the value of that. At a press conference announcing the deal, Hall of Fame sportscaster Bob Wolff (Rick Wolff's father) asked

Giamatti whether he, personally, believed Rose had bet on baseball. Giamatti answered that he did.

Rick Wolff was satisfied with chapter 10. "Because there was never a trial," he reflected, "and because Rose agreed to a deal with Major League Baseball, his book was really the only time that Rose's defense was open to the public. I felt that baseball fans could reach their own conclusion."[7]

The book was a commercial success. There were significant offers from magazines to run excerpts, but Macmillan turned them down to keep the focus on the book itself. *My Story* spent two weeks on the *New York Times* bestseller list.

Years later, after Rose admitted to having bet on baseball, Kahn admitted he was worried that their collaboration had tainted his legacy. In his 2006 memoir, *Into My Own*, Kahn wrote that Rose had been "evasive" and that he "lied a great deal, sounding sincere as he did."[8] As for Wolff, he said *My Story* was "the only book I ever edited that started out as nonfiction and ended up as fiction."[9]

◊ ◊ ◊

Like Rose, Trump early on mastered the art of publicity. Despite his later denunciations of the mainstream media, the pre-presidential Trump clearly enjoyed talking to—and manipulating—reporters. He was eminently quotable, especially about himself. And despite his dislike of reading, Trump clearly saw his own books as ways to burnish his image as a businessman with a Midas touch and to extend his fame beyond readers of New York's tabloids. Indeed, when he decided to run for president, he explained it was because we need a leader who wrote *The Art of the Deal.*

Random House paid a half million-dollar advance for *The Art of the Deal* and earned that back many times over. The book topped the *New York Times* bestseller list for thirteen weeks, spending a total of forty-eight weeks on the list, selling more than a million copies, and turning Trump from a largely New York celebrity into a national figure.

The book made clear that Trump, like Rose, had mastered not just the art of the deal but also the art of the lie. "A little hyperbole never hurts," he and Schwartz wrote in *The Art of the Deal.* "People want to believe that something is the biggest and greatest and the most spectacular." Trump and Schwartz referred to this as "truthful hyperbole."[10] Such hyperbole may not have been as untruthful as what Trump aide Kellyanne Conway later called "alternative facts,"[11] but it sure wasn't strictly truthful.

Trump and Schwartz rewrote Trump's failures as anyone's fault but his own. One of Trump's forays into the sports world, for example, was his unsuccessful stint as an owner of a team in the United States Football League. This investment, he explained in *The Art of the Deal*, would have paid off if only his fellow owners hadn't been afraid to directly challenge the NFL by moving USFL games from the spring to the fall. The book chronicled success after success, even though by the time it was published in 1989 Trump was deeply in debt, and a year later he declared bankruptcy.

Also untruthful was Trump's presentation of himself as a self-made man. He made fun of those born to wealth, calling them in *The Art of the Deal* members of the "Lucky Sperm Club."[12] For Trump to stress his humble origins, however well that might play to his blue collar admirers, was a much greater stretch than it was for Rose. Trump's father had made millions in real estate, and Fred Trump's loans and co-signings made possible many of his son's early deals.

As a political liberal, Schwartz was as unlikely a collaborator for Trump as Kahn was for Rose. Like Kahn, Schwartz came to regret his involvement in the book, despite the millions in royalties he earned. "I put lipstick on a pig," he told Jane Mayer for a July 2016 article in *The New Yorker.* "I feel a deep sense of remorse that I contributed to presenting Trump in a way that brought him wider attention and made him more appealing than he is."[13]

Trump's next coauthor, Charles Leerhsen, ended up as disturbed by the experience as Schwartz had been. Leerhsen and Trump wrote *Trump: Surviving at the Top*, which Random House published in 1990 and which, though not as huge a phenomenon as *The Art of the Deal*, still spent seven weeks on the *Times* bestseller list including two weeks at number one. Like Schwartz, Leerhsen portrayed Trump as a dealmaker with unerring instincts. But in a 2019 piece for the *Huffington Post*, Leerhsen wrote that in reality during most of the time they spent together Trump did nothing but flip through fabric swatches. "It was true that the carpets and drapes at his properties needed to be refreshed frequently," Leerhsen noted. "But the main thing about fabric swatches was that they were within his comfort zone—whereas, for example, the management of hotels and airlines clearly wasn't."[14]

Trump overcame his financial setbacks and again trumpeted his successes in subsequent books with an array of coauthors. In 1997 there was *The Art of the Comeback*. In 2004 there were *How to Get Rich* and *Think Like a Billionaire*. In 2006 there was *Why We Want You to Be Rich*. In 2007 there was *Think Big and Kick Ass in Business and Life*. In 2011 there was *Midas Touch: Why Some Entrepreneurs Get Rich—and Why Most Don't*.

Amidst the tales of his business success, many of which were repeated in book after book, Trump's thoughts about politics began to creep into his books. *Think Big and Kick Ass* noted, ironically in light of Trump's later position, that Bill Clinton "has the ability to think big, and his wife, Hillary, who is a fantastic person, also has the ability to think big."[15]

Trump's political ambitions were most evident, of course, in books released as he considered running and as then as he ran for president. There was *The America We Deserve* in 2000. There was *Time to Get Tough* in 2011. And there was *Crippled America: How to Make America Great Again* in 2015. Trump set forth his political positions, but his pitch harkened back to *The Art of the Deal*. What America needed, he consistently asserted, was a president who knew how to make a deal, and dealing with China or Mexico would be no different than dealing with real estate in New York or Atlantic City. *Crippled America* outsold every other candidate's book published that year.

◊ ◊ ◊

Rose was increasingly unhappy with the deal he had cut with Giamatti. He had hoped Major League Baseball might, with time, relent and allow him back into the game. That hadn't happened.

Perhaps, many suggested, MLB would relent if Rose admitted that, yes, he had bet on baseball. Rose decided to confess and again chose a book to tell his story.

My Prison Without Bars, coauthored by actor and screenwriter Rick Hill, was published in 2004 by Rodale, a company best known for its health and wellness magazines. Steve Murphy, who became CEO in 2002, was moving the company aggressively into other areas, and Rodale reportedly paid a one million dollar advance for the book and printed half a million copies.

My Prison included Rose's confession that he'd gambled on baseball games and even on Reds games he'd managed. But Rose was quick to point fingers elsewhere. The Dowd report, he and Hill wrote, had "more goddamn holes than Swiss cheese."[16]

Overall, *My Prison* had a lot more excuses than apologies for Rose's gambling. Rose and Hill quoted Dr. David Comings, director of medical genetics at the City of Hope National Medical Center in Duarte, California, who explained that Rose suffered from Attention Deficit Hyperactivity Disorder. The ADHD meant he was very strong-willed and it helped him become one of the greatest hitters in baseball history. Comings compared Rose to Albert Einstein. Both had trouble focusing on subjects that didn't interest them, Comings said, but both were great successes when they found something they loved.

Rose stressed that he never bet *against* the Reds. "I knew that I broke the letter of the law," he and Hill wrote. "But I didn't think I broke the 'spirit' of the law, which was designed to prevent corruption. During the times I gambled as a manager, ... I never allowed my wagers to influence my baseball decisions."[17] What drove him to bet, he explained, was not greed but his desire to win—the same desire that accounted for his 4,256 hits.

My Prison also argued that Rose's punishment didn't fit the crime. None of the players found to have used drugs, including performance enhancing drugs, were permanently banned from baseball. "Steve Howe and Darryl Strawberry violated baseball's drug policy— numerous times," Rose and Hill wrote. "Both men got suspended— numerous times. Baseball paid for their rehabilitation—numerous times. Yet I'm banned for life?"[18]

Rose was not only largely unapologetic about his gambling but also about his having failed to pay taxes on some gambling winnings as well as on cash he'd earned from selling memorabilia and autographs. For this he was sentenced to five months in prison. "I'm probably the only person in America to go to jail for under-paying his taxes by four percent,"[19] he said in *My Prison*. Always good for a one-liner, he added: "I'm better at breaking records than I am with keeping them."[20]

As was later the case for Trump, the more Rose flouted establishment norms, the more his admirers loved him. The same went for his sometimes-crude behavior, for example in his reality TV series. Unlike *The Apprentice*, which Trump starred in for 14 seasons, Rose's series lasted only six episodes. One of the plots in the series involved whether Rose's then-fiancé, a former Playboy model, should get breast reduction surgery. Rose was against it. He was for calling the series "Tits and Hits" but settled for *Pete Rose: Hits and Mrs.*

Off the set, Rose's behavior was equally brazen. He sometimes reserved seats at Cincinnati's Riverfront Stadium for both his wife and his girlfriend. He showed off his Rolls-Royce and talked about all the money he made. But this too didn't hurt his popularity, any more than Trump's boasting about women and money hurt his. For Rose's admirers and later for Trump's admirers, anything that offended critics merely proved the anti-establishment bonafides of their champions. Even Rose's tax evasion appealed to many tax-hating Americans.

My Prison made a splash, at least initially. The week the book was published, Rose appeared on *Good Morning America* and an excerpt appeared in *Sports Illustrated*. Thousands lined up at book signings, and the book spent five weeks on the *Times* bestseller list. But sales soon slowed and the book reportedly did not sell nearly as many as Rodale printed.

For Rose, the bigger disappointment was that Major League Baseball was unmoved by his confession. Rose and Hill compared the Dowd report to Swiss cheese. But, as Rose's 2014 biographer Kostya Kennedy put it, Rose's confession proved that Dowd's conclusions had been "as solid as hunk of petrified Gouda."[21] In a *New York Times* op-ed piece, Fay Vincent, who had become commissioner after Giamatti died in 1989, snidely remarked that St. Augustine had established a high bar for confessional tomes and that between Rose and Augustine, "there is little doubt whose book will last longer."[22] Bud Selig had replaced Vincent as commissioner in 2002 but, whether because he agreed with Vincent that Rose's confession was unsatisfactory or because of loyalty to Giamatti or for some other reason, Selig did not reinstate Rose.

To Giamatti's admirers, their hero was as much of a martyr as Rose. More so, for when Giamatti died of a heart attack just eight days after announcing Rose's ban and just five months after becoming commissioner, many blamed Rose. True, Giamatti was a smoker and overweight, but, as Vincent put it, "I don't think one can overestimate the pressure the Rose issue put on Bart."[23]

Rose's critics were also annoyed by the fact that he could not or would not see the dangers of betting on games which he played in or managed. Even if Rose had never bet against the Reds—and no evidence has emerged that he ever did—what if, for example, he'd been tempted to bring in a relief pitcher to assure a win on a game he'd bet on rather than saving that pitcher for the next game? Or what if he accumulated losses and a bookie then demanded to be paid back with a dubious managerial decision? There are good reasons to prohibit anyone in baseball from gambling on baseball games, and Rose wouldn't concede this.

The commissioners who succeeded Giamatti as well as Giamatti's many admirers viewed Rose's continued popularity with much the same combination of dismay and disgust as Trump's opponents later viewed Trump. Despite the attempts by Rose and Kahn to portray the commissioner as a pretentious intellectual who didn't understand the reality of baseball, Giamatti loved the game. His love for baseball may have differed from Rose's but it was just as deep.

Giamatti's admirers were bewildered by the anti–Giamatti rhetoric. Why, Vincent asked, would Giamatti want to pick a fight with someone as popular as Rose? Giamatti was physically and temperamentally unsuited to take on someone as unafraid as Rose to play—and fight—hard. Giamatti's kind of fight, Vincent said, "was over the proper interpretation of Dante."[24]

Above all, Giamatti's admirers were offended by the way Rose could change his story without ever seeming to alienate his fans. First Rose said he didn't bet on baseball. Then he said he bet only occasionally. Then he said he bet a lot but never on games he played in or managed. Finally, he said he bet on Reds games but always on the Reds to win. And when he finally apologized, it never seemed all that sincere. Sometimes he only seemed sorry he'd been caught. Other times, he only seemed to act sorry in the hope that Giamatti's successors would let him back into the game. Like Trump, Rose seemed able to lie without consequences, at least among his admirers.

Rose's lies were not, of course, as damaging as Trump's. And as a gambling addict, Rose may not have fully controlled what he was doing. Nor were all of Rose's supporters duped because they were stupid or uneducated; witness, for example, the strong defenses of Rose from Rick Wolff in the chapter he drafted for *My Story* or Bill James in *The Baseball Book 1990*. Many of Rose's supporters thought Rose was guilty but concluded—with some evidence—that Dowd and Giamatti were biased against Rose. Many thought he was guilty but still belonged in the Hall of Fame.

And so the gap widened between Rose's admirers and detractors, categories which certainly greatly overlapped with those who would become Trump's admirers and detractors. Neither side could make sense of the other side's positions or feelings.

Given Rose's interest in gambling and Trump's in casinos and in sports, it was perhaps inevitable that the two men would meet. They were first introduced when Rose appeared at autograph shows at Trump Plaza and Hotel in Atlantic City. But their longest meetings came after Rose was released from prison. Banned from baseball and looking for a new way to make money, Rose decided to get into the business of breeding thoroughbred horses. Rose and his partners, his friend Wayne Lyster and the well-known trainer D. Wayne Lukas, decided to ask Trump for a $30 million investment.

Rose and Lyster set up a meeting with Trump in New York, and in *My Prison* Rose described his pre-meeting jitters:

9. Pete Rose *(Rose; Kahn) and* My Prison... *(Rose; Hill)*

I played in 17 All-Star games and won three World Championships, yet I was nervous as hell.... Deep down, in a place where I didn't want to go, I was concerned that Mr. Trump might not want to invest with an ex-con who had been kicked out of baseball. But Wayne reassured me that everything would be fine. He was the technical expert who could answer all of Mr. Trump's questions, D. Wayne Lukas was the world-class trainer, and I was ... well, I was Pete Rose.[25]

Rose arrived at Trump Tower on Fifth Avenue, where he was impressed with the marble and waterfall in the lobby:

I knew that I was in the right place. Mr. Trump was very gracious and well-prepared. He asked all the right questions and even complimented us on what he thought was a first-class proposal. ... Mr. Trump was a big baseball fan and well aware of my hitting records. I didn't need to try and impress him. The meeting went far better than expected.[26]

Two weeks later, Rose reported, he met Trump again. Trump gave him a hug and expressed a desire to join him in the winner's circle of the Kentucky Derby. Alas:

Within days after returning to Cincinnati, we read in the newspaper that Ivana Trump had just caught The Donald in the company of a young beauty named Marla Maples. The scandal got front-page coverage and also cost us a chance at completing our deal. Later, a spokesman told us that Mr. Trump would not be getting involved with any new business ventures until after his pending divorce was final.[27]

A deal never happened, perhaps because of Trump's divorce or perhaps because he decided it was too risky an investment. But, though Trump never invested in Rose's business, he continued to be a Rose supporter. In February 2020, Trump tweeted:

Pete Rose played Major League Baseball for 24 seasons, 1963–1986, and had more hits, 4,256, than any other player (by a wide margin). He gambled, but only on his own team winning, and paid a decades long price. GET PETE ROSE INTO THE BASEBALL HALL OF FAME. It's Time![28]

Trump's supporters at Fox were also loyal to Rose. Rose's latest book, *Play Hungry*, was published in 2019 by Penguin Press. *Play Hungry* was in no way a book about politics, despite any connections there might be between Rose and Trump. Penguin Press editor Christopher Richards did note, however, that "the Fox networks were particularly keen to interview him and that they portrayed him in an especially positive light."[29]

What about Rose's and Trump's opponents? Were there any secret alliances on that side? Since some of their followers have been prone to conspiracy theories, let them connect these dots:

In 2017, John Dowd, the lawyer who wrote the report on Rose's gambling that led to Rose being banned from the game, represented Donald Trump during the Robert Mueller investigations. Also in 2017, Dowd introduced Trump to another lawyer who soon joined the Trump team: Ty Cobb, a distant relative of the player whose all-time hit record Rose surpassed. Both Dowd and Cobb were ultimately replaced because they were pushing Trump to cooperate with Mueller's investigation and had failed to deliver on promises to bring the investigation to a quick end.

Did Dowd, having ended the baseball career of the player beloved by blue collar Americans, then turn his sights on the president whose base consisted largely of the same demographic? Was Cobb part of the same vendetta?

There's no doubt Dowd and Cobb were more eager to cooperate with Mueller than others on Trump's legal team. A *New York Times* reporter overheard a lunch conversation between the two at a steakhouse near the White House. "Our view is we're not hiding anything," Cobb told Dowd, according to a *Times* report that suggested Cobb and Dowd wanted to turn over to Mueller more documents. Cobb then called another lawyer on the president's team a "McGahn spy,"[30] referring to White House counsel Donald McGahn, who was among those reluctant to turn over documents. Later, Trump strategist Steve Bannon called Cobb's willingness to waive executive privilege "reckless."[31]

Does that amount to a conspiracy against Trump? Certainly not. There's nothing unusual about lawyers disagreeing about the best strategy for their client. And to suggest a conspiracy aimed at both Trump *and* Rose is absurd. That Dowd had a role in both investigations suggests only that he had a knack for high profile cases. Even

Trump, who has not hesitated to embrace other conspiracy theories, has never suggested Dowd and Cobb conspired against him, let alone that it had anything to do with Rose.

But for those who like meaningless coincidences, here's one more: Charles Leerhsen, who coauthored *Trump: Surviving at the Top*, also wrote a biography of Ty Cobb.

10

Other Influential Books

Beadle's Dime Base-Ball Player
by Henry Chadwick
(New York: Irwin P. Beadle & Company, 1860)

Chadwick was baseball's first true reporter; indeed, before Chadwick newspapers and magazines barely covered sports. Starting in the late 1850s, Chadwick wrote for dailies and weeklies including the *New York Times, Brooklyn Eagle,* and *New York Clipper,* and in 1860 he produced *Beadle's Dime Base-Ball Player,* the game's first annual guide. This first edition included a history of baseball, which the British-born Chadwick believed had evolved from the English game of rounders. Chadwick included the rules for rounders as well as the much more complicated rules for baseball, which he had helped draft at an 1857 convention of baseball players from the New York area. Chadwick also included descriptions of the roles of players at each baseball position.

It was the 1861 edition of *Beadle's,* however, that introduced Chadwick's most influential innovations—methods for scoring baseball and statistical records for players and teams. His scoring system has been replaced by others, but scoring games is still a key part of how many fans experience games, and most scorers still record strikeouts with a "K," as did Chadwick. (Chadwick thought K and not S was the most memorable letter in "strike.")

Statistics have of course become key to how everyone—commentators, managers and general managers, players, and fans—analyze baseball. The stats Chadwick introduced in the 1861 *Beadle's* included runs and average, though Chadwick's batting average was calculated very differently from today's average. Chadwick divided the number of runs a player scored by the number of games in which he played.

Chadwick was convinced that statistical analysis was the best way to gauge a player's contributions. "Many a dashing player," he wrote in the 1864 *Beadle's*, "who carries off a great deal of éclat in prominent matches, has all 'the gilt taken off the gingerbread,' as the saying is, by these matter-of-fact figures, given at the close of the season; and we are frequently surprised to find that the modest but efficient worker, who has played earnestly and steadily through the season, apparently unnoticed, has come in, at the close of the race, the real victor."[1]

Chadwick's conviction that statistics mattered was very much of his time. Innovators in other fields were increasingly relying on quantitative analysis, and these included Chadwick's brother Edwin, who remained in England and became secretary to a royal commission tasked with reforming laws that provided relief to the poor and who relied on statistics to change the system.

Henry Chadwick later went on to edit other baseball annuals, including, starting in 1882, *Spalding's Official Base Ball Guide.* A.G. Spalding drew on Chadwick's papers in writing his history of baseball; see Chapter 1 for more on that book, *America's National Game.*

Chadwick and Spalding feuded, mostly amiably, over Spalding's claim that Abner Doubleday invented the game. Chadwick never backed away from his belief, as set forth in *Beadle's*, that baseball evolved from rounders, but it should be noted that he also wrote in that first annual that rounders was "entirely devoid of the manly features that characterize Base Ball."[2]

Chadwick was elected to the Hall of Fame in 1938.

The Great Match, and Other Matches
by Anonymous
(Boston: Roberts Brothers, 1877)

Was this the first novel about baseball? It depends how you look at it. William Everett's earlier novels, *Changing Base* (Boston: Lee & Shepard, 1868) and *Double Play* (Boston: Lee & Shepard, 1871), included some baseball action as did Caroline E. Kelly Davis's *The Yachtville Boys* (Boston: Henry Hoyt, 1869). But *The Great Match* was the first whose main plot revolved around a game, in this case between teams representing the fictional New England towns of Milltown and Dornfield.

The novel, though satirical, offered a look at small-town culture during the era. "Milltown had the money, and Dornfield the aristocracy,"[3] wrote the anonymous author, and both were deeply invested in their baseball teams: "The ministers of both towns found it necessary to preach sermons on brotherly love, and the sin of excitement in all things; but each town wanted to whip just once, and then would, perhaps, think of what their pastors inculcated."[4]

What generated the attention around the novel and thus ensured its influence was the decision to publish the book anonymously. *The Great Match* was the fifth in Roberts Brothers' "No Name" series. The publisher's gimmick led reviewers to speculate about the identity of the author, especially since Roberts Brothers advertised that some of the writers were well known. One was later identified as Louisa May Alcott, author of *Little Women*. Some reviewers, noting the baseball action in *The Great Match*, assumed it must have been written by a man; others noted that the plot also included romances between women of the towns and players on the teams and assumed it must have been written by a woman. (The romances give the title a double meaning.) In a 2010 article, literary scholar Geri Strecker argued convincingly that, though many in the nineteenth and twentieth century had settled on a man and the Library of Congress still credited John Trowbridge, the author was actually Mary P. Wells Smith. Among the evidence Strecker cited was that Smith was a strong supporter of women's rights, and the novel's heroine rejected traditional gender roles and, to the consternation of some novel's characters and some contemporary reviewers, wished she could play baseball.

Some scholars consider the first baseball novel not to be *The Great Match* but Noah Brooks' *Our Baseball Club and How it Won the Championship* (New York: E.P. Dutton, 1884), which again featured a rivalry between two towns but had more play-by-play action. In his introduction to that book, A.G. Spalding wrote: "The tale here told very cleverly gives the reader a glimpse of the ups and downs, the trials and the triumphs of a base ball club.... While nothing is really needed to popularize the game, I am sure the story will commend itself to every lover of pure and wholesome literature."[5]

Frank Merriwell's School Days
by Burt L. Standish
(Philadelphia: David McKay, 1901)

The boy who would become as All American a hero as ever could be first appeared in the 1896 dime novel, *Frank Merriwell; or First Days at Fardale.* Arriving at the military academy he would attend before going on to Yale, Merriwell intervenes when a fellow student kicks a dog. The bully warns Frank not to meddle.

"I have a right to meddle," Frank responds, "because you just struck one who is smaller and weaker than yourself.... I can't help it. I always take the side of the underdog."[6] Frank doesn't smoke or drink. He is brave, handsome, smart, and athletic. He stands up to bullies, often (as in this case) turning them into loyal friends. He also stars at every sport he plays, above all baseball. His go-to pitch when the game is on the line is his double-shoot, which breaks in two directions.

Baseball doesn't play a big part in this first story but that would soon change. By the time four Merriwell stories, including *First Days*, were combined in Standish's 1901 *School Days*, Merriwell's pitching prowess was central to the story. His plebes take on the established cadets, led by another bully who, unable to hit his pitches, arranges for Merriwell to take a swig of some poisoned water. Merriwell survives to triumph on and off the field in 245 books. Some of these, it should be noted, starred Frank's younger brother Dick.

For the vast majority of the Merriwell stories Burt Standish was actually Gilbert Patten, who wrote under a contract with his publisher, Street & Smith, that initially paid him $60 a week and later $150. Standish delivered twenty thousand words a week for more than seventeen years. Ultimately the stories were read by hundreds of millions of kids. In the 1930s, Merriwell also starred in a comic strip and radio show.

Wrote the editor and critic George Jean Nathan in *American Mercury*: "I doubt in all seriousness if there was an American writer … who was so widely read by the boys of the time…. For one who read Mark Twain's *Huckleberry Finn* or *Tom Sawyer*, there were ten thousand who read Standish's *Frank Merriwell's Dilemma* or *Frank Merriwell at Yale*."[7] Wrote Stewart Holbrook in *American Heritage*: "Americans born too late to have met him in the glorious days of his long career may have difficulty understanding what a really superb creation Frank Merriwell was. At the turn of last century, he approximated the young god that almost every boy in the United States actually wanted to be."

Unlike Horatio Alger's, Holbrook noted, Merriwell's was not a rags-to-riches story. He was born into wealth and "represented not only manliness and success, but the more admirable attitudes and characteristics of the Anglo-Saxon 'ruling class' of the period."[8]

For more on Merriwell, see Chapter 1.

Sol White's Official Base Ball Guide
by Sol White
(Philadelphia: H. Walter Schlichter, 1907)

As both a player and manager during the late nineteenth and early twentieth century, White was uniquely qualified to write about the early years of Black baseball, and his book is, as baseball historian Jerry Malloy put it, "still invaluable as a primary and a secondary source, a chronicle and a memoir, an elegy and an alarum."[9]

White experienced first-hand the hardening of the color line. Early in his career, he played on minor league white teams as well as on Black teams that played against white teams. Later, as Jim Crow spread, he played—with much success—for Black teams that played other Black teams.

White identified 1887 as the turning point, and he placed much of the blame on Cap Anson, the manager and first baseman of the

Chicago White Stockings (and also the first player to get 3,000 hits). Anson refused to let his players take the field against a team whose catcher was a Black—Moses Fleetwood "Fleet" Walker. Anson's "repugnant feeling ... toward colored ball players," White wrote, "hastened the exclusion to the black man from the white leagues."[10] Later historians have agreed that Anson was racist but have spread the blame more widely.

Walker was the last Black to play in a major league until Jackie Robinson in 1947. His experiences in and out of baseball left him bitter, and in 1908 he published a booklet called *Our Home Colony; A Treatise on the Past, Present and Future of the Negro Race in America.* Walker advocated, as Marcus Garvey later would, that Blacks move to Africa.

White was more optimistic than Walker about the prospects for integration. Baseball, he wrote, "should be taken seriously by the colored player, as honest efforts with his great ability will open an avenue in the near future wherein he may walk hand-in-hand with the opposite race in the greatest of all American games."[11] He even reported a rumor that a National League manager was pushing to sign a Black player. But White could not—how could he?—ignore the obstacles Blacks faced. "In no other profession has the color line been drawn more rigidly than in base ball,"[12] he wrote. And of course the discrimination took place off the field as well: White could remember a time when he stayed in the same hotels as whites, but now when Black teams arrive in a town "all hotels are generally filled from the cellar to the garret."[13]

The book's size did not reflect its importance. It was only 128 pages and that included fourteen pages of ads. By the 1920s, only a few copies were still around and White was unable to find a publisher for a second edition. If a manuscript of that second edition exists, it has not been found. But when interest in the early years of Black baseball grew in the last decades of the twentieth century, White's book was not only reprinted but also recognized as what baseball historian Lawrence D. Hogan called "an indispensable record."[14] Wrote Malloy: "Sol White's *Guide* is the Dead Sea Scrolls of black professional baseball's pioneering community."[15]

The National Game
by Alfred H. Spink
(St. Louis: National Game Publishing Company, 1910)

This history of the game was primarily a biographical encyclopedia, and Spink's loyalties were clear from his dedication: "to the professional base ball players of America, to the silent army, to the force that is in the field to-day, and to the legions that are to follow in years to come."[16]

The entries were organized by position, and then alphabetically within each section. For some of the game's early superstars Spink included not just basic biographical information but also the praise of others. On Napoleon Lajoie, the Philadelphia and Cleveland second baseman, Spink quoted White Sox manager Hugh Duffy on how he thought he had discovered that Lajoie's weakness was a high and inside pitch. The day after Duffy came to this conclusion, he instructed his pitcher accordingly. Lajoie promptly hit the pitch over the left field fence. Duffy decided he had previously "caught Larry on one of his few off-days and that weakness hunch was all a hallucination."[17] On Honus Wagner, the Pittsburgh shortstop, Spink quoted Omaha *Daily News* writer Tip Wright, who called him "a Dreadnaught, powerful, majestic, all-compelling—a leviathan of the sea, with the latent power of unaccounted volcanoes behind her steel sides—frisking at thirty knots, starting, stopping, turning, darting, dodging like a destroyer."[18]

The National Game was praised by many baseball officials, and the American League endorsed it as "the standard work on baseball."[19] Spink hoped that it would be updated annually, and an expanded second edition was published in 1911. After that, however, the book faded into obscurity. A.G. Spalding's *America's National Game*, which was published a year after Spink's book, was more generally accepted as the semi-official history of the game to date. In contrast to Spink, Spalding's interests and sympathies lay more with owners than with players; see Chapter 1.

Spink's influence lasted, however, not just through later encyclopedias and annuals but also through the weekly he founded in

1886, *The Sporting News.* Ownership of *The Sporting News* ultimately passed to his nephew, J.G. Taylor Spink, and later in the twentieth century it became known as "the bible of baseball."

Pitching in a Pinch
by Christy Mathewson
(New York: Putnam, 1912)

Mathewson was not the first baseball player to write a book. George Wright wrote *Record of the Boston Base Ball Club, Since Its Organization* (Boston: Rockwell and Company, 1874) and Mike "King" Kelly wrote the game's first memoir, *Play Ball: Stories of the Ball Field* (Boston: Emery and Hughes, 1888). Others followed. But Mathewson's book mattered to his readers because he was the first player to fully embody the image of an All-American hero. He was, to be sure, a great pitcher, one of five players chosen during the Hall of Fame's first election. The "pinch" of the book's title referred to clutch situations, and Mathewson was deservedly acclaimed for rising to an occasion. In eleven World Series games, he had an ERA of 1.15. But Mathewson was more famous for his image than his exploits. In an era when baseball was considered a barely respectable career, Mathewson had gone to college, spoke out against drinking, didn't play on Sundays, and rarely argued with umpires. It also helped that he was tall, blonde, and handsome, and that he managed, despite all this, not to incur the resentment of his teammates. Said Chief Meyers, his longtime catcher on the New York Giants: "We'd break our necks for that guy. If you'd make an error behind him, or anything of that sort, he'd never get mad or sulk. He'd come over and pat you on the back."[20]

"Matt was worshiped," wrote the critic Jonathan Yardley. "Men and women of all classes held him up as a model for their children."[21] There was even a special edition of *Pitching in a Pinch* for Boy Scouts.

Mathewson was often compared to Frank Merriwell, baseball's first flawless (and fictional) model for kids. Merriwell appeared in hundreds of dime novels, starting in 1896. That was four years before

Mathewson made it to the National League, so no one could accuse Gilbert Patten, Merriwell's creator, of exploiting the pitcher's image. The same could not be said for the Stratemeyer syndicate, which created Nancy Drew, the Hardy Boys, and starting in 1912, a character named Baseball Joe. Baseball Joe clearly drew on Mathewson; he played for the Giants and his manager was named McRae, which sounded suspiciously like the actual Giant manager John McGraw. Matthewson himself wrote a series of children's books with titles like *Pitcher Pollock* (New York: Grosset and Dunlap, 1914), *Catcher Craig* (New York: Grosset and Dunlap, 1915), and *First Base Faulkner* (New York: Grosset and Dunlap, 1916).

Despite his college education, Mathewson had a ghostwriter. John Wheeler, a reporter for the *New York Herald*, wrote some articles with Mathewson during the 1911 World Series between the Giants and Philadelphia Athletics and then the syndicated columns on "inside baseball" that became *Pitching in a Pinch*. The book mixed anecdotes about players, managers, and umpires with discussions of strategies and even ethics. Some of the latter are still timely. For example, Mathewson distinguished between honest and dishonest sign stealing and illustrated the latter by telling of a wire that ran from a clubhouse, where a spy was equipped with binoculars, across the outfield to a buzzer on a chunk of wood outside of third base. The plot was uncovered because the Philadelphia third base coach never budged, even though at one point he was standing in a puddle.

Baseball Joe of the Silver Stars
by Lester Chadwick
(New York: Cupples & Leon, 1912)

Like Frank Merriwell, "Baseball Joe" Matson was too good to be true. Joe starred in fourteen novels, starting with this one in 1912 and finishing in 1928. The books were produced by the Stratemeyer Syndicate. Stratemeyer might have chosen the name of Chadwick for the books' author to conjure up a connection to Henry Chadwick, who was well known for his early writings about baseball. The first baseball novel attributed to Lester Chadwick was *The Rival Pitchers* (New York: Cupples & Leon, 1910), but that wasn't about Baseball Joe.

Like Merriwell, Joe was as humble as he was good. In the final scene of *Silver Stars*, after the fifteen-year-old Joe struck out the final batter of his team's rival to win the county championship, his teammates celebrated.

"Great work, old man! Great!" yelled Darrell in Joe's ear. "You saved the day for us."

"Nonsense!" exclaimed Joe modestly.[22]

Like Merriwell, Joe went to prep school in *Baseball Joe on the School Nine* (New York: Cupples & Leon, 1912) and then to Yale in *Baseball Joe at Yale* (New York: Cupples & Leon, 1913). Unlike Merriwell, Joe then turned pro and played in the minors in *Baseball Joe in the Central League* (New York: Cupples & Leon, 1914) and in the majors in a series of books. These included *Baseball Joe in the World Series* (New York: Cupples & Leon, 1917), in which he foiled a plot to fix the Series, *Baseball Joe, Home Run King* (New York: Cupples & Leon, 1922), in which he followed Babe Ruth from pitching to hitting, and *Baseball Joe, Pitching Wizard* (New York, Cupples, & Leon, 1928), in which he struck out all twenty-seven batters. "Presumably unable to top this," wrote Andy McCue is his bibliography of baseball fiction, "the Baseball Joe series was not revived."[23]

When baseball eventually became a subject for serious novelists (see Chapter 4), they tended to distance themselves from juvenile fiction like the *Baseball Joe* books. When Mark Harris' *The Southpaw* appeared in 1953, the jacket copy stressed that the book's hero, Henry Wiggen, "has nothing in common with Frank Merriwell or Baseball Joe, just as 'The Southpaw' has nothing in common with the sentimental, saccharine and completely improbably sagas which keep bobbing up under the general category of 'baseball books.'" But Harris himself later wrote that as a boy he had read and undoubtedly been influenced by stories about boys who were good and who made good, like those by Horatio Alger and like those in the Baseball Joe series. Henry Wiggen is certainly a much more complex character than Baseball Joe but, Harris wrote, Wiggen "does succeed, does grow rich, does protect and preserve a moral virtue. For, of course, my novel had a great deal in common with that success tradition from which I emerged as a boy reader."[24]

The Kid from Tomkinsville
by John R. Tunis
(New York: Harcourt, Brace, 1940)

In his 2016 book, *Young Adult Literature: From Romance to Realism*, Michael Cart argued that Tunis was one of three writers who could claim to be the first to write fiction for young adults. Tunis' heroes may have triumphed, but they faced obstacles, internal and external, that couldn't be pushed aside as easily as those Frank Merriwell encountered. In *The Kid from Tomkinsville*, Tunis' first baseball book, Roy Tucker's rookie season as a Dodger pitcher was derailed, first when the veteran catcher who was mentoring him was cut and then when Tucker fell in a shower and injured his arm. In subsequent books featuring Tucker and the Dodgers, societal problems came to the fore: In *Keystone Kids* (New York: Harcourt, Brace, 1943), the brothers who played shortstop and second base were torn apart by the latter's anti–Semitic attitudes toward the team's Jewish catcher. In *The Kid Comes Back* (New York: William Morrow, 1946), Tucker returned to the Dodgers after having been injured during World War II.

Tunis himself didn't like being characterized as a YA author. He recalled in an interview sending his first novel, which was about a track star, to Alfred Harcourt, the founder of the publisher Harcourt, Brace. Harcourt told him he wanted to publish it as a book for boys. "I was shocked and disappointed," Tunis said. "I continued writing these so-called boys' books, but I've never considered them that. They can be read by adults. Oh, well, they sold."[25]

The Kid from Tomkinsville influenced writers of adult as well as young adult fiction. The hero of Bernard Malamud's 1952 novel *The Natural* was, like Tucker, forced to turn from pitcher to outfielder after being injured. It's unclear whether Malamud consciously drew on Tunis but Philip Roth certainly did so: the hero of Roth's 1997 novel *American Pastoral* was a star athlete who faced Job-like problems—and who as a child, Roth's narrator reported, kept on a shelf by his bed *The Kid from Tomkinsville.*

Wrote journalist Pete Hamill in 1999: "One thing that strikes me about this short novel: Virtually every sportswriter I know remembers reading it as a boy."[26]

Ball, Bat and Bishop: The Origin of Ball Games
by Robert W. Henderson
(New York: Rockport Press, 1947)

The Mills Commission, which was formed to investigate the origins of baseball, proclaimed in December 1907 that the game had been invented by Abner Doubleday, but from the start there were doubters. One of the earliest and most thorough debunkers was Henderson, a librarian. Amidst preparations in 1939 to celebrate the opening of the National Baseball Hall of Fame and Museum and the supposed centennial of Doubleday's invention, Henderson published an article in the *Bulletin of the New York Public Library* with descriptions of games that sounded much like baseball and that had appeared before 1839. Henderson followed up with *Ball, Bat and Bishop*, which pointed out the many holes in the case for Doubleday and added many examples of bat-and-ball games through the ages. Among the intriguing examples was one from *Female Robinson Crusoe*, a novel published in 1837 in which Indians played a baseball-like game using a ball made of a sturgeon's head covered with deerskin. Another was a twelfth-century Easter ceremony in France that included the Archbishop throwing a ball; hence the "bishop" in Henderson's title.

Taking up where Henderson left off, Harold Peterson's *The Man Who Invented Baseball* (New York: Scribner's, 1973) added more examples of baseball-like games through the centuries. Peterson substituted Hoboken for Cooperstown as baseball's birthplace and Alexander Cartwright for Doubleday as the game's inventor, based on Cartwright, as a member of New York's Knickerbocker club, having supposedly written down in 1845 the rules for a game much like today's baseball. Peterson was not the first to put forward Cartwright as an alternative to Doubleday, but he buttressed the case by following Cartwright as he traveled west to California and Hawaii, spreading his version of the game. The case for Cartwright has since been largely discredited by baseball historian John Thorn, who presented evidence that other members of the Knickerbockers played greater roles in shaping the rules. More thorough than Peterson was David Block, whose *Baseball Before We Knew It: A Search for the Roots of the Game* (Lincoln: University of Nebraska Press, 2005) added more examples of baseball-like games from across the globe. Those played in England and early America included club-ball, stool-ball, trap-ball, and tip-cat.

For more on the Doubleday myth, see Chapter 1.

Baseball: A Historical Narrative of the Game, the Men Who Have Played It, and Its Place in American Life
by Robert Smith
(New York: Simon & Schuster, 1947)

Though Harold Seymour and Jules Tygiel later demonstrated the benefits of a scholarly approach to the game's history, no true baseball fan—or baseball writer—would denigrate a more casual approach. Smith's remains one of the most enjoyable anecdotal histories of the game and especially its early years. Here you can read about how Mike "King" Kelly, in the days before there was a rule about runners passing each other on the base paths, would have the runner ahead of him stop in front of home plate so that Kelly could slide between the man's feet. Or how Toad Ramsey struck out 355 batters in 1887, thanks to having had bricks dropped on his left hand; this prevented him from flexing his middle finger and led him to throw a natural knuckleball. Or how Pete Browning believed the best way to pack hits into his eyeballs was to stare straight into the sun, a practice that instead of blinding him somehow led to a .341 average over thirteen seasons. Or how John McGraw, while playing third base, would slip his fingers inside a runner's belt to keep him from tagging up. Browning put a stop to this by loosening his belt so that when he headed home, he left McGraw holding the belt in his hand.

McGraw also figured in a story Smith told about Fred Merkle, who infamously failed to touch second base and thus cost the Giants the 1908 pennant. McGraw, then the Giant manager, reportedly sneaked Merkle into the ballpark later that night so that Merkle could truthfully swear he had touched second base on the fateful date. "Although I am a man who will believe almost anything any-one tells me about baseball," Smith wrote, "I somehow cannot quite ingest this particular fable."[27] That did not stop Smith from telling the story, nor should it have done so. For as Daniel Okrent and Steve Wulf wrote in the preface to their 1989 collection of baseball anec-dotes, "if you don't show a willingness to hear at least *something* in the obvious tall-tale, you're missing out on the game's very music."[28]

A revised and expanded edition of *Baseball* was published in 1970.

Jackie Robinson: My Own Story
by Jackie Robinson as told to Wendell Smith
(New York: Greenberg, 1948)

Robinson's first book was published in May 1948, just a little over a year after he had broken major league baseball's color line, and it reflected and enhanced the image he and Branch Rickey, the Brooklyn Dodgers' general manager, had carefully cultivated. Robinson came across as a man with a Gandhi-like patience, one whose answer to racism was to turn the other cheek. More militant Blacks later criticized Robinson as an Uncle Tom, and the book's non-confrontational tone provided ammunition for such attacks. See Chapter 3 for a discussion of how these attacks failed to take into account the many ways Robinson fought, aggressively, for civil rights on and off the field.

Robinson never shrugged off racism. The tone of *My Own Story* was partly the result of the limits placed on him by Rickey and by the times. It was also partly the work of his collaborator. Wendell Smith was one of the most influential of the era's Black sportswriters, and his reporting in the Pittsburgh *Courier* played an important role in pressuring baseball executives that the time had come to integrate the game and that Robinson was the player to do so. But Smith very much agreed with Rickey that Robinson had to do so by being polite in the face of whatever insults were hurled at him. Robinson, Smith wrote in the *Courier* in December 1945, "has the hopes, aspirations and ambitions of thirteen million black Americans heaped upon his broad, sturdy shoulders."[29]

In the years after the book was published, as Robinson became more assertive, Smith turned on him. When Robinson complained the press was treating him unfairly—and reporters did tend to jump all over and sometimes exaggerate Robinson's run-ins with other players—Smith lectured him in a tone that made clear he ought to appreciate what reporters (and Smith) had done for him. Wrote Smith in the *Courier*: "If it had not been for the press—the sympathetic press—Mr. Robinson would have probably still been t[r]amping around the country with Negro teams.... Mr. Robinson's memory, it seems, is getting shorter and shorter. That is especially true in the case of the many newspapermen who have befriended him throughout his career."[30]

Clearly the pressure to turn the other cheek, as Robinson did when he first came up to the majors and in his first book, came not just from whites but also from many Blacks.

The Year the Yankees Lost the Pennant
by Douglas Wallop
(New York: W.W. Norton, 1954)

Two years after Bernard Malamud's *The Natural* injected Arthurian and other myths into a novel about baseball, Douglas Wallop did the same for the legend of Faust, the scholar who sold his soul to the devil in return for magic powers. In this case, the devil was named Applegate and the magic powers were purchased by Joe Boyd, a middle-aged real estate salesman dissatisfied with his job, his wife, and above all the losing ways of the Washington Senators. Applegate transforms Joe Boyd into Joe Hardy, a twenty-one-year-old phenom who less than two months later has hit 48 home runs with a batting average of .545 and who has led the Senators into contention. But the devil, it turns out to the surprise of very few readers, is a Yankee fan, and Joe Boyd, it turns out to the surprise of even fewer, loves his wife and wants to go home. In the climactic scene, Applegate turns Hardy back into Boyd, but Boyd manages to slide under the Yankee catcher's tag to win the pennant. And, Wallop wrote, "not even the devil could force an umpire to change his decision."[31]

Other than drawing on a venerable legend, Wallop's approach was completely different from Malamud's. Wallop did not take his book too seriously; it's lighthearted throughout and often very funny. The jacket cartoon was drawn by Willard Mullin, best known for drawing the Brooklyn Bum, symbol of a team even more famous than the Senators for its losing ways.

The book was turned into the hit musical *Damn Yankees*, which won eight Tony Awards including for best musical, best leading actor (Ray Walston as Applegate), best leading actress (Gwen Verdon as Lola, the temptress Applegate enlists to seduce Joe), and best choreography. The choreographer was Bob Fosse, and in the 1958 movie version of *Damn Yankees* Fosse danced with Verdon, who again starred alongside Walston. Wallop co-wrote the book for the musical with George Abbott.

After the 1969 Mets won the World Series—almost as improbably as the Senators' win in Wallop's book—many of the Mets, including Tom Seaver, appeared on the *Ed Sullivan Show* to sing "You Gotta Have Heart," the song the Senators sang in the musical. A 1997 revival of the show starred Maggie Gyllenhaal as Lola and Whoopi Goldberg as Applegate. A 1985 revival starred former Cincinnati Red catcher Johnny Bench as Boyd and Hardy.

Fear Strikes Out: The Jim Piersall Story
by Jim Piersall and Al Hirshberg
(Boston: Little, Brown, 1955)

At a time when mental illness was rarely discussed openly, Piersall's story of his breakdown, hospitalization, and recovery resounded well beyond the sports world. "I want the world to know that people like me who have returned from the half-world of mental oblivion are not forever contaminated," he wrote. "We don't have to talk about our sickness in whispers or prowl about on the edge of society with our hands to our ears to block out the whispers of others."[32]

The breakdown occurred in 1952, while Piersall was the rookie shortstop for the Red Sox. Piersall's illness manifested itself in ways that often entertained fans. He imitated Dom DiMaggio's stride in the outfield and Satchel Paige's motions on the mound, and he hitched rides on the jeep carrying relievers from the bullpen. But the illness also led to more serious incidents, such as fistfights with other players and repeatedly getting thrown out of games by umpires.

One symptom of Piersall's illness was that he remembered nothing of the six months prior to his hospitalization. In *Fear Strikes Out*, he told the stories not as he remembered them but as he learned of them from his wife, doctor, and newspaper clippings.

Piersall's successful return to the Red Sox in 1953 undoubtedly inspired many. So did a 1955 television show starring Tab Hunter as Piersall and a 1957 movie starring Anthony Perkins as Piersall and Karl Malden as his father. Piersall himself didn't like the movie, partly because it portrayed his father negatively (though the book also presented the pressure his father put on him to succeed as one of the reasons for Piersall's breakdown). Piersall also complained that Perkins "danced around the outfield like a ballerina, and he was supposed to be depicting me, a major league baseball player."[33]

Some of Piersall's later work treated his mental illness more lightly than *Fear Strikes Out*. In 1965 he was a guest star on *The Lucy Show*, and after meeting Lucy he quipped: "And they call me a kook."[34] His later memoir, coauthored with Richard Whittingham,

The Truth Hurts (Chicago: Contemporary Books, 1984), recounted numerous incidents which Piersall presented as funny but which, in light of his earlier episodes, indicated a continuing struggle to control his emotions. What Piersall suffered from would probably today be diagnosed as bipolar disorder, for which symptoms often recur even in patients who seem to have recovered as well as Piersall did. But if Piersall later downplayed how serious and long-lasting his symptoms were, his honest account in *Fear Strikes Out* remained a breakthrough. Sixty years after the book was published, Barron H. Lerner, a professor of medicine, wrote that Piersall "did a world of good for people who had long suffered in silence."[35]

The Hot Stove League
by Lee Allen
(New York: A.S. Barnes, 1955)

Decades before Bill James and the Elias Sports Bureau started publishing previously obscure statistics, one could find out in *The Hot Stove League* what states sent the most players to the major leagues (California, with the top five states producing 36.8 percent of all players) or what the average rookie weighed (184.6 pounds in 1953, up from 174.0 in 1929). Any aspect of the game's history might catch Allen's attention, and his work inspired future statisticians and future historians.

In his foreword to a collection of Allen's columns from *The Sporting News*, Paul D. Adomites, the publications director of the Society for American Baseball Research, wrote that "before there was a SABR, Lee Allen was a SABR member ... holding forth on the births and deaths of 19th century stars, describing players who died in plane crashes, relishing stories of fat pitchers, elucidating his all-Lithuanian team."[36] John Thorn, major league baseball's official historian, described Allen as "the Sherlock Holmes of baseball— the finder of lost players, connoisseur of curious facts, debunker of well-entrenched myths."[37]

Allen collected stories as well as facts, and *The Hot Stove*

League offers a great selection. In a chapter on players' nicknames, one learns that Aloysius Szymanski became outfielder Al Simmons because he saw the name Simmons on a billboard, and infielder Jack Atz said he was once named Zimmerman but decided to change his name because players on a financially struggling team were paid in alphabetical order. Always a researcher as well as a storyteller, Allen checked out Atz's story with his widow and learned that "her husband's name was never Zimmerman, never, in fact, anything but Atz."[38] Allen also enjoyed debunking the tales told by various players who claimed to be the model for "Casey at the Bat." These included a Daniel M. Casey who played for the Phillies from 1886 through 1899 and who presented as evidence his recollection that the neighborhood where the Phillies played was often referred to as Mudville, the setting for Ernest Thayer's poem, and that he once struck out and stranded two runners in the ninth, just as Thayer's Casey did. Daniel Casey's claim was undercut, Allen noted, by the fact that he had never posted a batting average higher than .183.

Allen was the historian for the Hall of Fame's library from 1959 until his death in 1969. (His predecessor in that job thought the phrase "hot stove league"—meaning off-season baseball talk—originated with a Cincinnati sportswriter named Ren Mulford around the turn of the twentieth century.) Allen's files were crucial sources for *The Baseball Encyclopedia*, published the year he died.

A Day in the Bleachers
by Arnold Hano
(New York: Crowell, 1955)

Hano was the first to devote an entire book to a single game, in this case the first game of the 1954 World Series between the New York Giants and the Cleveland Indians. The game is most often remembered for what's still referred to as "the catch"—Willie Mays' game-saving-on-the-run-over-the-shoulder-seemingly-impossible catch of Vic Wertz's hit to deep center field. From the bleachers, where Hano sat, it did not seem quite so impossible, because Mays had turned so quickly and run so fast to get there. Hano was more impressed by the throw, which kept the runners from advancing: "This was the throw of a giant, the throw of a howitzer made human."[39]

As he recounted the progress of the game, Hano provided background on players and strategies, a loose structure that others later followed, most notably Daniel Okrent in *Nine Innings* (New York: Ticknor & Fields, 1985). But what was most remarkable was how Hano described what it was like to sit in the bleachers: the waiting in line for tickets, the banter between strangers, the memories of previous games that popped into his mind, even the temptation to decide whether a pitch was a ball or strike, without waiting for the umpire's call and while sitting more than five hundred feet away from home plate: "Once in a while I'm mistaken, but then, I remind myself, umpires are human."[40]

Wrote Roger Kahn in his introduction to a 1982 reprint: "This was what it was like to sit in the cheap seats and follow a ball game as a knowledgeable fan. This was how it was when Willie Mays was young and all the grass was real and the bleachers were a haven."[41] In writing from the perspective of a fan—a fan whose prose was always elegant and often lighthearted—Hano was a forerunner of Roger Angell.

The Fireside Book of Baseball
edited by Charles Einstein
(New York: Simon & Schuster, 1956)

Einstein's superb mix of autobiography, fiction, history, poems, profiles, spot reporting, and miscellaneous other baseball writings confirmed to any who might have doubted it that baseball was a game for writers. Rather than organize his anthology by categories or chronology, Einstein just placed the entries alphabetically by author, with the category besides it. This was, he later wrote, sort of like when Casey Stengel in his final year as a manager assembled his rookies and told them, "Line up in alphabetical order according to height."[42] The results placed famous names next to obscure ones and also led to some appealing juxtapositions. Ernest L. Thayer's famous "Casey at the Bat," for example, was followed by Fred W. Thayer's letter to A.G. Spalding about the invention of the catcher's mask, which included a rhyme as apt as anything in "Casey": "Thatcher was the catcher."[43]

It was not difficult, Einstein wrote in his preface, to choose between good writing and writing about memorable moments or famous players: "Time and again, the three show up together.... Good writers 'come up' to good material. Like good ballplayers, they can hit in the clutch."[44]

Einstein followed up the success of *Fireside* with equally worthy sequels: *The Second Fireside Book of Baseball* (New York: Simon & Schuster, 1958), *The Third Fireside Book of Baseball* (New York: Simon & Schuster, 1968), and *The Fireside Book of Baseball* (New York Simon & Schuster, 1987, fourth edition). Einstein's became the standards against which other anthologies would be judged, and given the amount of good baseball writing to draw from, others did indeed follow, with some but by no means too much overlap. The best were John Thorn's *The Armchair Book of Baseball* (New York: Scribner's, 1985) and *The Armchair Book of Baseball II* (New York, Scribner's, 1987) and Nicholas Dawidoff's *Baseball: A Literary Anthology* (New York: Library of America, 2002). The most offbeat were edited by Richard Grossinger and Kevin Kerrane and culminated in *Into the Temple of Baseball* (Berkeley, California: Celestial Arts, 1990), which included mystical as well as more standard approaches to the game. An example of the former was Rob Brezsny's "Qabalistic Sex* Magick for Shortstops and Second Basemen."

Baseball: The Early Years
by Harold Seymour
(New York: Oxford University Press, 1960)

Seymour's doctoral dissertation for Cornell University was the first one on baseball to be accepted by a university history department, and his book went a long way toward making base-ball a respectable subject for academic books, journals, and courses. *Baseball: The Early Years*, the first volume in a trilogy, chroni-cles the sport from its evolution from a child's game to an amateur sport for gentlemen to an organized business monopoly. The focus is less on teams and players and more on how the game reflected eco-nomic and social aspects of American society. The book ends with the American League in place and with baseball America's lead-ing spectator sport. The second volume, *Baseball: The Golden Age* (New York: Oxford, 1971), carries the story through the period when baseball fully captured the American imagination, including the organizational changes that ended with the rule of baseball's first commissioner, Kenesaw Mountain Landis. The third volume, *Base-ball: The People's Game* (New York: Oxford, 1990), departs from the chronological approach to cover baseball outside the major and minor leagues with sections on the game as played, prior to World War II, in colleges, prisons, and the military, and by women and Blacks.

Among the scholars who followed in Seymour's footsteps was David Quentin Voigt who wrote his own admirable three-volume history: *American Baseball: From Gentleman's Sport to the Commis-sioner System* (Norman: University of Oklahoma Press, 1966), *Amer-ican Baseball: From the Commissioners to Continental Expansion* (Norman: Oklahoma, 1970), and *American Baseball: From Postwar Expansion to the Electronic Age* (University Park: Pennsylvania State University Press, 1983).

Despite Seymour's success in making baseball a respectable sub-ject for academics and academic publishers, Oxford University Press was quick to point out in its author biography that Seymour had firsthand experience with the game which included being a batboy for the Brooklyn Dodgers. And despite Seymour's academic reputa-tion, he in one case failed to give proper attribution. His wife played a substantial role in preparing the books, and in 2010, almost twenty years after he died, Oxford University Press began crediting Dorothy Seymour Mills as co-author of the three books.

The Long Season
by Jim Brosnan
(New York: Harper & Row, 1960)

The Long Season is often described as a predecessor to *Ball Four*; see Chapter 5 for a discussion of Brosnan's book in the context of Bouton's. Both were diaries of a season by a pitcher and both were far more candid than the average as-told-to book, though Brosnan's was much less salacious. But Brosnan deserves attention in his own right, not only because he wrote the book on his own but also because he captured, as well as anyone before or after, both the ways a pitcher approached each batter and also the ways a player approached the ups and downs of what is indeed a long season. This particular season was 1959, during which Brosnan pitched first for the St. Louis Cardinals and then for the Cincinnati Reds.

On May 6 Brosnan entered a game against Philadelphia in the ninth with a three-run lead. The first batter he faced was infielder Willie Jones. "I knew I could get him out if I kept everything away, and wasted maybe one pitch inside," Brosnan wrote. "But he hit a pitch that was just not quite far enough away from him."[45] After giving up a hit to Phillies outfielder Dave Philley, Brosnan was relieved, and after the Phillies scored the winning run, "the locker room steamed nervously, the damp walls reflecting every player's breath."[46] Twenty-four hours later Brosnan was again pitching in the ninth and again gave up a hit to Jones before again facing Philley. He told himself: "Nothing but power this time. I'm going to throw this ball right by him."

"And I did."[47]

Brosnan followed *The Long Season* with *Pennant Race* (New York: Harper & Brothers, 1962), a diary of his 1961 season with the Reds. That book had the added excitement of a race which the Reds won.

Veeck As in Wreck: The Autobiography of Bill Veeck
by Bill Veeck with Ed Linn
(New York: Putnam, 1962)

Veeck is best known as the man who, as owner of the St. Louis Browns in 1951, sent up to bat the three-foot seven-inch Eddie

Gaedel. When the pitcher, understandably, couldn't come close to the strike zone, Gaedel walked. But Gaedel was merely the most famous of Veeck's ingenious promotions, or as more traditional owners tended to brand them, cheap stunts.

In his autobiography, Veeck answered his critics. "I have never objected to being called vulgar," Veeck wrote. "The word ... comes from the Latin *vulgaris*, which means—students?— 'the common people.'"[48] Veeck was a fan as well as owner, and he was happier in the bleachers than in the owner's box.

For Veeck, a baseball game was entertainment, not sacred ritual. He introduced circus acts and fireworks between games of doubleheaders, and scoreboards that would explode after home runs. "In what way does a fireworks display intrude upon a baseball game?" he argued. "Baseball loves to wrap itself in that phrase 'The National Game,' but what's so un–American about fireworks?"[49]

Some of Veeck's innovations, he readily admitted, stretched the bounds of sportsmanship. As owner of a minor league team in Milwaukee that couldn't run, his infield was made up of a loose, sandy mixture that was so much like running on a beach that the team's opponents couldn't run either. And because the same team also didn't have much in the way of hitting, he installed motorized fences that were lowered for the home team and raised for the visitor's half of the inning. (The league quickly and reasonably made this practice illegal.) Veeck's descriptions of such efforts on behalf of "closer competition"[50] are very funny.

Many of Veeck's ideas were not jokes, however, and many were ultimately adopted despite the initial resistance of the baseball establishment. Veeck was an early advocate of interleague play and of amending the reserve clause that bound players to a single team. And he signed the American League's first Negro League player in Larry Doby and its most famous one in Satchel Paige. In fact, before the Dodgers signed Jackie Robinson, Veeck planned to buy the Phillies and stock the team with multiple Negro Leaguers, but when he informed Commissioner Kenesaw Mountain Landis of his plan the commissioner quickly arranged for the Phillies to be sold to someone else.

How might the causes Veeck championed fared without him, or without his book? It's impossible to say for sure. But, as his coauthor Ed Linn wrote in 1986, the year Veeck died, "at what Bill Veeck did, he wasn't only the first, and he wasn't only the best. He was the only."[51]

Maybe I'll Pitch Forever
by LeRoy (Satchel) Paige as told to David Lipman
(Garden City, New York: Doubleday, 1962)

Paige's 1948 memoir *Pitchin' Man* was among the most influential baseball books written; see Chapter 4. It was published just one year after Jackie Robinson joined the Brooklyn Dodgers and the same year that Paige joined the Cleveland Indians—at a time when it was by no means certain that the integration of baseball would be successful or lasting. But if *Pitchin' Man* was published when Paige could still change the course of history, the 1962 *Maybe I'll Pitch Forever* offered a fuller and more honest view of that history.

As in the earlier book, Paige filled *Forever* with entertaining stories, usually at least partly true, about his records and his age, his confrontations with the slugger Josh Gibson and the Dominican dictator Rafael Trujillo, his rules for staying young like "don't look back. Something might be gaining on you."[52] But in *Forever* Paige allowed more of his bitterness to seep through. About his childhood in Alabama: "I found out what it was like to be a Negro in Mobile. Even if you're only seven, eight, or nine, it eats at you when you know you got nothing."[53] Or about traveling on Black teams in the Jim Crow era: "There'd be some white folks in the stands. Some of them'd call you nigger, but most would cheer you.... But I still remember those, 'Sorry, we can't serve you here.'"[54] Or about his feelings when Jackie Robinson was called up to the majors: Unlike Robinson, Paige wrote, he wouldn't have been willing to start in the minors and he would have demanded a higher salary. "But signing Jackie like they did still hurt me deep down. I'd been the guy who started all that big talk about letting us in the big time. I'd been the one who'd opened up the major league parks to the colored teams. I'd been the one who the white boys wanted to barnstorm against. I'd been the one who everybody'd said should be in the majors."[55]

Eight Men Out: The Black Sox and the 1919 World Series
by Eliot Asinof
(New York: Holt, Rinehart & Winston, 1963)

Asinof's classic history proved that a story about baseball could benefit from intensive reporting, with as satisfying a payoff as a story about anything else. Since its publication, some critics have questioned whether Asinof's reconstructions of scenes bordered on fiction. But in this sense, too, Asinof was in the vanguard: in the years that followed the book's publication, writers like Tom Wolfe would apply literary techniques to non-fiction in what Wolfe called the "New Journalism." And Asinof's version of how and why eight members of the 1919 White Sox threw the Series has largely withstood the test of time—and of later investigations.

The players who threw the Series are not the villains of Asinof's story. They were guilty, yes, but they were also grossly underpaid by White Sox owner Charles Comiskey. Indeed, part of the book's appeal is that so many of its characters are portrayed sympathetically. Asinof's sympathy for underpaid players was also apparent in his first novel, *Man on Spikes* (New York: McGraw-Hill, 1955), a story about a struggling minor leaguer.

John Sayles' superb 1988 movie further increased public sympathy for the eight men out—the eight players, most famously "Shoeless Joe" Jackson, who were permanently banned from baseball. So did the movie *Field of Dreams*, which was released a year after Sayles' movie and in which the hero builds a ballpark on his Iowa farm so that Jackson, or perhaps Jackson's ghost, can emerge from the corn field.

Asinof titled a later book *1919: America's Loss of Innocence* (New York: Donald I. Fine, 1990). That book went beyond baseball to include the Senate's rejection of the League of Nations, anti-communist panic and violence, and the corruption that followed Prohibition. But what most clearly disillusioned Americans was the Black Sox scandal.

"If baseball was corrupt, then *anything* might be—and probably was," Asinof wrote. "There is no way to gauge the extent of the damage on the American psyche. It is impossible to add up bitterness like a batting average."

Asinof then repeated the famous lines with which a boy supposedly approached Jackson. "'Say it ain't so, Joe ... say it ain't so.' It was like a last, desperate plea for faith itself."

A week later, Asinof added, instead of "Play ball," Chicago kids were hollering, "Play bail."[56]

The Glory of Their Times: The Story of the Early Days of Baseball Told by the Men Who Played It
by Lawrence S. Ritter
(New York: Macmillan, 1966)

Ritter has sometimes been credited with inventing oral history. That's an overstatement. Decades before Ritter traveled around the country recording the words of long-retired baseball players, John and Alan Lomax had done the same for folk singers. But Ritter certainly was a master of the art of interviewing and of the subsequent editing of first-person accounts, in his case from those who played the game in the last years of the nineteenth century and the early years of the twentieth. In the process, he went a long way toward establishing our idea of "the good old days," both for baseball and for America.

This was an era, as described by the players Ritter interviewed, in which the country was imbued with optimism and energy. Teenagers who ran away from home ended up not as missing persons but as major leaguers. Stanley Coveleski told Ritter that as a twelve year old he was too busy working as a miner to play much baseball, but every evening after he got home, he threw stones. "Just for something to do," Coveleski mused. "Heck, we didn't have any television then, or radio, or automobiles, or even a telephone or electric lights. Had to do *something*. So I threw stones."[57] Ultimately, this paid off in more than two hundred wins for Coveleski, mostly for Cleveland.

It was a more rugged game. Fields and equipment were primitive. Infielder Hans Lobert was playing for Cincinnati in 1907 when he was beaned and knocked out for ten minutes. He stayed in the game. But Lobert, like the others Ritter interviewed, loved the game, especially the focus on speed instead of power.

"In *my* book the most exciting play in baseball is a three-bagger, or an inside-the-park home run," said Tommy Leach, an outfielder and third baseman who spent much of his career in Pittsburgh. "You used to see a fair number of them in the old days, but now they're the rarest plays in baseball. For sheer excitement, I don't think anything can beat when you see that guy go tearing around the bases and come sliding into third or into the plate, with the ball coming in on a line from the outfield at the same time."[58]

Davy Jones, who played outfield for various teams until 1918, put it this way: "Oh, the game was very different in my day from what it's like today. I don't mean just that the fences were further back and the ball was deader and things like that. I mean it was more *fun* to play."

The game was full of colorful characters. "Back at the turn of the century," Jones explained, "we didn't have the mass communication and mass transportation that exist nowadays. We didn't have as much schooling, either. As a result, people were more unique then."[59]

Certainly unique was Germany Schaefer, an infielder for various teams until 1916. Schaefer and Jones were playing for Detroit in 1908 when Schaefer was on first and Jones on third. Schaefer flashed Jones the sign for a double steal, hoping to draw a throw to second so Jones could steal home. Schaefer reached second, but the catcher held onto the ball so Jones held at third.

On the next pitch, Schaefer yelled, "'Let's try it again,'" Jones recalled. "And with a blood-curdling shout he took off like a wild Indian *back to first base*, and dove in headfirst in a cloud of dust." The catcher was too stunned to do anything, so Jones was still stuck on third. But on the next pitch Schaefer again took off for second. By this time the catcher "evidently had enough because he finally threw to second to get Schaefer, and when he did I took off for home and *both* of us were safe."[60]

Ritter started work on a sequel but never finished it, in part because of the press of his duties as a professor of economics. (His best known book, besides *Glory*, was titled *Principles of Money, Banking, and Financial Markets*.) He turned over the three new interviews he'd done to baseball writer Donald Honig, who put them to good use in *Baseball When the Grass Was Real: Baseball from the Twenties to the Forties Told by the Men Who Played It* (New York: Coward, McCann and Geoghegan, 1975). Honig followed that with *Baseball Between the Lines: Baseball in the Forties and Fifties* (New York: Coward, McCann and Geoghegan, 1976), *The Man in the Dugout: Fifteen Big League Managers Speak Their Minds* (Westchester, Illinois: Follett, 1977), and *The October Heroes: Great World Series Games Remembered by the Men Who Played Them* (New York: Simon & Schuster, 1979).

Danny Peary organized his work by year rather than by the person interviewed in *We Played the Game: 65 Players Remember Baseball's Greatest Era, 1947–1964* (New York: Hyperion, 1994) as did Peter Golenbock in *Dynasty: The New York Yankees, 1949–1964* (Englewood Cliffs, New Jersey: Prentice-Hall, 1975), the first of his popular oral histories on teams. John Holway collected *Voices from the Great Black Baseball Leagues* (New York: Dodd, Mead, 1975). Others branched out to interview non-players. Jerome Holtzman interviewed sports writers for *No Cheering in the Press Box* (New York: Holt, Rinehart and Winston, 1974). Curt Smith did the same for play-by-play and color men in *The Storytellers: From Mel Allen to Bob Costas: Sixty Years of Baseball Tales from the Broadcast Booth* (New York: Macmillan, 1995). Mike Bryan's *Baseball Lives: Men and Women of the Game Talk About Their Jobs, Their Lives, and the National Pastime* (New York: Pantheon, 1989) included everyone from bus drivers to beer vendors, and his interview with the director of marketing for the San Diego Padres captures, perhaps better than anything else written, the passion of a fan.

The Universal Baseball Association, Inc.
J. Henry Waugh, Prop.
by Robert Coover
(New York: Random House, 1968)

Coover's novel about an accountant who escaped his drab life by inventing and becoming obsessed with an imaginary baseball league whose results are determined by rolls of his dice followed in the tradition of Bernard Malamud's *The Natural* by playing with the connections between baseball and mythology; see Chapter 4 for a discussion of the book in that context. But Coover was in the forefront of another literary tradition. Along with such postmodernist writers as John Barth, Donald Barthelme, William Gass, Thomas Pynchon, Tom Stoppard, and Kurt Vonnegut, Coover also played with the lines between fantasy and reality. In the final chapter of *The Universal Baseball Association*, Waugh—the accountant who created the league—has disappeared, leaving his players and his readers to wonder whether he, like God, ever existed, or perhaps was dead. Or perhaps, as one character suggested, "that God exists and he is a nut."[61]

In a 2011 interview, Coover said he and other experimental novelists of the late 1960s "didn't launch forth like a school, announcing manifestos and so on," but that "there was a desire for renewal, and desire does sometimes take somewhat experimental forms."[62] But other writers certainly acknowledged Coover's influence. The novelist Hari Kunzru, writing in 2011, said Coover (and others) "broke open the carapace of postwar American realism to reveal a fantastical funhouse of narrative possibilities." Of Coover in particular, Kunzru wrote: "His relentless experimentalism, combined with a sly and often bawdy humour, have made him a writer's writer."[63]

The Baseball Encyclopedia: The Complete
and Official Record of Major League Baseball
by Information Concepts, Inc.
(New York: Macmillan, 1969)

The Baseball Encyclopedia was certainly not the first book of baseball statistics. Starting in 1862, Henry Chadwick compiled basic stats in the annual *Beadle's Dime Base-Ball Player* (New York: Sinclair-Tousey, 1862), and just about ninety years later Hy Turkin and S.C. Thompson pulled together players' stats in *The Official Encyclopedia of Baseball* (New York: A.S. Barnes, 1951). But what came to be known as "Big Mac" (because it was published by Macmillan) far surpassed previous works in scope and accuracy.

The Baseball Encyclopedia originated with statistician David Neft, who enlisted about twenty researchers and the data processing capabilities of Information Concepts, Inc. The work was painstaking and sometimes controversial. For example, ICI decided to increase Babe Ruth's home run total from 714 to 715, after realizing that a 1918 home run had been counted as a triple. (The rules then in effect credited batters who hit what today would be called a walk-off home run with only as many bases as it took for a runner on base to score.) Faced with an uproar from traditionalists, ICI backed away and Ruth's total remained 714.

The *Encyclopedia* weighed in at 2,337 pages and six and a half pounds. It was, wrote Alan Schwarz in *The Numbers Game*, his entertaining history of baseball statistics, "the national pastime's equivalent of the *Oxford English Dictionary*."[64] The book included year-by-year and total statistics. For hitters, these were games, at bats, hits, doubles, triples, home runs, home run percentage, runs, RBIs, walks, strikeouts, steals, batting average, pinch hit at-bats, pinch hits, and games by position played. The little-used home run percentage (homers per 100 at-bats) was included, Schwarz noted, because as a boy Neft had invented a game for which he figured all stats per 100 at-bats. For pitchers, the stats were wins, losses, winning percentage, ERA, games, games started, games completed, innings pitched, hits, walks, strikeouts, and shutouts, as well as some categories for relief appearances, including saves.

The Baseball Encyclopedia was ultimately supplanted by John Thorn's and Pete Palmer's *Total Baseball* (New York: Warner, 1989), which corrected many old statistics and added many new statistical categories, and in 1996 Macmillan stopped printing the book. But in its day Big Mac reigned supreme, and even its limitations were valuable fuel for the innovations that in the 1980s and 1990s revolutionized thinking about baseball statistics.

My Turn at Bat: The Story of My Life
by Ted Williams with John Underwood
(New York: Simon & Schuster, 1969)

No coauthor has better captured a player's voice than Underwood did Williams.' Williams spent much of his life seething with resentment—at his neglectful mother, at fickle fans, above all at reporters who he believed treated him unfairly—and here was his chance to express his anger. Few other great athletes would look back on their career and state, as Williams did in his opening line: "I'm glad it's over."[65] Years after retiring, he could still say: "Oh, I hated that Boston press," and gloat that "I've outlived the ones who were really vicious, who wrote some of the meanest, most slanderous things you can imagine."[66] Indeed, that Williams trusted his life's story to a reporter underlined just how special was his relationship with Underwood. Leigh Montville, who wrote a biography of Williams, summed up how unlikely a relationship this was with the mock headline: "Williams Befriends Sportswriter! Man Bites Cocker Spaniel!"[67]

Underwood not only set a standard for as-told-to books but also produced a work on which all future writing about Williams would draw—and Williams has perhaps attracted more good writing than any other player. Fine books about him include Richard Ben Cramer's *The Seasons of the Kid* (New York: Prentice Hall Press, 1991), which included an essay by Cramer originally published in *Esquire* and photo essays by John Thorn; Michael Seidel's *Ted Williams: A Baseball Life* (Chicago: Contemporary Books, 1991); Ed Linn's *Hitter: The Life and Turmoils of Ted Williams* (San Diego: Harcourt Brace, 1993); Montville's *Ted Williams: The Biography of an American Hero* (New York: Doubleday, 2004); and Ben Bradlee, Jr.'s *The Kid: The Immortal Life of Ted Williams* (Boston: Little, Brown, 2013). Lawrence Baldassaro's *The Ted Williams Reader* (New York: Fireside, 1991) includes two classic works on Williams' last game: John Updike's "Hub Fans Bid Kid Adieu" and Linn's "The Kid's Last Game." Dick Johnson's and Glenn Stout's *Ted Williams: A Portrait in Words and Pictures* (New York: Walker, 1991) includes essays by Stephen Jay Gould, Donald Hall, George Higgins, and others.

Williams and Underwood collaborated on two other books, one on fishing and one an instructional manual on hitting. Many major leaguers continue to swear by *The Science of Hitting* (New York: Simon & Schuster, 1970).

Only the Ball Was White: A History of Legendary Black Players and All-Black Professional Teams
by Robert Peterson
(New York: Oxford University Press, 1970)

The integration of baseball meant the Negro Leagues were finished and, to some extent, forgotten. But the 1970s brought new interest in their history, and Peterson's book was in the forefront of that movement. Part I chronicles nineteenth-century Black players and teams; some played each other and some played with and against whites in an era when race relations were in flux and Jim Crow not yet firmly established. Part II covers Black teams between 1900 and 1930, especially the beginnings of organized major Negro Leagues and the seemingly endless shifting of franchises. Some minor Negro Leagues and barnstorming are also covered. Part III moves on to the integration of the Major League Baseball and the demise of the Negro Leagues. *Only the Ball Was White* also includes profiles of players and managers.

Black baseball before integration was at once, Peterson wrote, "a gladsome thing and a blot on America's conscience."[68]

Other writers quickly followed Peterson's lead. John Holway's *Voices from the Great Black Baseball Leagues* (New York: Dodd, Mead, 1975) featured oral histories of Negro League stars. Donn Rogosin, in *Invisible Men: Life in Baseball's Negro Leagues* (New York: Atheneum, 1983), argued that Negro Leagues were an integral part of African American communities and that they—more than Branch Rickey or Jackie Robinson—were ultimately responsible for baseball's integration.

Peterson's book was also notable for its appendices, which included league standings, box scores of All-Star games, and a register of players. Others, especially those in the Society for American Baseball Research, have since done considerably more research on Negro League statistics as well as history. The statistical research will surely continue in light of Major League Baseball's 2020 announcement that more than 3,400 players from seven Negro Leagues that operated between 1920 and 1948 would be recognized as major leaguers.

I Never Had It Made: An Autobiography
by Jackie Robinson as told to Alfred Duckett
(New York: Putnam, 1972)

Like Satchel Paige's second book, Robinson's later memoir was more honest about racism than his first—both the racism he'd faced and what Blacks continued to face. "Everything I ever got I fought hard for," he wrote, explaining the book's title, "but I know that I haven't got the right to say truthfully that I have it made. I cannot possibly believe I have it made while so many of my black brothers and sisters are hungry, inadequately housed, insufficiently clothed, denied their dignity as they live in slums or barely exist on welfare. I cannot say I have it made while our country drives full speed ahead to deeper rifts between men and women of varying colors."[69]

Long after he retired, more militant Blacks still resented Robinson for having tolerated the abuse thrown at him when he first broke the color line. In *I Never Had It Made*, Robinson printed an exchange of letters with Malcolm X. Malcolm accused Robinson of consistently pleasing his "white boss." Robinson responded by accusing Malcolm of failing to engage with most whites and Blacks, writing "your militancy is mainly expressed in Harlem where it is safe."[70] But Robinson also wrote that, though they disagreed about how to combat racism, "many of the statements [Malcolm] made about the problems faced by our people and the immorality of the white power structure were naked truth."[71]

Even after he died in 1972, the year this book was published, some continued to criticize Robinson. But he remained an inspiration to much of the nation, including some of those who followed in his footsteps. Hank Aaron, who encountered plenty of racism as he pursued Babe Ruth's all-time home run record, wrote this in an introduction to a 1995 reprint of *I Never Had It Made*: "I knew this was only the tip of the iceberg of what Jackie Robinson had gone through. I said to myself I would be doing him an injustice if I quit. And this gave me the strength to continue."[72]

See Chapter 3 for a broader discussion of Robinson's books.

The Summer Game
by Roger Angell
(New York: Viking, 1972)

Writing for *The New Yorker* and without the constant deadlines of regular reporters and columnists, Angell had the luxury of choosing what games to watch and then reflecting on them at length. The resulting essays—in this and his subsequent collections—were elegant and often profound. His perspective was generally that of a fan, albeit one with an extraordinary ability to reveal to his fellow fans new ways to see players, teams, games (and the game itself). *The Summer Game* covers, unsystematically, the ten seasons before its publication.

Angell is almost universally acknowledged to be one of the best writers of baseball non-fiction, perhaps challenged only by Roger Kahn among his contemporaries and Red Smith among his predecessors. So acclaimed is Angell that one could argue that he was *not* influential, since he could not be imitated. In that sense, the only books that followed in the wake of *The Summer Game* were Angell's subsequent collections: *Five Seasons: A Baseball Companion* (New York, Viking, 1977), *Late Innings: A Baseball Companion* (New York:

Simon & Schuster, 1982), *Season Ticket: A Baseball Companion* (Boston: Houghton Mifflin, 1988), *Once More Around the Park: A Baseball Reader* (New York: Ballantine, 1991), and *Game Time: A Baseball Companion* (Orlando: Harcourt, 2003). Yet Angell surely inspired others to turn baseball coverage into literature. Thomas Boswell, whose essays have often been compared to Angell's, is sometimes as graceful and often punchier. Boswell's baseball collections are *How Life Imitates the World Series* (Garden City, New York: Doubleday, 1982), *Why Time Begins on Opening Day* (Garden City: Doubleday, 1984), *The Heart of the Order* (New York: Doubleday, 1989), and *Cracking the Show* (New York: Doubleday, 1994).

The Great American Novel
by Philip Roth
(New York: Holt, Rinehart and Winston, 1973)

Roth's title, like the rest of his novel, is satirical. *The Great American Novel* was not Roth's, let alone America's, greatest novel. The story about a mythical third baseball league poked fun at much of what America held sacred, including baseball. But Roth was most certainly a serious novelist, and by writing about baseball he more firmly established it as a subject worthy of serious fiction; see Chapter 4 for a discussion of the novel in that context.

Roth made fun of those who mythologized baseball by, among much else, giving the players in his league the names of ancient gods and heroes. But this did not mask his love for the game any more than the notorious scene in his earlier novel, *Portnoy's Complaint*, in which the narrator masturbated into his baseball glove. After all, Alexander Portnoy was never happier than in center field, "standing without a care in the world in the sunshine ... just waiting there for the ball to fall into the glove I raise to it."[73]

In a *New York Times* essay published soon after *The Great American Novel* was published, Roth put aside all satire to explain why he loved the game: "For someone whose roots in America were strong but only inches deep, and who had no experience, such as a Catholic child might, of an awesome hierarchy that was real and felt, base-ball was a kind of secular church that reached into every class and region of the nation and bound us together in common concerns, loyalties, rituals, enthusiasms, and antagonisms. Baseball made me understand what patriotism was about, at its best."[74]

Babe: The Legend Comes to Life
by Robert W. Creamer
(New York: Simon & Schuster, 1974)

The mid–1970s saw a rush of Ruth biographies, probably because Hank Aaron was then challenging Ruth's lifetime home-run record. These included Ken Sobol's *Babe Ruth and the American Dream* (New York: Random House, 1974), Kal Wagenheim's *Babe Ruth* (Westport, Conn: Praeger, 1974), and Marshall Smelser's *The Life That Ruth Built* (New York: Quadrangle, 1975). Creamer's was the best. In fact, Creamer established a standard that future biographers of sports figures aspired to match.

Part of the appeal of *Babe* is that Creamer didn't just debunk the myths surrounding Ruth. He told various versions of stories before suggesting what was most likely true. This was the perfect approach for a figure who Smelser called "our Hercules, our Samson, Beowulf, Siegfried."[75] Take, for example, what came to be known as the belly-ache heard the world. That Ruth might sometimes have suffered from indigestion was hardly surprising; this was a man who could down between twelve and eighteen hot dogs at a time. But when he collapsed in 1925 it was clearly more than that, and explanations then and later ranged from syphilis to poison. Ruth's doctor said he had an intestinal abscess, an imprecise term that fueled speculation. But Ruth did return to the team with a long scar on the left side of his abdomen and, Creamer noted, "abdominal surgery is not standard procedure for correction of venereal disease."[76] Of the most famous myth about Ruth—that in the 1932 World Series between the Yan-kees and the Cubs he pointed his finger at the center field bleach-ers before hitting a home run to that very spot—Creamer concluded that Ruth did not point but argued that what he did do was worthy enough of becoming a legend: "He did challenge the Cubs before 50,000 people, did indicate he was going to hit a home run and did hit a home run. What more could you ask?"[77]

Among the superb biographers who followed in Creamer's footsteps in chronicling both myth and reality were Richard Ben Cramer with *Joe DiMaggio: The Hero's Life* (New York: Simon & Schuster, 2000), Allen Barra with *Yogi Berra: Eternal Yankee* (New York: W.W. Norton, 2009) and *Mickey and Willie: Mantle and Mays, The Parallel Lives of Baseball's Golden Age* (New York: Crown, 2013), and Jane Leavy with *Sandy Koufax: A Lefty's Legacy* (New York: HarperCollins, 2002), *The Last Boy: Mickey Mantle and the End of America's Childhood* (New York: Harper, 2010), and *The Big Fella: Babe Ruth and the World He Created* (New York: Harper, 2018). Creamer followed *Babe* with *Stengel: His Life and Times* (New York: Simon & Schuster, 1984).

A False Spring
by Pat Jordan
(New York: Dodd, Mead, 1975)

Jordan has often been compared to Jim Brosnan and Jim Bouton, other pitchers whose memoirs offered an inside look at the game. But unlike Brosnan and Bouton, who recounted their ups and downs on the mound, Jordan's story has mostly downs, which came steadily and plentifully. Though a high school star sought after by many teams, he fell apart in the Milwaukee Braves' minor league system and never made it to the majors. He is less interested than Brosnan and Bouton in telling stories about other players than in understanding himself, especially why he failed to live up to his promise. He considers various possibilities: his inability to get along with others (as manifested, for example, in a fight with the then-minor league catcher Joe Torre), a change to his motion that never felt natural, an uncertainty about whether to go for speed or control. None of it adds up to a fully satisfying explanation.

"I wondered where I'd lost it," Jordan writes. "But it was like trying to read isolated, disconnected points on a graph."[78]

Jordan is brutally honest about his failures, as a person as well as a pitcher. In this sense *A False Spring* is closer to an addiction memoir than a baseball one. It would be a stretch to say the spate of confessions from rock stars and actors were a result of Jordan's, but he was certainly in the vanguard of those who were fearless about their flaws. Jordan portrayed himself as a self-obsessed teenager, one who could without too much thought leave behind another teen whom he got pregnant.

Though Jordan never made it as a pitcher, he certainly made it as a writer. His later work included magazine profiles (about failures more than successes) and another memoir, *A Nice Tuesday* (New York: Golden Books, 1999). That his ambitions had moved on from baseball to books was clear from the title of *A False Spring*. Not only did it suggest the fading of his youthful promise but it was drawn from a line in *A Moveable Feast* by Ernest Hemingway.

The Chrysanthemum and the Bat: Baseball Samurai Style
by Robert Whiting
(New York: Dodd, Mead, 1977)

The huge success of Japanese players in America, especially Ichiro Suzuki and Shohei Ohtani, has made Japanese baseball seem less foreign to Americans, and perhaps even made Japan seem less foreign. But in the 1970s, when the Japanese were taking control over companies that made everything from cars to movies, Japanese baseball provided one window through which to view a culture that seemed both a threat and a model. Whiting described a game that was in some ways familiar and in other ways very unfamiliar.

While Americans prized individualism, the Japanese generally placed teamwork above all else. A good baseball team, Whiting wrote, was like a Japanese garden: "Every tree, every rock, every blade of grass has its place.... The rocks and trees viewed individually might be pleasing to look at, but when organized properly, the garden becomes more than just the sum of its parts. It becomes a work of art."[79]

The Chrysanthemum and the Bat was the first of three books that Whiting, a journalist based in Japan, wrote about Japanese baseball. That's not counting *Slugging It Out in Japan* (Tokyo: Kodansha International, 1991), which Whiting coauthored with Warren Cromartie, an outfielder with the Montreal Expos who moved to Japan to join the Tokyo Giants. *Slugging It Out* was a hit in Japan.

In America, Whiting's most successful baseball book was *You Gotta Have Wa* (New York: Macmillan, 1989), which focused on the struggles of Americans who, like Cromartie, played in Japan. Their struggles with *wa*—the concept and practice of group harmony—turned baseball from play to work for many of these Americans abroad and also made for entertaining stories. The Japanese, for example, placed a high value on tactics that involved teamwork, like the hit-and-run play. But even those American players who wanted to follow their managers' instructions sometimes couldn't always understand them. One translator who was sent to the on-deck circle to talk to the American batter there later reported: "Well, I went out there and looked in my dictionary and under hit-and-run it said something about an auto accident."[80]

In *The Meaning of Ichiro* (New York: Grand Central, 2004), Whiting reversed directions to follow Japanese players who came to America.

The 1979 Sport Americana Baseball Card Price Guide
by James Beckett and Dennis W. Eckes
(Laurel, Maryland: Den's Collectors Den, 1979)

Card collecting was still largely a hobby for kids in the late 1970s. Adults were buying and selling cards, but that business was hampered by the lack of a guide that let them know what might be a fair price. Eckes, who owned a sports memorabilia shop in Laurel, Maryland, published a price list between 1975 and 1978. But it was not until 1979, when Eckes teamed up with Beckett, a professor of statistics at Bowling Green University, that the *Sport Americana Baseball Card Price Guide*—and the values of cards—took off. Updated annually and renamed *Beckett Baseball Card Price Guide*, the books and Beckett's magazines sold millions of copies and ended up not just estimating prices but in many cases setting them. By the early 1990s, sales of new cards passed a billion dollars. Hockey star Wayne Gretzky and Los Angeles Kings owner Bruce McNall paid almost half a million dollars for a rare Honus Wagner card. Baseball cards were by then considered a serious investment: "A Grand Slam Profit May be in the Cards,"[81] trumpeted a *New York Times* headline.

To some, it seemed like baseball cards had gone the way of baseball, turning from an innocent game into a big business. But, as journalist Dave Jamieson wrote in his entertaining history of baseball cards, "that arc is too tidy in either case. Baseball cards have always been … about making money."[82] In the nineteenth century they were produced by tobacco companies to encourage smoking, and during the Depression candy and gum makers included cards with their products.

The bubble burst in the 1990s, a result of a number of factors. Card companies overprinted. Kids started collecting other things instead, such as Pokémon cards. Baseball fans were disillusioned by the 1994 players' strike. And bursting is just something bubbles do. Still, some rare cards (such as the Wagner one) continued to sell for millions, and though Beckett sold his company in 2005 the guides continue to be published annually as well as online.

Those who long for a time when collecting cards was just for fun can turn to books other than Beckett's. Kids can read Dan Gutman's *Honus and Me* (New York: Avon, 1998), whose hero always thought about cards that "there was something—oh, *magical*—about them,"[83] and then discovered they had the power to transport him back in time to meet Honus Wagner, and in sequels Jackie Robinson, Babe Ruth, Willie Mays, and others. And adults can turn to Brendan C. Boyd's and Fred C. Harris' *The Great American Baseball Card Flipping, Trading, and Bubble Gum Book* (Boston: Little, Brown, 1973), which will conjure up "the sweet pleasant smell of the bubble gum, and the sweet pleasant melting of it in your mouth. And the secure feel of the cards in your pocket, and the knowledge that they were yours and yours alone."[84] In other words, Boyd and Harris will remind adults, at least those born in the 1950s, of their childhoods, as well as the one other thing they remember about baseball cards: "that your mother threw them out one sunny summer morning. And there was no possible way to get them back."[85]

The Ultimate Baseball Book
edited by Daniel Okrent and Harris Lewine
(Boston: Houghton Mifflin, 1979)

Editor-author Okrent and art director Lewine did not invent the baseball coffee table book but they packaged one that merited its boastful title. The book has more than eight hundred well-chosen and often previously unseen photos and more than two hundred works of graphic art, including programs, pennants, buttons, and cards. The history of baseball by David Nemec is interspersed by original essays by superb writers: Robert Creamer on the Orioles of John McGraw, Jonathan Yardley on Christy Mathewson (the "real Frank Merriwell"), Wilfred Sheed on a very unsaintly Connie Mack, Red Smith on Pepper Martin's astounding World Series of 1931, Roy Blount, Jr., on how Joe DiMaggio made things look easy, Tom Wicker on the hustle that made Enos Slaughter, John Leonard on rooting for the Dodgers, Mordecai Richler on baseball in Montreal, and George Higgins on Fenway Park and broken hearts.

Among the many books that followed in the wake of *Ultimate* were two literary coffee-table books done with Baseball's Hall of Fame: *The Baseball Hall of Fame 50th Anniversary Book* (New York: Prentice Hall Press, 1988) and *Baseball as America: Seeing Ourselves through Our National Game* (Washington, D.C.: National Geographic, 2002). The former followed the *Ultimate* format especially closely, with a history of the game by Gerald Astor interspersed with original essays by big-name writers, including two—Blount and Creamer—who contributed to *Ultimate*. It would be unfair to characterize as a copycat any book with original essays and well-chosen art, but the influence of *Ultimate* surely included showing publishers that there was a large market for such books.

An updated and expanded edition of *Ultimate* was published in 2000.

Shoeless Joe
by W.P. Kinsella
(Boston: Houghton Mifflin, 1982)

Lest anyone doubt Kinsella believed baseball was an American religion, filled with an array of magic and myth, the narrator of his novel states early on that his birthstone is a diamond and his astrological sign is hit and run. It's a funny line, but it's more than a joke. And when the narrator hears a voice telling him to build a field on his Iowa farm, only for a moment does he wonder whether he can ignore "the great god Baseball."[86]

For a discussion of how *Shoeless Joe* (and *Field of Dreams*, the movie based on the novel) turned a baseball field into a sacred space for other writers and for millions of Americans, see Chapter 4.

Kinsella's narrator built his field so that Shoeless Joe Jackson and his teammates, long exiled from baseball, could play there, as could the narrator's long-dead father, and the movie ends with a father-son game of catch that's portrayed as a near-sacred ritual. For a discussion of fathers and sons and baseball (and books), see Chapter 6.

Baseball's Great Experiment: Jackie Robinson and His Legacy
by Jules Tygiel
(New York: Oxford University Press, 1983)

Harold Seymour's 1960 history of baseball's early years established the sport as a respectable subject for academics, but it wasn't until Tygiel retold the story of baseball's integration that a history professor showed the full potential of a scholarly approach. Previous accounts had underscored the drama of Robinson's story. Tygiel's version was as dramatic as any but added historical context. On the question of what motivated Branch Rickey to sign Robinson, for example, Tygiel gave due consideration to the possibilities that the Dodger president was idealistically striking a blow against racism and that he was greedily trying to win the pennant or attract Black fans. But Tygiel also highlighted factors outside of Rickey's control, such as the pressure the Black press was putting on baseball to integrate.

Tygiel's broad focus also extended the story beyond the Dodgers to include the Black players who entered the majors soon after Robinson, as well as the impact of integration on minor leagues and the Negro Leagues. To cover all this, Tygiel drew on a scholar's full array of sources, including archives, newspapers, and interviews.

Later works that took on the topic of baseball's integration acknowledged their debt to Tygiel. Wrote Arnold Rampersad in *Jackie Robinson: A Biography* (New York: Knopf, 1997): "All serious scholarly work on Jackie Robinson builds on Jules Tygiel's landmark study."[87] And Tygiel was generous to other scholars; he shared notes and hundreds of pages of transcribed interviews with Jonathan Eig as Eig worked on *Opening Day: The Story of Jackie Robinson's First Season* (New York: Simon & Schuster, 2007).

For a discussion of the influence of Robinson's own books, see Chapter 3.

The Hidden Game of Baseball: A Revolutionary Approach to Baseball and Its Statistics
by John Thorn and Peter Palmer
(Garden City, New York: Doubleday, 1984)

Statistician Palmer and writer Thorn were of course not the first to look at baseball numbers in new ways. Indeed, their book included a history of baseball statistics from Henry Chadwick's in the nineteenth century to Bill James' in the twentieth. But Thorn and Palmer approached strategy and history systematically and creatively, and their challenges to previously-established wisdom have held up remarkably well. They argued, for example, that steals were generally too risky to be of value and that walks were more valuable than generally recognized—positions managers and general managers have come to embrace. And, using their new measures of performance, which took into account among other factors a player's era and home park, they listed the top players of all time. A 2015 edition included an updated list of the top 500, of whom the top ten were Barry Bonds, Babe Ruth, Nap Lajoie, Walter Johnson, Ted Williams, Rogers Hornsby, Ty Cobb, Willie Mays, Hank Aaron, and Tris Speaker.

One reason the book was so influential was that, though Palmer's formulas were often complex, Thorn made them accessible for those without a background in math. As Keith Law, then of ESPN, put it in his foreword to the 2015 edition: "They begin by eviscerating sacred cows like RBIs, but gently, so that the cow barely knows what hit her, tearing down the reader's resistance to such heretical ideas as ditching batting average for on-base percentage or valuing a pitcher's performance without considering whether his team won the game."[88] Thorn's writing is not only clear but often eloquent: "Statistics are not the instruments of vivisection," he wrote, "taking the life out of a thing in order to examine it; rather, statistics are themselves the vital part of baseball, the only tangible and imperishable remains of game played yesterday or a hundred years ago." For readers of *The Hidden Game*, numbers "take on reality and, sometimes, beauty."[89]

See Chapter 7 for a fuller discussion of the revolution in baseball statistics during the 1980s.

The Bill James Historical Baseball Abstract
by Bill James
(New York: Villard Books, 1985)

Like his annual *Abstract*s, James' historical one was not just statistical analysis. It included a decade-by-decade history of baseball and position-by-position entries on notable players. The book covered anything and everything from changing rules to changes in the ethnic backgrounds of players. Much of it was revealing and entertaining, and even what seemed like trivia was often not trivial. Who was the only catcher in history to have 4,000 total bases? Answer: No one; Carlton Fisk retired with 3,999. For James, this was a launching pad for an essay on why Fisk was among the greatest catchers of all time.

That analysis of Fisk was in *The New Bill James Historical Baseball Abstract* (New York: Free Press, 2001). One of James's strengths was his willingness to look anew at old ways of thinking, including his own. The 2001 *Historical Abstract* was not just updated but substantially revised.

Fisk may have been underrated but was certainly not unknown. Others James wrote about were much more obscure. Outfielder Bill Lange, for example, "was probably the greatest athlete to play major league baseball in the nineteenth century,"[90] though the play for which he was once most remembered—crashing through a wooden fence to make a game-saving catch—probably never happened. And pitcher Ed Reulbach was "one of the Dangerfields of baseball history, a player whose name commands little respect today."[91] Even in his own time, Reulbach was unappreciated: In 1907, he won 17 games and lost four, but the 1908 *Spalding Guide* described him as "effective at times but extremely wild and unreliable."[92]

To reduce James's work to a list of the greatest players of all time is to miss the pleasure of his analyses, statistical and otherwise. But it's hard to resist mentioning his top ten, this again from the revised edition: Babe Ruth, Honus Wagner, Willie Mays, Oscar Charleston, Ty Cobb, Mickey Mantle, Ted Williams, Walter Johnson, Josh Gibson, Stan Musial. The list diverged from the consensus of the time by including Charleston and Gibson, two Negro Leaguers. Explained James: "It's not like one person saw Oscar Charleston play and said that he was the greatest player ever. *Lots* of people said he was the greatest player they ever saw."[93] As for Mantle, who James rated higher than most other list-makers: "My argument would be that there has been too much talk about Mantle's drinking and too little about the impact of his career on base percentage, .421."[94]

For a broader discussion of James' influence, see Chapter 7.

Nine Innings
by Daniel Okrent
(New York: Ticknor & Fields, 1985)

Thirty years after Arnold Hano's *A Day in the Bleachers*, Okrent revived the book-about-a-single-game structure. Unlike Hano, who wrote about the first game of the 1954 World Series, Okrent chose a seemingly insignificant game: a June 10, 1982, Milwaukee Brewers win over the Baltimore Orioles. And unlike Hano, who wrote from the perspective of a fan sitting in the bleachers, Okrent delved into behind-the-scenes strategies and histories that even sophisticated fans couldn't see from their seats.

As it turned out, the game was significant, since the Brewers ended up winning the American League East by one game over the Orioles. But that was not Okrent's point; he was more interested in describing what pitchers and hitters were thinking (often pitch-by-pitch) and how the teams were put together. His book was filled with insights from and about players, managers, general managers, owners, reporters, even groundskeepers. Brewer Paul Molitor, who played third in this game and was successful at every position he played, was "the dreamboat that every 17-year-old girl in greater Milwaukee pined for"[95]; Brewer center fielder Gorman Thomas was "the hero that every 47-year-old brewery worker idolized"[96] because they came to see him strike out or homer or run into a fence and, as Thomas put it, "I try to accommodate them at least one way every game."[97] Okrent's digressions often took him back months and years, but he generally managed to connect them to the game at hand. George Blaeholder of the St. Louis Browns, Okrent told readers, perfected the slider in the 1930s—and Rollie Fingers, who was credited with the win against the Orioles, built his success on the slider.

Among those who followed in Okrent's footsteps were Robert Benson with *The Game: One Man, Nine Innings, A Love Affair with Baseball* (New York: Tarcher/Putnam, 2001). Benson's alleged topic was a minor-league game between the Iowa Cubs and Nashville Sounds but his real interest was in baseball as a metaphor for life. As he approached the age of fifty, Benson saw himself as "somewhere in the neighborhood of the seventh-inning stretch,"[98] and he dished out wisdom along the lines of everyone being like Mighty Casey and sometimes striking out and everybody having to leave home and then "doing the things that you must to get home again, some of them simple and routine, some of them occasionally heroic and glorious."[99]

Okrent's structure was extended to three games in Buzz Bissinger's *Three Nights in August: Strategy, Heartbreak, and Joy Inside the Mind of a Manager* (Boston: Houghton Mifflin, 2005), which focused on a series between the St. Louis Cardinals and the Chicago Cubs as seen through the eyes of Cardinal manager Tony La Russa. It was extended to basketball in Bob Ryan's and Terry Pluto's *48 Minutes: A Night in the Life of the NBA* (New York: Macmillan, 1988) about a game between the Boston Celtics and Cleveland Cavaliers.

More recently, Rob Neyer's *Power Ball: Anatomy of a Modern Baseball Game* (New York: Harper, 2018) took as its official subject a September 8, 2017, game between the Oakland A's and Houston Astros and as its actual theme the way the game has changed. Those changes include, to name a few: the increased use of the defensive shift, the preponderance of strikeouts and homers, and the influx of foreign born players (and the decreasing numbers of U.S.–born Black players). In other words, Neyer wrote, "the stuff that's changed since Arnold Hano and Dan Okrent ... wrote about the modern game."[100]

Total Baseball
edited by John Thorn and Pete Palmer
(New York: Warner, 1989)

Just as in 1969 Macmillan's *Baseball Encyclopedia* supplanted Hy Turkin's and S.C. Thompson's 1951 *Official Encyclopedia of Baseball*, in 1989 *Total Baseball* supplanted "Big Mac." Thorn and Palmer corrected many old statistics, but their biggest changes were the addition of new statistical categories developed by Bill James, Palmer, and others. These included PRO+ or production plus (on base percentage plus slugging average, normalized to league average and adjusted to factor in the influence of home park), Runs Created (James's measure of a hitter's contribution), Batting Runs (Palmer's measure of a hitter's contribution), and Pitching Runs (Palmer's measure of runs saved beyond what a league-average pitcher might have saved). These measures were part of the statistical analysis James dubbed sabermetrics, a name meant to honor the Society for American Baseball Research, many of whose members aided Thorn and Palmer. By *Total*'s fourth edition in 1995 it had become the official encyclopedia of Major League Baseball.

Unlike the Turkin-Thompson and Macmillan encyclopedias, *Total Baseball* also included hundreds of pages of prose, with essays by experts in a variety of fields. These included, to mention just a few, team histories, ballpark information, profiles of selected players, Black ball, women in baseball, and collecting. Later editions added prose as well as numbers. For example, as baseball was increasingly seen as an international sport, essays covered its history and culture in other countries.

Ultimately, *Total Baseball* was itself supplanted—as were reference books in other fields—by online sources. But through the turn of the twenty-first century it was the most authoritative (and at nearly 3,000 pages the largest) baseball encyclopedia published, and it played a key part in changing the way the game was analyzed. See Chapter 7 for more on the sabermetric revolution.

The Dickson Baseball Dictionary
edited and compiled by Paul Dickson
(New York: Facts on File, 1989)

The Dickson Baseball Dictionary is that rare reference work: it's both definitive and fun. Take for example Dickson's entry on "fungo," a word the pioneering baseball writer Henry Chadwick used as early as 1867 to describe when a batter throws a ball up in the air himself and then hits it. Dickson considers five theories on the word's etymology, all seemingly reasonable. Perhaps it was a compound word made out of "fun" and "go." Or it could have come from "fungible," which means something that can be substituted as a thin fungo stick sometimes replaced a conventional bat. Then there's the fungus theory, since fungo bats were sometimes made with a lighter, softer wood, like a fungus, or since the end of a fungo bat resembled a mushroom. And then there were the foreign etymologies—*fangen* is German for "to catch" and someone has to catch a ball after it's hit, and *fung* is Scottish for "to pitch" or "to toss."

In addition to its etymologies, the *Dictionary* is well worth reading for its tracking of the non-baseball uses of many baseball terms. Some are obvious, such as home run as a metaphor for any action that has become a clear success, or as slang for sex—on a scale that starts at first base. Others are less so. Hit-and-run was a baseball term before it came to describe an accident in which a driver leaves the scene. Bonehead described unintelligent baseball players or plays before coming to mean unintelligent people or actions in general. The broader meanings of baseball terms, Dickson rightly argues, demonstrate baseball's influence on American culture. Or, as Reggie Jackson put it: "The country is as American as baseball."[101]

The book expanded over the years. The first edition had more than five thousand entries. By the third edition (New York: W.W. Norton, 2011), there were more than ten thousand. Even in an era when so many reference books have migrated from print to online, Dickson's remains one of the few—like Roget's and Webster's—that merit not only keeping it in print but also keeping its compiler's name in its title.

Everything Baseball
by James Mote
(New York: Prentice Hall, 1989)

That baseball had found its way into pretty much every nook and cranny of American culture was clear well before James Mote's comprehensive—indeed, obsessive—compendium. But Mote drove home baseball's omnipresence by including absolutely every baseball song, novel, play, movie, TV and radio show, painting, sculpture, and comic strip—or at least everything as of 1989. As one review noted, the book was "accurately titled"[102] and filled with an "embarrassment of riches."[103] The book represented, as Mote put it, "the canon of an original American mythology."[104]

Most fans, for example, would have been able to recite at least a few lines from Ernest Thayer's 1888 poem, "Casey at the Bat." Some might even have seen Walt Disney's 1946 classic cartoon treatment. But only those who studied *Everything Baseball* were likely to know about the 1986 TV production that starred Elliot Gould as Casey and featured Howard Cosell, Bob Uecker, Bill Macy, and Carol Kane. Or the 1954 recording of the poem by Lionel Barrymore. Or the 1953 radio drama in which Casey struck out deliberately. Or the full scale-opera of that same year by the Pulitzer Prize-winning composer William Schuman. Or the 1927 silent film starring Wallace Beery in which Casey was accused of taking a bribe, though it turned out gamblers had framed him and it was an illegal pitch that did him in.

Mote celebrated the abundance of material, but his commentary—especially in his captions to the many revealing photos and in his incisive essays scattered throughout the book—recognized that many of the works he catalogued were by no means masterpieces. Early baseball movies like *The Babe Ruth Story* of 1948, starring William Bendix, "nearly made cricket fans of us all,"[105] and "even the great Irving Berlin struck out occasionally,"[106] as he did with the 1913 song, "Jake, Jake (The Yiddisha Ball Player)."

The Physics of Baseball
by Robert K. Adair
(New York: Harper & Row, 1990)

Does a curveball really curve? In 1941, *Life* magazine enlisted two top curveballers, Cy Blanton of the Phillies and Carl Hubbell of the Giants, to answer the question. The magazine arranged for three cameras to photograph a pitch at intervals of one-thirtieth of a second. The photos, as *Life* interpreted them, showed that gravity forced the ball to turn downward but a horizontal curve was an optical illu-sion. Understandably, many batters swore otherwise, and baseball writer Martin Quigley recounted a joke that circulated at the time: "'What did you hit?' 'A hanging optical illusion,' the home run hit-ter would tell his mates. 'Well, that's *Life* for you.'"[107] *Life*'s rival *Look* conducted its own experiment in 1949 and decided that balls did indeed curve.

The semi-official answer of Major League Baseball came from Adair, a professor of physics at Yale and a friend and former colleague of Bart Giamatti, who had been president of Yale before becoming president of the National League and then commissioner of baseball. In 1987, Giamatti named Adair "Physicist to the National League." Adair's report to Giamatti, which was expanded into *The Physics of Baseball*, explained not only how a ball curved but also how *Life* had misinterpreted its own photos.

Adair delved into other questions as well: What is the ideal tra-jectory of the bat? Thirty-five degrees. How many more feet will a 400-foot homer travel for every inch a barometer drops? About six feet. What advantage do bats stuffed with cork have? Not much, and in any case none that couldn't be achieved legally by choking up or using a bat made of slightly lighter wood. Adair's technical expla-nations are sometimes slow-going for non-physicists, but his analy-ses of the physical laws governing pitching, batting, running, fielding and throwing remain as close to definitive as science can determine.

The book was slightly revised and expanded in 1994 and 2002.

Girls of Summer: The Real Story of the All-American Girls Professional Baseball League
by Lois Browne
(New York: HarperCollins, 1992)

What made most people aware of the history of women in base-ball was not a book but the 1992 movie, *A League of Their Own*. The movie was fiction but the league—the All-American Girls Professional Baseball League—was real. The AAGPBL operated in mid-sized American cities from 1943 to 1954. Hollywood producer and director Penny Marshall was inspired to make the movie after seeing a 1987 documentary, also titled *A League of Their Own*. Marshall's movie, which starred Geena Davis as the star catcher of the Rockford Peaches and Tom Hanks as the team's manager, grossed over $100 million.

A number of books on women in baseball came out around the same time as the movie and reinforced the message that yes, Virginia, there were women in baseball. Browne's *Girls of Summer* was arguably the most influential since it came out the same year as the movie and told the real story of the AAGPBL. The book's approach was chronological, starting with the league's origins in the mind of Philip Wrigley, who owned the Chicago Cubs and worried that as major league players went off to fight in World War II, Wrigley Field, home of the Cubs, might sit empty. Wrigley's original idea was for a women's softball league and the league originally played a slightly faster version of softball but eventually turned to hardball. The AAGPBL continued to draw fans after World War II but ultimately couldn't survive the 1950s. As Susan E. Johnson, a sociologist and author of a book on the AAGPBL, put it: it was made clear to women that "they should leave the factories, offices, and ballparks to the men and return to their proper place, the kitchen and the nursery."[108]

Johnson's book, *When Women Played Hardball: The Story of the All-American Girls Professional Baseball League* (Seattle, Washington: Seal Press, 1994), took as its focus the championship series in 1950 between the Peaches and Fort Wayne Daisies. (The Peaches won the seventh and deciding game.) Also published soon after the movie was released was Sue Macy's *A Whole New Ball Game* (New York: Henry Holt and Company, 1993) for young adults.

Other books are worthy of mention here because they went beyond the AAGPBL to tell the stories of women throughout baseball's history. That history included the barnstorming "Bloomer Girl" teams that formed in 1869, just after men started playing professionally. Named after the clothing they wore, hundreds of these teams played men's semi-pro and minor league teams as well as each other. The last of the Bloomer Girl teams disbanded in the 1930s, partly because women chose to play softball instead of baseball. The history of women playing with and against men also included such figures as Lizzie Arlington, who just before the turn of the twentieth century became the first woman to play in the minor leagues, and Jackie Mitchell, who in a 1931 exhibition struck out both Babe Ruth and Lou Gehrig. A newspaper report had Ruth throwing his bat after the third strike, though it's unclear whether he was truly disgusted or playing his role in a publicity stunt.

Of the two books that came out soon after *A League of Their Own* and covered more than the league, Barbara Gregorich's *Women at Play: The Story of Women in Baseball* (San Diego, Harcourt Brace, 1993) was aimed at a general audience and Gai Ingham Berlage's *Women in Baseball: The Forgotten History* (Westport, Connecticut: Praeger, 1994) was for a more academic audience.

Whether because of the movie or books or the general progress of society, women have made inroads into professional baseball, including as coaches and in 2020 as a major league general manager. In addition to her history of women in baseball, Gregorich also wrote *She's on First* (Chicago, Contemporary Books, 1987), a novel about the first woman to play in the major leagues. That, so far, remains fiction.

Baseball and Billions: A Probing Look Inside the Big Business of Our National Pastime
by Andrew Zimbalist
(New York: Basic Books, 1992)

Economist Zimbalist sliced through the propaganda that owners (and sometimes players) tended to propagate with an objective analysis of the business of baseball. His book was filled with insights about how teams were often more profitable than their owners claimed, how free agency had not undercut competitive balance as small-market teams often claimed, and how problematic it could be for cities to pay for stadiums. Zimbalist followed up *Baseball and Billions* with *May the Best Team Win: Baseball Economics and Public*

Policy (Washington, D.C.: Brookings Institution Press, 2003), which blamed many of Major League Baseball's problems on its status as a monopoly, and *In the Best Interests of Baseball: The Revolutionary Reign of Bud Selig* (Hoboken, New Jersey: Wiley, 2006), which placed much of the blame for baseball's problems on the game's commissioners prior to Selig, whom he credited with uniting the owners so they could more sensibly negotiate with players and plan for the future.

Selig may have influenced some team owners to approach baseball's problems more sensibly, though he of course did not head off the 1994 strike, which cancelled more than nine hundred games. It was that strike that actually jolted owners and players into compromises that allowed the business of baseball to flourish in the following decades.

Others followed Zimbalist in writing seriously about the business of baseball. Journalist John Helyar, in *Lords of the Realm: The Real History of Baseball* (New York: Villard Books, 1994) chronicled how billionaire and millionaire owners repeatedly bungled their battles with players. Helyar quoted Atlanta Braves owner Ted Turner explaining the situation to his fellow magnates: "Gentlemen, we have the only legal monopoly in the country and we're fucking it up."[109] Lawyer Henry D. Fetter, in *Taking on the Yankees: Winning and Losing in the Business of Baseball* (New York: W.W. Norton, 2003), made a strong case that management, more than money, made the difference for the Yankees and their rivals. Economist J.C. Bradbury, in *The Baseball Economist: The Real Game Exposed* (New York: Dutton, 2007) argued that Major League Baseball wasn't really a monopoly— taking issue not only with Zimbalist but also with economists James Quirk and Rodney Fort, who had concluded in *Hard Ball: The Abuse of Power in Pro Team Sports* (Princeton, New Jersey: Princeton University Press, 1999) that the problems of professional sports could be solved by eliminating the leagues' monopoly powers.

Here should also be mentioned two men whose lives, though not their books, changed the course of the business of baseball. Outfielder Curt Flood refused to accept a trade from the St. Louis Cardinals to the Philadelphia Phillies in 1969. He lost his case in the

Supreme Court but in the process, as Zimbalist put it, "shook the foundations of the reserve system."[110] Flood told his story, though before the Supreme Court handed down its decision, with Richard Carter in *The Way It Is* (New York: Trident Press, 1970). Marvin Miller, who as head of the Players' Association from 1966 to 1982 ultimately brought down that reserve system, told his story in *A Whole Different Ball Game: The Sport and Business of Baseball* (New York: Birch Lane Press, 1991).

Cobb: A Biography
by Al Stump
(Chapel Hill: North Carolina: Algonquin Books, 1994)

Well before Stump's biography, Ty Cobb was generally considered one of the greatest players of all time if not the greatest—and also one of the most vicious. This was a man who had no qualms about sharpening his spikes so as to intimidate and bloody any fielder who might dare to tag him out as he slid into a base. Cobb not only fought with opponents but also with fans and with his own teammates. But though Stump didn't create Cobb's image he certainly solidified it. Witness the blurbs on the back jacket. This from essayist and newspaper editor Hal Crowther: "With the possible exception of Adolf Hitler, Ty Cobb must be the most frightening human being I ever encountered in a biography."[111] And this from Ed Linn, author of among other books *The Life and Turmoils of Ted Williams*: "What Stump gives us is the portrait of a monster."[112]

Stump's credibility was enhanced by his personal relationship to Cobb. He coauthored Cobb's autobiography, *My Life in Baseball: The True Record* (Garden City, New York: Doubleday, 1961). Cobb saw the autobiography as a chance to tell his side of the story, but what Stump saw convinced him that he ought eventually to tell a different story. Here's how Stump described his time working with the dying Cobb: "I put him to bed, prepared his insulin, picked him up when he fell down, warded off irate taxi drivers, bill collectors, bartenders, waiters, clerks, and private citizens whom Cobb was inclined to punch, cooked what food he could digest, drew his bath, got drunk with him, and knelt with him in prayer on black nights when he knew death was near. I ducked a few bottles he threw, too."[113] Stump concluded that throughout his baseball career Cobb had been psychotic, and Stump's view of Cobb was further popularized by the 1994 movie *Cobb*, which starred Tommy Lee Jones as Cobb and Robert Wuhl as Stump.

Yet Stump was unfair to Cobb and to his readers. Charles Leerhsen's *Ty Cobb: A Terrible Beauty* (New York: Simon & Schuster, 2015) offered a compelling defense of Cobb, who Leerhsen saw as a far more complex figure, flawed but no monster. Leerhsen surely understood the pressure coauthors feel to tell the true story after having told a celebrity's version; he coauthored Donald Trump's 1991 book *Trump: Surviving at the Top*, and he later came to regret his role enhancing Trump's image. Perhaps that led Leerhsen to investigate Stump's work and to conclude that the autobiography Stump wrote with Cobb and the biography Stump wrote about Cobb were both "highly fictionalized."[114]

Shut Out: A Story of Race and Baseball in Boston
by Howard Bryant
(New York: Routledge, 2002)

Inspirational stories about Jackie Robinson have far outnumbered those about continuing racism in baseball, an imbalance Bryant worked to correct with his book about the team that waited until 1959—after every other major league team had integrated—to add a Black player to its roster. Bryant chronicled how the Red Sox chose not to sign both Jackie Robinson and Willie Mays, as well as how Blacks who later played for the Sox struggled with the culture of the team and the city. Among those whose stories Bryant told in detail were Reggie Smith, Jim Rice, Ellis Burks, and Mo Vaughn. *Shut Out* also told the stories of Boston journalists who reported on racism (or, more often, didn't). The book ended on a hopeful note, with new ownership for the Red Sox that would not only work to change the culture but would also, two years after the publication of *Shut Out*, bring a championship to Boston.

Bryant's subsequent books offered additional insights into racism in baseball. *The Last Hero: A Life of Henry Aaron* (New York: Pantheon, 2010) told how Aaron overcame everything from Jim Crow to death threats, as he surpassed Babe Ruth's record for life-time home-runs. Bryant portrayed Aaron as a civil rights advocate, albeit one who preferred working behind the scenes, thus debunking the myth of Aaron as politically ignorant and apathetic. Aaron himself had gone a long way toward correcting that image in his autobiography, written with Lonnie Wheeler, *I Had a Hammer: The Hank Aaron Story* (New York: HarperCollins, 1991). Bryant's *The Heritage: Black Athletes, A Divided America, and the Politics of Patriotism* (Boston: Beacon Press, 2018) expanded the field beyond baseball to chronicle the evolution of athlete activism, including how some, like Robinson and Muhammad Ali, embraced the role of activist; how others, like Michael Jordan and Tiger Woods, later backed away from activism; and how, more recently, Colin Kaepernick, LeBron James, and others have revived "the heritage."

Moneyball: The Art of Winning an Unfair Game
by Michael Lewis
(New York: W.W. Norton, 2003)

Lewis' book and the 2011 movie based on it portrayed how Oakland A's general manager Billy Beane used sabermetric analysis—such as that pioneered by Bill James—to create winning teams on a limited budget. The book and movie encouraged businesses other than baseball to apply new forms of statistical analysis. Within the sport, other teams responded by hiring analysts who sometimes outnumbered the players on the field. See Chapter 7 for a broader discussion of the sabermetric revolution.

The book's lasting influence could also be seen in the ways later books defined themselves in comparison to *Moneyball*. Sheldon Hirsch's and Alan Hirsch's *The Beauty of Short Hops: How*

Chance and Circumstance Confound the Moneyball Approach to Baseball (Jefferson, North Carolina: McFarland, 2011) bemoaned the "attitude exemplified in *Moneyball*, the best-selling book which announced and accelerated the success of the sabermetrics revolution." Hirsch and Hirsch wrote, somewhat unfairly, that Beane "grew up a Strat-O-Matic fanatic and can't stand the actual games."[115] Rob Neyer's *Power Ball: Anatomy of a Modern Baseball Game* (New York: HarperCollins, 2018), argued that "today you must look far beyond on-base percentage," since the importance of that stat and others Beane appreciated "aren't any sort of secret these days."[116] In the course of a book-long description of a single game between the A's and the Houston Astros, Neyer explained the rise of post–*Moneyball* measurements such as a pitcher's spin rate. The jacket copy of Ben Lindbergh's and Travis Sawchik's *The MVP Machine: How Baseball's New Nonconformists are Using Data to Build Better Players* (New York: Basic Books, 2019) proclaimed that "the *Moneyball* era is over,"[117] and that with every team having gotten smart about statistical analyses, front offices could no longer out-draft or out-trade rivals and were instead turning to new technologies that improved the performances of the players they already had.

Juiced: Wild Times, Rampant 'Roids, Smash Hits, and How Baseball Got Big
by Jose Canseco
(New York: Regan Books, 2005)

As Mark McGwire and Barry Bonds shattered seemingly unbreakable home run records, rumors abounded steroids were behind the power surge throughout the game. Baseball's management took no strong measures to investigate or curb steroid use, partly because of resistance from the players' union and partly because the homers brought back fans who had been disgruntled since the 1994 strike that led to the cancellation of the World Series. Canseco's book forced baseball to take steroids seriously. He admitted that steroids had powered his career, and he presented himself as a "Typhoid Mary"[118] who spread steroids to the various teams on which he played. Among the users Canseco named were such stars as McGwire and Jason Giambi, both of whom played with Canseco on the Oakland Athletics, and Rafael Palmeiro, Ivan Rodriguez, and Juan Gonzalez, who played with him on the Texas Rangers.

Many initially mocked and dismissed the book as lurid gossip, and Canseco did come across as almost as proud of his relationship with Madonna as of his on-field accomplishments. But *Juiced* became a bestseller and attitudes soon changed. Pressure from Congress and the press led baseball to turn to Senator George Mitchell to investigate steroid use. Mitchell's report named a lot more names than Canseco's book—89 major and minor-league players. That in turn led Major League Baseball to introduce stricter testing and stronger punishments.

Canseco's wasn't the only book to force a reckoning with steroids. Most influential was Mark Fainaru-Wada's and Lance Williams' *Game of Shadows: Barry Bonds, BALCO, and the Steroids Scandal That Rocked Professional Sports* (New York: Gotham Books, 2006). *San Francisco Chronicle* reporters Fainaru-Wada and Williams focused on the investigation into BALCO which stood for Bay Area Laboratory Co-Operative and which supplied steroids to athletes. The book presented circumstantial but damning evidence that Bonds was among these athletes. Like *Juiced*, *Game of Shadows* became a bestseller and added doubts—if not asterisks—to Bonds' single-season and lifetime home run records. Also worthy of note was Howard Bryant's *Juicing the Game: Drugs, Power, and the Fight for the Soul of Major League Baseball* (New York: Viking, 2005). Bryant's revelations were less sensational than those of Fainaru-Wada and Williams, but his book provided more background about the culture that allowed the use of steroids to spread.

Later books on steroids didn't have the same impact on baseball's steroid policies but did provide additional revelations and context. These included *American Icon: The Fall of Roger Clemens and the Rise of Steroids in America's Pastime* by the New York *Daily News* team of Teri Thompson, Nathaniel Vinton, Michael O'Keefe and Christian Red (New York: Knopf, 2009) and *Blood Sport: Alex*

Rodriguez, Biogenesis, and the Quest to End Baseball's Steroid Era by Tim Elfrink of the *Miami New Times* and Gus Garcia-Roberts of Long Island's *Newsday* (New York: Dutton, 2014).

Canseco himself produced a sequel, *Vindicated: Big Names, Big Liars, and the Battle to Save Baseball* (New York: Simon Spotlight, 2008). He described how reporters initially dismissed him as the "NotCredible Hulk"[119] with "the kind of credibility not even nanotechnology could find or measure."[120] And he gloated about how they came around to recognizing, as one reporter put it, that "the most maligned book since *Ball Four* may turn out to be just as important."[121]

Baseball in the Garden of Eden: The Secret History of the Early Game
by John Thorn
(New York: Simon & Schuster, 2011)

Well before Thorn wrote his history of the game's early years, knowledgeable fans already knew that Abner Doubleday did not invent baseball in 1839. Many even knew that Alexander Cartwright's claim to fame—for having formally set down the game's rules in 1845 when he was a member of the New York Knickerbockers baseball club—was also suspect. What was most important about *Eden*, then, was not so much Thorn's debunking of baseball's most famous myths but his placing them in the context of other misleading myths about the game's rise. Far from being a game played by gentlemen purely for sport, baseball in its early years was closely tied to gambling, class tensions, and racism. Indeed, gambling was "the vital spark that in the beginning made it worthy of adult attention and press coverage."[122]

No one invented baseball; it evolved from earlier bat-and-ball games. But several figures emerge from *Eden* with a stronger claim than Doubleday or Cartwright. It was Louis Fenn Wadsworth, for one, and not Cartwright, who pushed for the game to have nine innings. Wadsworth's descent into obscurity, tracked down by

Thorn, included becoming a drunk and dying in a poorhouse. And Daniel Lucius Adams, a doctor, played baseball as early as 1839 with clubs whose rules were likely very similar to those the Knickerbockers later adopted. Adams became president of the Knickerbockers and presided over a meeting of three clubs that set rules and regulations including ending games after a set number of innings rather than after one team scored twenty-one runs. When Adams retired and moved to Connecticut, his teammates passed a resolution naming him the "Nestor of Ball Players."[123]

Some of the most interesting figures in *Eden* are not those who played some role in the game's creation but rather those who created the game's mythology, especially the player-turned-entrepreneur A.G. Spalding. After all, wrote Thorn: "In the Garden of Eden.... Adam and Eve are bores; it is the serpent who holds our attention."[124]

The same year *Eden* was published, Major League Baseball named Thorn its official historian.

Chapter Notes

Chapter 1

All quotes from *America's National Game* (*ANG*) are from the Bison Book edition: Albert G. Spalding, *America's National Game: Historic Facts Concerning the Beginning, Evolution, Development and Popularity of Base Ball with Personal Reminiscences of Its Vicissitudes, Its Victories and Its Votaries* (Lincoln: University of Nebraska Press, 1992).

1. *ANG*, 4.
2. *ANG*, 7.
3. *ANG*, 7.
4. *ANG*, 13.
5. *ANG*, 361.
6. *ANG*, 6.
7. George F. Will, *Bunts: Curt Flood, Camden Yards, Peter Rose and Other Reflections on Baseball* (New York: Scribner, 1988), 172.
8. *ANG*, 193.
9. *ANG*, 423.
10. *ANG*, 427.
11. *ANG*, 429.
12. *ANG*, 49.
13. *ANG*, 51.
14. *ANG*, 288.
15. *ANG*, 281.
16. Paul Goldberger, *Ballpark: Baseball in the American City* (New York: Knopf, 2019), 48.
17. *ANG*, 302.
18. Bill James, *Bill James Historical Baseball Abstract* (New York: Villard Books, 1988), 45.
19. Richard Peterson, *Extra Innings: Writing on Baseball* (Urbana and Chicago: University of Illinois Press 2001), 57.
20. *ANG*, 288.

21. Bryan Di Salvatore, *A Clever Base-Ballist: The Life and Times of John Montgomery Ward* (New York: Pantheon, 1999), 314.
22. *ANG*, 528.
23. Quoted in Geoffrey C. Ward, *Baseball: An Illustrated History* (New York, Knopf, 1994), 28.
24. *Spalding's Official Baseball Guide 1909* (New York: American Sports Publishing Co., 1909), 139. https://library.si.edu/digital-library/book/spaldings base19091910chic
25. Daniel Okrent, "Always Right on Time" in Ward, *Baseball*, 468.
26. *ANG*, 541.
27. H. Addington Bruce, "Baseball and the National Life," *The Outlook*, May 17, 1913, 106. https://www.unz.com/print/Outlook-1913may17-00104/
28. *ANG*, 259.
29. *ANG*, 263.
30. Quoted in Mark Lamster, *Spalding's World Tour: The Epic Adventure That Took Baseball Around the Globe—and Made It America's Game* (New York: Public Affairs, 2006), xvi.
31. Quoted in Mike Shannon, *Baseball: The Writer's Game* (Washington, D.C.: Brassey's, 2002), 257.
32. *ANG*, 19.
33. Alan Taylor, *William Cooper's Town* (New York: Knopf, 1995), 384.
34. *ANG*, 52.
35. Stephen Jay Gould, *Triumph and Tragedy in Mudville: A Lifelong Passion for Baseball* (New York: W.W. Norton, 2003), 203, 204.
36. Quoted in Peter Levine, *A.G. Spalding and the Rise of Baseball* (New York: Oxford University Press, 1986), 120.

37. Alfred H. Spink, *The National Game* (Carbondale and Edwardsville, Illinois: Southern Illinois University Press, 2000), 29. This is a reprint of the second edition of the book, originally published in 1911.

38. *Ibid.*, 54.

39. *ANG*, xviii–xix.

40. Levine, *A.G. Spalding and the Rise of Baseball*, 116.

41. Quoted in John Thorn, *Baseball in the Garden of Eden* New York: Simon& Schuster, 2011), 269.

Chapter 2

All quotes from *You Know Me Al* and other Lardner baseball stories are, unless otherwise specified, from *The Annotated Baseball Stories of Ring W. Lardner (ABS), 1914–1919*, edited by George W. Hilton (Stanford: Stanford University Press, 1995).

1. Burt L. Standish, *Frank Merriwell at Yale*, 1903. http://www.gutenberg.org/files/11115/11115-h/11115-h.htm#CH1

2. "Charles Dryden Dies," *New York Times*, Feb. 13, 1931.

3. *Sporting News*, Jan. 12, 1911 in *The Lost Journalism of Ring Lardner*, edited by Ron Rapoport (Lincoln: University of Nebraska Press, 2017), 19.

4. *Ibid.*, 20.

5. Jeff Silverman, editor, *Lardner on Baseball* (Guilford, Connecticut: Lyons Press, 2002), xii.

6. *ABS*, 130.

7. *ABS*, 51–52.

8. Donald Elder, *Ring Lardner: A Biography* (Garden City, NY: Doubleday, 1956), 114.

9. H. L. Mencken, *The American Language* (New York: Knopf, 1919). http://www.gutenberg.org/files/43376/43376-h/43376-h.htm

10. *ABS*, 189

11. *ABS*, 320. This was from "The Busher Pulls a Mays," which was not included in *YKMA*. The story appeared in *The Saturday Evening Post* in 1919.

12. Mencken, *American Language*.

http://www.gutenberg.org/files/43376/43376-h/43376-h.htm

13. *ABS*, 462.

14. Ring Lardner, *The Real Dope*. http://www.gutenberg.org/files/7405/7405-h/7405-h.htm

15. Ring W. Lardner, Jr., *The Young Immigrunts* (Indianapolis: Bobbs-Merrill, 1920), 19. The actual author was of course Senior, not the four-year old Junior. https://babel.hathitrust.org/cgi/pt?id=cool.ark:/13960/t1xd1g67t&view=1up&seq=42

16. *Ibid.*, 38.

17. Quoted in Jonathan Yardley, *Ring: A Biography of Ring Lardner* (New York: Random House, 1977), 244.

18. Quoted in Yardley, *Ring*, 170.

19. Quoted in Yardley, *Ring*, 391.

20. Quoted in Yardley, *Ring*, 182.

21. Quoted in Elder, *Ring Lardner*, 183.

22. Clifford M. Caruthers, ed. *Letters from Ring*. (Flint, MI: Waldon Press, 1979), 231.

23. Christian K. Messenger, *Sport and the Spirit of Play in American Fiction: Hawthorne to Faulkner* (New York: Columbia University Press, 1981), 206.

24. Quoted in Yardley, *Ring*, 393.

25. Quoted in Yardley, *Ring*, 5.

26. Quoted in Yardley, *Ring*, 276–277.

27. Ernest Hemingway to Arnold Gingrich, April 3, 1933, in *Ernest Hemingway: Selected Letters* edited by Carlos Baker (New York: Scribner, 1981), 385.

28. Caruthers, *Letters*, 226.

29. Ring W. Lardner, *How to Write Short Stories (With Samples)* New York, Scribner's, 1925), vi.

30. *Ibid.*, 1.

31. A. Scott Berg, *Max Perkins: Editor of Genius* (New York: E. P. Dutton, 1978), 203.

32. Caruthers, *Letters*, 226.

33. Ring Lardner, Jr., *The Lardners: My Family Remembered* (New York: Harper and Row, 1976), 4.

34. *Ibid.*, 175.

35. Yardley, *Ring*, 5.

36. Quoted in Yardley, *Ring*, 170.

37. Quoted in Elder, *Ring Lardner*, 170.

38. Caruthers, *Letters*, 270.
39. Lardner Jr., *The Lardners*, 146.
40. *Ibid.*, 147.

Chapter 3

All quotes from *Pitchin' Man* (*PM*) are from the 1992 reprint of *Pitchin' Man: Satchel Paige's Own Story* by Satchel Paige as told to Hal Lebovitz (Westport: Connecticut: Meckler, 1992). The first edition was published in 1948.

1. Quoted in Larry Tye, *Satchel: The Life and Times of an American Legend* (New York: Random House, 2009), 203.
2. Buck O'Neil with Steve Wulf and David Conrads, *I Was Right on Time* New York, Simon & Schuster, 1996), 113.
3. *PM*, 64.
4. *PM*, 46–47.
5. O'Neil, *Right on Time*, 134.
6. *PM*, 55–56.
7. LeRoy (Satchel) Page as told to David Lipman, *Maybe I'll Pitch Forever* (New York: Grove Press, 1962), 103.
8. O'Neil, *Right on Time*, 104.
9. Spink, "The Ill-Advised Moves," *Sporting News*, July 14, 1948.
10. Bill Veeck with Ed Linn, *Veeck as in Wreck* (New York: Simon & Schuster, 1989, originally published in 1962), 185.
11. *1949 Cleveland Indians Sketchbook* quoted in Tye, *Satchel*, ix.
12. John Lardner, "The Old Man in the Chair," *Newsweek*, July 7, 1952, quoted in Tye, *Satchel*, ix.
13. *PM*, 7.
14. Quoted in Tye, *Satchel*, 256.
15. *PM*, 8.
16. Quoted in Tye, *Satchel*, 190.
17. Quoted in Tye, *Satchel*, 254.
18. Paige, *Maybe I'll Pitch Forever*, 220.
19. Veeck, *Wreck*, 181.
20. Quoted in Tye, *Satchel*, 95.
21. *PM*, quoted in foreword by John Holway, xiv.
22. *PM*, 63.
23. *PM*, 16.
24. *PM*, 17.
25. *PM*, 16.
26. Quoted in Tye, *Satchel*, 191.

27. Quoted in Mark Ribowsky, *Don't Look Back: Satchel Paige in the Shadows of Baseball* (New York: Da Capo Press, 1994), 207.
28. Quoted in Ribowsky, *Don't Look Back*, 208.
29. Quoted in Tye, *Satchel*, 193.
30. Robert Peterson, *Only the Ball Was White: A History of Black Players and All-Black Professional Teams* (New York: Oxford University Press, 1970), 142–143.
31. O'Neil, *Right on Time*, 76.
32. *Ibid.*, 3.
33. *Ibid.*, 101.
34. Tom Meany, "$64 Question: Paige's Age," *New York Star*, July 21, 1948, quoted in Tye, *Satchel*, 207.
35. *PM*, 80.
36. Ribowsky, *Don't Look Back*, 265.
37. Paige, *Maybe I'll Pitch Forever*, 201. The quote originally appeared in "Satch Makes the Majors," *Collier's*, 55.
38. *Ibid.*, 201
39. *Ibid.*, 215.
40. *Ibid.*, 216.
41. *Ibid.*, 217.
42. Jackie Robinson as told to Wendell Smith, *Jackie Robinson: My Own Story* (Los Angeles: Allegro Editions, 2013, originally published in 1948), 160–161.
43. *Ibid.*, 151.
44. *Ibid.*, 23.
45. *Ibid.*, 86.
46. *Ibid.*, 89.
47. *Ibid.*, 141.
48. Roger Kahn, *Rickey & Robinson: The True, Untold Story of the Integration of Baseball* (Emmaus, Pennsylvania: Rodale, 2014), 167.
49. Robinson, *My Own Story*, 124.
50. Jackie Robinson as told to Alfred Duckett, *I Never Had It Made: An Autobiography* (Hopewell, New Jersey: Ecco Press, 1995, originally published in 1972), xxii.
51. *Ibid.*, 140.
52. *Ibid.*, 80.
53. *Ibid.*, 97.
54. Quoted in Jules Tygiel, *Baseball's Great Experiment: Jackie Robinson and His Legacy* (New York: Oxford University Press, 1983), 323.

55. Quoted in Arnold Rampersad, *Jackie Robinson: A Biography* (New York: Knopf, 1997), 7.

56. Red Barber and Robert Creamer, *Rhubarb in the Catbird Seat* (Lincoln: University of Nebraska Press, 1997, originally published in 1968), 275.

57. Tygiel, *Great Experiment*, 9.

58. Geoffrey C. Ward and Ken Burns, *Baseball: An Illustrated History* (New York: Knopf, 1994), 291.

59. Roger Kahn, *The Boys of Summer* (New York: Harper & Row, 1972), xvii.

60. Quoted in Tye, *Satchel*, 189.

Chapter 4

All quotes from *The Natural* (*TN*) are from a paperback reprint (New York: Pocket Books, 1973). The book was originally published in 1952.

1. Quoted in Jonathan Yardley, *Ring: A Biography of Ring Lardner* (New York: Random House, 1977), 5.

2. Daniel Stern, "The Art of Fiction: Bernard Malamud," in *Conversations with Bernard Malamud*, edited by Lawrence M. Lasher, Jackson: University Press of Mississippi, 1991), 61.

3. *TN*, 217.

4. *TN*, 37.

5. *TN*, 24.

6. *TN*, 212.

7. *TN*, 152.

8. *TN*, 153.

9. *TN*, 25.

10. *TN*, 25.

11. *TN*, 25.

12. Norman Podhoretz, "Achilles in Left Field," *Commentary*, March 1953.

13. Jonathan Baumbach, "The Economy of Love," in *Bernard Malamud*, edited by Harold Bloom (New York: Chelsea House, 1986), 29. Baumbach's essay originally appeared in *The Kenyon Review* 3, vol. 25.

14. Alan Warren Friedman, "The Hero as Schnook," in *Bernard Malamud*, edited by Harold Bloom (New York: Chelsea House, 1986), 114. Friedman's essay originally appeared in *Southern Review* 4, vol. 4.

15. Earl R. Wasserman, "'The Natural': Malamud's Word Ceres," in *Bernard Malamud*, edited by Harold Bloom (New York: Chelsea House, 1986), 48. Wasserman's essay originally appeared in *Centennial Review* 4, vol. 9.

16. Peter Carino, "History as Myth in Bernard Malamud's The Natural," *NINE: A Journal of Baseball History and Culture*, vol. 14, no. 1 (Fall 2005) 76.

17. Roger Angell, "No, But I Saw the Game," *The New Yorker*, July 31, 1989, 49.

18. Mark Harris, "Horatio at the Bat, or Why Such a Lengthy Embryonic Period for the Serious Baseball Novel?" *Aethlon*, vol. 14, no. 1 (Fall 1996), 37.

19. *Ibid.*, 40.

20. Mark Harris, *Henry Wiggen's Books* (New York: Avon, 1977), 313. *Henry Wiggen's Books* includes in one volume the first three of Harris's novels about Wiggen: *The Southpaw*, originally published in 1953, *Bang The Drum Slowly*, originally published in 1956, and *A Ticket for a Seamstitch*, originally published in 1957.

21. Robert Coover, *The Universal Ball Association, Inc., J Henry Waugh, Prop.* (New York: Random House, 1968), 69.

22. *Ibid.*, 219.

23. *Ibid.*, 223–224.

24. Albert Einstein to Max Born, Dec. 4, 1926, *The Collected Papers of Albert Einstein*, Document 426. https://einsteinpapers.press.princeton.edu/vol15-doc/766?highlightText=%22play+dice%22. Einstein's actual words to Born, translated from the German, were "He does not play dice."

25. Philip Roth, *The Great American Novel* (New York: Holt, Rinehart and Winston, 1973), 115.

26. *Ibid.*, 1.

27. *Ibid.*, 27.

28. *Ibid.*, 28.

29. Philip Roth, *Reading Myself and Others* (New York: Farrar, Straus and Giroux, 1975), 89 90.

30. Roth, *Great American Novel*, 16.

31. W. P. Kinsella, *Shoeless Joe* (Boston: Mariner Books, 1999; originally published by Houghton Mifflin in 1982), 3.

32. *Ibid.*, 3.

33. *Ibid.*, 84.

34. *Ibid.*, 160.

35. *Ibid.*, 253.

36. Roger Angell, "No, But I Saw the Game," *The New Yorker*, July 31, 1989, 55.

37. Kenneth S. Robson, editor, *A Great and Glorious Game: Baseball Writings of A. Bartlett Giamatti* (Chapel Hill: Algonquin Books, 1998), 13. Giamatti's essay, "The Green Fields of the Mind," was first published in the *Yale Alumni Magazine* in 1977.

Chapter 5

All quotes from *Ball Four (BF)* are from the 2014 printing of *Ball Four: The Final Pitch* (Nashville: Turner, 2014). This edition includes "Ball Five," written ten years after the original 1970 edition, "Ball Six," written twenty years after, and "Ball Seven," written thirty years after.

1. *BF*, xi.

2. *BF*, 40.

3. *BF*, xii.

4. Jim Bouton, *I'm Glad You Didn't Take It Personally* (New York: William Morrow, 1971), 127.

5. Quoted in Bouton, *Personally*, 139.

6. Quoted in Mitchell Nathanson, *Bouton: The Life of a Baseball Original* (Lincoln: University of Nebraska Press, 2020), 119.

7. Nathanson, *Bouton*, 71.

8. Jim Brosnan, *The Long Season* (New York: Harper & Row, 1975, originally published in 1960), 39.

9. Quoted in Nathanson, *Bouton*, 86.

10. *BF*, 85.

11. *BF*, 283.

12. *BF*, 283.

13. *BF*, 200.

14. *BF*, 42.

15. *BF*, 84.

16. *BF*, 106.

17. *BF*, 110.

18. Nathanson, *Bouton*, 145.

19. *BF*, 397.

20. Dick Young, "Young Ideas," *New York Daily News*, May 28, 1970, quoted in Nathanson, *Bouton*, 155.

21. Robert Lipsyte, "Crack in the Clubhouse Wall," *New York Times*, June 1, 1970.

22. Rex Lardner, "The Oddball with the Knuckleball," *New York Times Book Review*, July 26, 1970.

23. Quoted in *New York Times*, July 10, 2019.

24. "Does an Athlete Have the Right to Tell It Like It Is?" *Sport*, August 1970, quoted in Nathanson, *Bouton*, 163.

25. Jim Bouton, edited by Leonard Shecter, *I'm Glad You Didn't Take It Personally* (New York: Morrow, 1971), 83.

26. *Ibid.*, 84.

27. *BF*, xiii.

28. Nathanson, *Bouton*, 166.

29. John Florio and Ousie Shapiro, *One Nation Under Baseball: How the 1960s Collided with the National Pastime* (Lincoln: University of Nebraska Press, 2017), 190.

30. *BF*, 408.

31. *Personally*, 67.

32. *BF*, 445.

33. Nathanson, *Bouton*, 174.

34. *Ibid.*, 174.

35. *BF*, 406.

36. Curt Flood with Richard Carter, *The Way It Is* (New York: Trident Press, 1971), 18.

37. Maury Allen, *Bo: Pitching and Wooing* (New York: Dial Press, 1973), jacket.

38. *Ibid.*, 119.

39. Sparky Lyle and Peter Golenbock, *The Bronx Zoo* (New York: Crown, 1979), 47.

40. Whitey Ford, Mickey Mantle, and Joseph Durso, *Whitey and Mickey: An Autobiography of the Yankee Years* (New York: Viking, 1977), 136.

41. *BF*, 416.

42. Nathanson, *Bouton*, 211.

43. *BF*, 404.

44. Bouton, *Personally* 11–12.

45. *BF*, 500.

Chapter 6

All quotes from *The Boys of Summer (BOS)* are from the 2006 Harper Perennial Modern Classics edition; the book was originally published in 1972.

1. Paul Goldberger, *Ballpark: Baseball in the American City* (New York: Knopf, 2019), 170.

2. *BOS*, ix. "I see the boys of summer" was included in Dylan Thomas' first book of poetry, *18 Poems* (London: Fortune Press, 1934).

3. *BOS*, 210.

4. Wilfred Sheed, *My Life as a Fan: A Memoir* (New York: Simon & Schuster, 1993), 65.

5. *BOS*, 441.

6. *BOS*, 447.

7. Roger Kahn, *Into My Own: The Remarkable People and Events That Shaped a Life* (New York: St. Martin's, 2006), 160.

8. David Krell, *"Our Bums": The Brooklyn Dodgers in History, Memory and Popular Culture* (Jefferson, North Carolina: McFarland & Company, 2015), 119.

9. Peter Golenbock, *Bums: An Oral History of the Brooklyn Dodgers* (New York: Putnam's, 1984), 347–348.

10. Dick Young, "To Hell with the Los Angeles Dodgers, *Sport* 24 (August 1957), 83.

11. Neil J. Sullivan, *The Dodgers Move West* (New York: Oxford University Press, 1987), 18–19.

12. Carl E. Prince, *Brooklyn's Dodgers: The Bums, the Borough, and the Best of Baseball* (New York: Oxford University Press, 1996), 118.

13. Golenbock, *Bums*, 448.

14. *Ibid.*, 445.

15. Sheed, *My Life*, 204.

16. Golenbock, *Bums*, 81.

17. *BOS*, 196.

18. Roger Kahn, *A Season in the Sun* (New York: Harper & Row, 1977), 7.

19. Roger Kahn, *Good Enough to Dream* (Garden City, New York: Doubleday, 1985), 190.

20. Roger Kahn, *Memories of Summer: When Baseball Was an Art, and Writing About It a Game* (New York: Hyperion, 1997), 5.

21. Donald Hall, *Fathers Playing Catch with Sons: Essays on Sport (Mostly Baseball)* (San Francisco: North Point Press, 1985), 30.

22. Doris Kearns Goodwin, *Wait Till Next Year: A Memoir* (New York: Simon & Schuster, 1997), 255–256.

23. Golenbock, *Bums*, 158–159.

24. quoted in Roger Kahn, *The Passionate People: What It Means to Be a Jew in America* (New York: William Morrow, 1968), 105.

25. *Ibid.*, 105.

26. *BOS*, 21.

27. *Good Enough*, 25.

28. Roger Kahn, *The Era, 1947–1957: When the Yankees, the Giants, and the Dodgers Ruled the World* (New York: Ticknor & Fields, 1993), 327.

29. Kahn, *Into My Own*, 148.

30. Alex Belth, "The Two Rogers," *SB Nation*, Oct. 25, 2012, https://www.sbnation.com/longform/2012/10/25/3553752/the-two-rogers

31. *Ibid.*

32. *Ibid.*

33. Henry D. Fetter, *Taking on the Yankees: Winning and Losing in the Business of Baseball, 1903–2003* (New York: W. W. Norton, 2005), 281.

34. Kahn, *The Era*, 299.

35. Jerald Podair, *City of Dreams: Dodger Stadium and the Birth of Modern Los Angeles* (Princeton: Princeton University Press, 2017), 4.

36. Harvey Frommer, *New York City Baseball: The Last Golden Age, 1947–1957* (Madison: University of Wisconsin Press, 2004, originally published in 1980), 2–3.

37. *BOS*, 447.

38. *BOS*, 447.

Chapter 7

The *Bill James Baseball Abstract* is abbreviated below as *BJBA*. The annuals were first self-published (1977–1981) and then published by Ballantine (New York: 1982–1988).

1. Ben McGrath, "The Professor of Baseball," *The New Yorker*, July 14, 2003.

2. George F. Will, *Bunts: Curt Flood, Camden Yards, Pete Rose and Other Reflections on Baseball* (New York: Scribner, 1998), 54.

3. F. C. Lane, "Why the System of

Batting Averages Should Be Changed," *Baseball Magazine* vol. 16, no. 5 (March 1916), 41.

4. Alan Schwarz, *The Numbers Game: Baseball's Lifelong Fascination with Statistics* (New York: St. Martin's Press, 2004), 91.

5. Bill James, "Stats" in *Baseball: An Illustrated History* by Geoffrey C. Ward and Ken Burns (New York: Knopf, 1994), 101.

6. Schwarz, *Numbers Game*, 112.

7. *BJBA*, 1983, 96.

8. Mike Shannon, *The Writer's Game* (Washington, D.C.: Brassey's, Inc., 2002), 177.

9. Email to author from Daniel Okrent, March 16, 2021.

10. *BJBA*, 1982, 142.

11. *BJBA*, 1983, 162.

12. *BJBA*, 1983, 96.

13. Wilfred Sheed, *Baseball and Lesser Sports* (New York: HarperCollins, 1991), 83.

14. Bill James, *The Bill James Historical Baseball Abstract* (New York: Villard, 1988), ix.

15. *BJBA*, 1983, 161.

16. Scott Gray, *The Mind of Bill James: How a Complete Outsider Changed Baseball* (New York: Doubleday, 2006), 61.

17. *BJBA*, 1984, 8.

18. *BJBA* 1982, 34.

19. Schwarz, *Numbers Game*, 131.

20. Shannon, *Writer's Game*, 113.

21. *Ibid.*, 114.

22. John Thorn and Pete Palmer, *The Hidden Game of Baseball* (Garden City, New York: Doubleday, 1984), back jacket.

23. Michael Lewis, *Moneyball: The Art of Winning an Unfair Game* (New York: Norton, 2003), 37.

24. George Ignatin and Allen Barra, *Football by the Numbers 1987* (New York: Prentice Hall Press, 1987), back cover.

25. Interview with author, June 15, 2020.

26. Email to author from David Mannheim, June 11, 2020.

27. Schwarz, *Numbers Game*, 243.

28. Lewis, *Moneyball*, 72.

Chapter 8

Rotisserie League Baseball is abbreviated below as *RLB*. The annuals were edited by Glen Waggoner, sometimes with Robert Sklar. They were published by Bantam (New York, 1984–1993) and then by Little, Brown (Boston: 1994–1997).

1. *RLB*, 1984, 4. Okrent's piece first appeared in a different form in March 31, 1981, issue of *Inside Sports*.

2. *RLB*, 1984, 6.

3. Email to author from David Mannheim, June 11, 2020.

4. Email to author from Kevin Beatty, June 29, 2020.

5. Sam Walker, *Fantasyland: A Season on Baseball's Lunatic Fringe* (New York: Viking, 2006), 8.

6. *Ibid.*, 248.

7. Email to author from David Mannheim, June 11, 2020.

8. *RLB*, 1984, 15.

9. Walker, *Fantasyland*, 70.

10. *RLB*, 1995, 8.

11. Julies Tygiel, *Past Time: Baseball as History* (New York: Oxford University Press, 2000), 220.

12. "Baseball boors" and "It's unseemly..." Murray Chass, "Rotisserie Leagues: Fans in the Land of Oz," *New York Times*, September 22, 1991.

13. *RLB*, 1992, 1.

14. *RLB*, 1992, 2.

15. Tygiel, *Past Time*, 203.

16. *RLB*, 1984, 132.

17. *RLB*, 1991, 1–2.

18. Peter Golenbock, *How to Win at Rotisserie Baseball* (New York: Vintage, 1987), 8.

19. *Ibid.*, 9.

20. Tygiel, *Past Time*, 199.

21. Walker, *Fantasyland*, 332.

22. Steve Wulf, "For the Champion in the Rotisserie League, Joy Is a Yoo-Hoo Shampoo," *Sports Illustrated*, May 14, 1984.

23. Ben McGrath, "Dream Teams, *The New Yorker*, April 13, 2015.

24. "Old Jews Talking Baseball," https://soundcloud.com/user-50128 1864/old-jews-talking-baseball-daniel-okrent-and-john-thorn. Okrent's

comments were made during a 2014 presentation with baseball historian John Thorn at the National Museum of American Jewish History.

25. Mike Shannon, *The Writer's Game* (Washington, D.C.: Brassey's Inc., 2002), 169.

Chapter 9

Pete Rose: My Story by Roger Kahn and Pete Rose (New York: Macmillan, 1989) is abbreviated *MS*. *My Prison Without Bars* by Pete Rose with Rick Hill (Emmaus, Penn.: Rodale, 2004) is abbreviated *MPWB*.

1. John Fay, "Hit King" Pete Rose was funny, irreverent as ever for Reds Hall of Fame induction," June 25, WCPO Cincinnati, June 25, 2016. https://www.wcpo.com/news/insider/fay-hit-king-pete-rose-was-funny-irreverent-as-ever-for-reds-hall-of-fame-induction

2. *MS*, 136.
3. *MS*, 173.
4. Phone interview with Rick Wolff, Dec. 17, 2020.
5. Fay Vincent, *The Last Commissioner: A Baseball Valentine* (New York: Simon & Schuster, 2002), 123.
6. *MS*, 230.
7. Email to author from Rick Wolff, Jan. 14, 2021.
8. Roger Kahn, *Into My Own* (New York: Thomas Dunne Books, 2006), 272.
9. Phone interview with Rick Wolff, Dec. 17, 2020.
10. Donald L. Trump with Tony Schwartz, *Trump: The Art of the Deal* (New York: Warner Books, 1987, originally published by Random House in 1987).
11. NBC News, Jan. 22, 2017. https://www.nbcnews.com/meet-the-press/video/conway-press-secretary-gave-alternative-facts-860142147643
12. Trump and Schwartz, *Art of the Deal*, 237.
13. Jane Mayer, "Trump's Boswell Speaks," *The New Yorker*, July 25, 2016.
14. Charles Leerhsen, "Trump Ghostwriter Charles Leerhsen Says President

Was Bad at Business," *Huffington Post*, May 9, 2019.
15. Donald J. Trump and Bill Zanker, *Think Big and Kick Ass in Business and Life* (New York: Collins, 2007), 278.
16. *MPWB*, 164.
17. *MPWB*, 147–148.
18. *MPWB*, 225.
19. *MPWB*, 189.
20. *MPWB*, 309.
21. Kostya Kennedy, *Pete Rose: An American Dilemma* (New York: Sports Illustrated Books, 2014), 266.
22. Fay Vincent, "The Confessions of Pete Rose," *The New York Times*, Jan. 2, 2004.
23. Vincent, *Last Commissioner*, 133.
24. *Ibid.*, 114.
25. *MPWB*, 257.
26. *MPWB*, 258.
27. *MPWB*, 259.
28. @realDonaldTrump, Feb. 8, 2020.
29. Email to author from Christopher Richards, Dec. 18, 2020.
30. Peter Baker and Kenneth P. Vogel, "Trump Lawyers Clash Over How Much to Cooperate with Russia Inquiry" *New York Times*, September 17, 2017.
31. Matt Apuzzo and Michael S. Schmidt, "Trump Adds Clinton Impeachment Lawyer; Bracing for a Fight on Multiple Fronts," *New York Times*, May 2, 2018.

Chapter 10

1. Henry Chadwick, *Beadle's Dime Base-Ball Player* (New York: Beadle, 1864), 59–60 quoted in Andrew J. Schiff, *"The Father of Baseball": A Biography of Henry Chadwick* (Jefferson, North Carolina: McFarland, 2008), 84.
2. Henry Chadwick, *Beadle's Dime Base Ball Player* (New York: Irwin P. Beadle, 1860), 6.
3. Trey Strecker and Geri Strecker, editors, *The Great Match* and *Our Base Ball Club: Two Novels from the Early Days of Baseball* (Jefferson, North Carolina: McFarland & Company, 2010), 7. *The Great Match* was originally published in 1877 and *Our Base Ball Club* in 1884.
4. *Ibid.*, 44.

5. *Ibid.*, 163.

6. Burt L. Standish, *Frank Merriwell's School Days* (Philadelphia: David McKay, 1901), 10.

7. Quoted in Stewart H. Holbrook, "Frank Merriwell at Yale Again and Again and Again," *American Heritage*, vol. 12, no. 4 (June 1961).

8. *Ibid.*

9. Jerry Malloy, *Sol White's History of Colored Base Ball, with Other Documents on the Early Black Game 1886–1936* (Lincoln: University of Nebraska Press, 1995), xv.

10. *Ibid.*, 77.

11. *Ibid.*, 67.

12. *Ibid.*, 74.

13. *Ibid.*, 77.

14. Lawrence D. Hogan, *Shades of Glory: The Negro Leagues and the Story of African-American Baseball* (Washington, D.C.: National Geographic, 2006), 49.

15. Malloy, *Sol White's History*, 16.

16. Alfred H. Spink, *The National Game* (Carbondale and Edwardsville: Southern Illinois University Press, 2000), iii. This is a reprint of the second edition, originally published in 1911.

17. *Ibid.*, 202.

18. *Ibid.*, 232.

19. *Ibid.*, lxx.

20. Lawrence Ritter, *The Glory of Their Times: The Story of the Early Days of Baseball Told by the Men Who Played It* (New York: Macmillan, 1966), 168.

21. Jonathan Yardley, "Pitcher: The Real Frank Merriwell," in *The Ultimate Baseball Book*, edited by Daniel Okrent and Harris Lewine (Boston: Houghton Mifflin, 1979), 70.

22. Lester Chadwick, *Baseball Joe of the Silver Stars* (New York: Cupples & Leon, 1912), 242.

23. Andy McCue, *Baseball by the Books: A History and Complete Bibliography of Baseball Fiction* (Dubuque, Iowa: Wm. C. Brown, 1991), 108.

24. Mark Harris, "Bring Back That Old Sandlot Novel," *New York Times*, Oct. 16, 1988.

25. Jerome Holtzman, editor, *No Cheering in the Press Box* (New York: Holt, Rinehart and Winston, 1973), 271.

26. Pete Hamill, "In play: A legendary newspaperman picks five sports novels that really hit home" *Salon*, May 5, 1999.

27. Robert Smith, *Baseball* (New York: Simon & Schuster, 1970, originally published in 1947), 86.

28. Daniel Okrent and Steve Wulf, *Baseball Anecdotes* (New York: Oxford University Press, 1989), viii.

29. Pittsburgh *Courier*, December 29, 1945, quoted in Julies Tygiel, *Baseball's Great Experiment: Jackie Robinson and His Legacy* (New York: Oxford University Press, 1983), 75.

30. Pittsburgh *Courier*, March 19, 1949, quoted in Arnold Rampersad, *Jackie Robinson: A Biography* (New York, Knopf, 1997), 206–207.

31. Douglas Wallop, *The Year the Yankees Lost the Pennant* (New York: W. W. Norton, 1954), 234.

32. Jim Piersall and Al Hirsberg, *Fear Strikes Out: The Jim Piersall Story* (Boston: Little, Brown, 1955), 4–5.

33. Jimmy Piersall with Richard Whittingham, *The Truth Hurts* (Chicago: Contemporary Books, 1984), 29.

34. "Lucy at Marineland," *The Lucy Show*, broadcast June 10, 1965.

35. Barron H. Lerner, M.D., "Fighting Mental Illness on the Ball Field," https://well.blogs.nytimes.com/2015/04/09/fighting-mental-illness-on-the-ball-field/

36. Lee Allen, *Cooperstown Corner: Columns from The Sporting News* (Cleveland: SABR, 1990), vi.

37. John Thorn, editor, *The Armchair Book of Baseball* (New York: Scribner's, 1985), 1.

38. Lee Allen, *The Hot Stove League* (New York: A. S. Barnes, 1955), 5.

39. Arnold Hano, *A Day in the Bleachers* (New York: Da Capo, 1982, originally published in 1955), 124

40. *Ibid.*, 27.

41. *Ibid.*, vi.

42. Charles Einstein, editor, *The Fireside Book of Baseball* (New York: Simon & Schuster, 1987, 2. The line appeared in Einstein's preface to the fourth edition of *Fireside*.

43. *Ibid.*, 338.

44. *Ibid.*, xxi.

45. Jim Brosnan, *The Long Season* (New York: Harper & Row, 1960), 119.

46. *Ibid.*, 120.

47. *Ibid.*, 122.

48. Bill Veeck with Ed Linn, *Veeck as in Wreck: The Autobiography of Bill Veeck* (New York: Fireside, 1989, originally published in 1962), 20.

49. *Ibid.*, 117.

50. *Ibid.*, 60.

51. *Ibid.*, 398

52. LeRoy (Satchel) Paige as told to David Lipman, *Maybe I'll Pitch Forever* (New York: Grove Press, 1971, originally published in 1962), 201.

53. *Ibid.*, 16.

54. *Ibid.*, 43–44.

55. *Ibid.*, 151.

56. Eliot Asinof, *Eight Men Out: The Black Sox and the 1919 World Series* (New York: Henry Holt, 1987, originally published in 1963), 197–198.

57. Lawrence S. Ritter, *The Glory of Their Times: The Story of the Early Days of Baseball Told by the Men Who Played It* (New York: Macmillan, 1966), 110.

58. *Ibid.*, 33.

59. *Ibid.*, 34.

60. *Ibid.*, 43–45.

61. Robert Coover, *The Universal Baseball Association, Inc. J. Henry Waugh, Prop.* (New York: Random House, 1968), 233.

62. Jonathan Derbyshire, "The Books Interview: Robert Coover," *New Statesman*, May 12, 2011 https://www.newstatesman.com/books/2011/05/digital-world-myth-literature

63. Hari Kunzru, "Robert Coover: A Life in Writing," *The Guardian*, June 27, 2011 https://www.theguardian.com/culture/2011/jun/27/robert-coover-life-in-writing

64. Alan Schwarz, *The Numbers Game: Baseball's Lifelong Fascination with Statistics* (New York: St. Martin's, 2004), 90.

65. Ted Williams with John Underwood, *My Turn at Bat: The Story of My Life* (New York: Fireside, 1988), 7. This was a revised edition; the original was published in 1969.

66. *Ibid.*, 9.

67. Leigh Montville, *Ted Williams: The Biography of an American Hero* (New York: Doubleday, 2004), 316.

68. Robert Peterson, *Only the Ball Was White: A History of Legendary Black Players and All-Black Professional Teams* (New York: Oxford University Press, 1970), 15.

69. Jackie Robinson as told to Alfred Duckett, *I Never Had It Made: An Autobiography* (Hopewell, New Jersey: Ecco Press, 1995, originally published in 1972), 265.

70. *Ibid.*, 179.

71. *Ibid.*, 179.

72. *Ibid.*, xvi–xvii.

73. Philip Roth, *Portnoy's Complaint* (New York: Random House, 1967), 70–71.

74. Philip Roth, "My Baseball Years," *The New York Times*, April 2, 1973.

75. Marshall Smelser, *The Life That Ruth Built* (Lincoln, University of Nebraska Press, 1993, originally published in 1975), 560.

76. Robert Creamer, *Babe: The Legend Comes to Life* (New York: Fireside, 1992, originally published in 1974), 289.

77. *Ibid.*, 363.

78. Jordan, *A False Spring* (New York: Bantam, 1976), 244.

79. Robert Whiting, *The Chrysanthemum and the Bat: Baseball Samurai Style* (New York: Avon, 1983, originally published in 1977), 67.

80. Robert Whiting, *You Gotta Have Wa* (New York: Macmillan, 1989), 123.

81. *The New York Times*, November 13, 1988.

82. Dave Jamieson, *Mint Condition: How Baseball Cards Became an American Obsession* (New York: Grove Press, 2010), 9.

83. Dan Gutman, *Honus and Me* (New York: Avon, 1998), 2.

84. Brendan C. Boyd and Fred C. Harris, *The Great American Baseball Card Flipping, Trading, and Bubble Gum Book* (Boston: Little, Brown, 1973), 8–9.

85. *Ibid.*, 149.

86. W. P. Kinsella, *Shoeless Joe* (Boston: Mariner Books, 1999, originally published in 1982), 6.

87. Arnold Rampersad, *Jackie Robinson: A Biography* (New York: Knopf, 1997), 493.

88. John Thorn and Pete Palmer, *The Hidden Game of Baseball: A Revolutionary Approach to Baseball and Its Statistics* (Chicago: University of Chicago Press, 2015, originally published in 1984), xi.

89. *Ibid.*, 3–4.

90. Bill James, *The Bill James Historical Baseball Abstract* (New York: Villard Books, 1988, originally published in 1985), 49.

91. *Ibid.*, 73.

92. Quoted in James, *Historical Abstract*, 73.

93. Bill James, *The New Bill James Historical Baseball Abstract* (New York: Free Press, 2003, originally published in 2001), 359.

94. *Ibid.*, 360.

95. Daniel Okrent, *Nine Innings* (New York: Ticknor & Fields, 1985), 45.

96. *Ibid.*, 45.

97. *Ibid.*, 46–47.

98. Robert Benson, *The Game: One Man, Nine Innings, A Love Affair with Baseball* (New York: Tarcher/Putnam, 2001), 90–91.

99. *Ibid.*, 176.

100. Rob Neyer, *Power Ball: Anatomy of a Modern Baseball Game* (New York: Harper, 2018), xii.

101. Quoted in Paul Dickson, editor and compiler, *The Dickson Baseball Dictionary* (New York: Facts on File, 1989), xvi.

102. *Journal of Sports History*, vol. 16, no. 3 (Winter 1989), 305.

103. *Ibid.*, 306.

104. James Mote, *Everything Baseball* (New York: Prentice Hall Press, 1989), x.

105. *Ibid.*, 19.

106. *Ibid.*, 292.

107. Martin Quigley, *The Crooked Pitch: The Curveball in American Baseball History* (Chapel Hill, North Carolina: Algonquin Books, 1984), 23.

108. Susan E. Johnson, *When Women Played Hardball* (Seattle, Washington: Seal Press, 1994), xxiv.

109. John Helyar, *Lords of the Realm: The Real History of Baseball* (New York: Villard Books, 1994), 252.

110. Andrew Zimbalist, *Baseball and Billions: A Probing Look Inside the Business of Our National Pastime* (New York: Basic Books, 1994, originally published in 1992), 19.

111. Al Stump, *Cobb: A Biography* by Al Stump (Chapel Hill: North Carolina: Algonquin Books, 1994), back jacket.

112. *Ibid.*

113. *Ibid.*, 12.

114. Charles Leerhsen, *Ty Cobb: A Terrible Beauty* (New York: Simon & Schuster, 2015), 36.

115. Sheldon Hirsh and Alan Hirsch, *The Beauty of Short Hops: How Chance and Circumstance Confound the Moneyball Approach to Baseball* (Jefferson, North Carolina: McFarland, 2011), 3.

116. Neyer, *Power Ball*, 28.

117. Ben Lindbergh and Travis Sawchik. *The MVP Machine: How Baseball's New Nonconformists Are Using Data to Build Better Players* (New York: Basic Books, 2019), front flap.

118. Jose Canseco, *Juiced: Wild Times, Rampant 'Roids, Smash Hits, and How Baseball Got Big* (New York: Regan Books, 2005), 205. Canseco preferred to call himself the "Godfather of Steroids," though he may also have liked how reporter Selena Roberts characterized him in her biography, *A-Rod: The Many Lives of Alex Rodriguez* (New York: Harper, 2009). Roberts called Canseco "the Johnny Appleseed of Generation Steroid."

119. Jose Canseco, *Vindicated: Big Names, Big Liars, and the Battle to Save Baseball* (New York: Simon Spotlight, 2008), 8.

120. *Ibid.*, 9.

121. *Ibid.*, 85.

122. John Thorn, *Baseball in the Garden of Eden: The Secret History of the Early Game* (New York: Simon & Schuster, 2011), xiii.

123. *Ibid.*, 36.

124. *Ibid.*, xi.

Bibliographic Essay

Preface

There are far too many good histories of baseball, both scholarly and popular, to mention here. Three worth noting because of their efforts to place baseball in the broader context of American history are *National Pastime: U.S. History Through Baseball* by Martin C. Babicz and Thomas W. Zeiler (Lanham, Maryland: Rowman & Littlefield, 2017), which takes on the subject systematically; *A People's History of Baseball* by Mitchell Nathanson (Urbana: University of Illinois Press, 2002) which, as the title suggests, rejects the patriotic haze through which so much of baseball history has often been viewed; and *Past Time: Baseball as History* by Jules Tygiel (New York: Oxford University Press, 2000), a fascinating collection of essays on topics including baseball's emergence as the national pastime, its struggles during the Depression, and its connections to Jim Crow.

Books about baseball books and writers include Jerome Holtzman's anecdotal *Jerome Holtzman on Baseball: A History of Baseball Scribes* (Champaign, Illinois: Sports Publishing, 2005), Andy McCue's useful *Baseball by the Books: A History and Complete Bibliography of Baseball Fiction* (Madison, Wisconsin: Wm. C. Brown, 1991), and Mike Shannon's insightful *Diamond Classics: Essays on 100 of the Best Baseball Books Ever Published* (Jefferson, North Carolina: McFarland, 1989). Shannon's *Baseball: The Writer's Game* (Washington, D.C.: Brassey's, 2002) has revealing interviews with many of the writers discussed in this book, including Jim Brosnan, Peter Golenbock, John Holway, Roger Kahn, W.P. Kinsella, Daniel Okrent, and John Thorn. Richard Peterson's *Extra Innings: Writing on Baseball* (Urbana and Chicago: University of Illinois Press, 2001) examines how baseball writers of both fiction and nonfiction have been unable to resist transforming baseball into mythology.

Chapter 1: America's National Game

Peter Levine's *A.G. Spalding and the Rise of Baseball: The Promise of American Sport* (New York: Oxford, 1986) is a scholarly treatment of Spalding's role in baseball's rise. Arthur Bartlett's *Baseball and Mr. Spalding: The History and Romance of Baseball* (New York: Farrar, Straus and Young, 1951) is less scholarly but entertaining. Mark Lamster's *Spalding's World Tour: The Epic Adventure That Took Baseball Around the Globe— And Made It America's Game* (New York: Public Affairs, 2006) follows the game's missionaries on their thirty-thousand-mile journey. John Thorn's *Baseball in the Garden of Eden: The Secret History of the Early Game* (New York: Simon & Schuster, 2011) is the best study of baseball's early years.

The Bison books edition of *America's National Game* (Lincoln: University of Nebraska Press, 1992) includes a useful introduction by Benjamin G. Rader. A series called "Writing Baseball" made available the second edition of Alfred H. Spink's *The National Game* (Carbondale and Edwardsville, Illinois: Southern Illinois University Press, 2000); this second edition was originally published in 1911. Unlike Spalding, Spink focused on players more than owners; indeed, his book was the first big biographical encyclopedia of baseball.

Chapter 2: You Know Me Al

Both major biographies of Lardner—Donald Elder's *Ring Lardner: A Biography* (Garden City, New York: Doubleday, 1956) and Jonathan Yardley's *Ring: A Biography of Ring Lardner* (New York: Random House, 1977) are entertaining and insightful. Clifford M. Caruthers' collection, *Letters from Ring* (Flint, MI: Waldon Press, 1979), provides useful context as well as the letters themselves. Ring Lardner, Jr.'s *The Lardners: My Family Remembered* (New York: Harper and Row, 1976) demonstrates that the son as well as the father was a superb writer.

Ring Around the Bases: The Complete Baseball Stories of Ring Lardner, edited by Matthew J. Bruccoli (Columbia: University of South Carolina Press, 1992) has, as its subtitle promises, all of them. *The Annotated Baseball Stories of Ring W. Lardner, 1914–1919*, edited by George W. Hilton (Stanford: Stanford University Press, 1995) has, as its subtitle promises, annotations; these are especially helpful in identifying the actual players and events in the stories. *Lardner on Baseball* (Guilford, Connecticut;

Lyons Press, 2002), edited by Jeff Silverman, includes not only a selection of his short stories but also his columns during the 1919 World Series. Lardner's approach to that Series was lighthearted as usual but readers might have sensed he suspected something was amiss. This is from his October 1 report, after the White Sox lost the opening game of the Series 9–1:

> The big thrill come in the 4th innings when everybody was wondering if the Sox would ever get the 3rd man out. They finely did and several occupants of the press box was overcome. The White Sox only chance at that pt was to keep the Reds in there hitting till darkness fell and made it a illegal game but Heinie Groh finely hit a ball that Felsch could not help from catching and gummed up another piece of stratagem.

Chapter 3: Pitchin' Man

Of Paige biographies, Mark Ribowsky's *Don't Look Back: Satchel Paige in the Shadows of Baseball* (New York: Da Capo Press, 1994) presents the most negative view of Paige; his Paige was often looking out for himself, though as a way of coping with racism. Larry Tye's *Satchel: The Life and Times of an American Legend* (New York: Random House, 2009) is balanced and comprehensive. Donald Spivey's *"If You Were Only White": The Life of Leroy "Satchel" Paige* (Columbia: University of Missouri Press, 2012) is a scholarly work that places Paige in his historical context. John Holway's *Josh and Satch: The Life and Times of Josh Gibson and Satchel Paige* (New York: Carroll & Graf, 1991) is a season-by-season account of the Negro Leagues' greatest hitter and pitcher.

Pitchin' Man: Satchel Paige's Own Story by Leroy Satchel Paige as told to Hal Lebovitz (Westport, Connecticut: Meckler, 1992) includes a useful foreword by baseball historian Holway as well as, from the original 1948 edition, a preface by N.R. Howard, editor of the Cleveland *News*, a foreword by Indians owner Bill Veeck, a note from Indians manager Lou Boudreau, and an introduction by Lebovitz. Though *Pitchin' Man* better represents how Paige presented himself during the years leading up to baseball's integration and immediately after, Paige's second memoir, *Maybe I'll Pitch Forever* by LeRoy (Satchel) Paige as told to David Lipman (New York: Doubleday, 1962), tells a fuller version of his life and times. A version of Paige's own words can also be heard in William Price Fox's *Satchel Paige's America* (Tuscaloosa: University of Alabama Press, 2005). Price interviewed Fox in the 1970s, though he didn't publish his recollections of those interviews until thirty years later.

Bibliographic Essay

Valuable histories of Black baseball before integration include Robert Peterson's groundbreaking *Only the Ball Was White: A History of Legendary Black Players and All-Black Professional Teams* (New York: Oxford University Press, 1970); John Holway's *Voices from the Great Black Baseball Leagues* (New York: Dodd, Mead, 1975), which featured oral histories of Negro League stars; Donn Rogosin's *Invisible Men: Life in Baseball's Negro Leagues* (New York: Atheneum, 1983), which showed how important the Negro Leagues were to African American communities; and Lawrence D. Hogan's *Shades of Glory: The Negro Leagues and the Story of African-American Baseball* (Washington, D.C.: National Geographic, 2006), which was commissioned by the National Baseball Hall of Fame and Museum. Also worth reading is Buck O'Neil's touching memoir, *I Was Right on Time*, written with Steve Wulf and David Conrads (New York: Simon & Schuster, 1996).

Arnold Rampersad's *Jackie Robinson: A Biography* (New York: Knopf, 1997) is definitive. Histories of baseball integration include Julie Tygiel's masterful *Baseball's Great Experiment: Jackie Robinson and his Legacy* (New York: Oxford University Press, 1983) and Scott Simon's brief but nuanced *Jackie Robinson and the Integration of Baseball* (Hoboken, New Jersey: John Wiley & Sons, 2002). Roger Kahn's personal and elegant recollections of the Dodgers appear in many of his books, most notably *The Boys of Summer* (New York: Harper & Row, 1972) and *Rickey & Robinson: The True, Untold Story of the Integration of Baseball* (Emmaus, Pennsylvania: Rodale, 2014). *The Jackie Robinson Reader*, edited by Tygiel (New York: Dutton, 1997) includes important perspectives from Kahn, Wendell Smith, Malcolm X, and others. *Veeck as in Wreck: The Autobiography of Bill Veeck* by Bill Veeck with Ed Linn (New York: Simon & Schuster, 1989, originally published in 1962) presents Veeck's first-hand account of his role in integrating baseball, including how he might have done so before Rickey signed Robinson, had it not been for the interference of Commissioner Kenesaw Mountain Landis.

Jackie Robinson: My Own Story by Robinson as told to Wendell Smith (Los Angeles: Allegro Publications, 2013) was originally published in 1948. Smith was among the African American reporters who played an important role in pressuring the major leagues to integrate, and he was also among those who criticized Robinson when he became more assertive on and off the field. *I Never Had It Made: An Autobiography* by Robinson as told to Alfred Duckett (Hopewell, New Jersey: Ecco, 1995) was originally published in 1972. Duckett was a speechwriter for Martin Luther King, Jr.

Chapter 4: *The Natural*

The importance of Earl R. Wasserman's 1965 essay, "*The Natural*: World Ceres," can be gauged from its inclusion in two useful collections of Malamud criticism: *Bernard Malamud and the Critics*, edited by Leslie A. Field and Joyce Field (New York: New York University Press, 1970) and *Bernard Malamud*, edited by Harold Bloom (New York: Chelsea House, 1986). Ceres, by the way, was a Roman goddess. *Conversations with Bernard* Malamud, edited by Lawrence M. Lasher (Jackson: University of Mississippi Press, 1991), collects interviews with a writer who disliked them.

More general works covering baseball fiction include *Dreaming of Heroes: American Sports Fiction, 1868–1980* by Michael Oriard (Chicago: Nelson-Hall, 1982), in which Oriard argues that Malamud was the first novelist to recognize that sport was the most important repository for myth in America; *Home Games: Essays on Baseball Fiction* by John A. Lauricella (Jefferson, North Carolina: McFarland, 1999), which traces the theme of "home" through the works of Lardner, Malamud, Harris, and Coover; *Ground Rules* by Deanne Westbrook (Urbana: University of Illinois Press, 1996), which argues that baseball provides America with a mythology and which includes chapters on Malamud, Harris, Coover, and Kinsella; *Extra Innings: Writing on Baseball* by Richard Peterson (Urbana: University of Illinois Press, 2001), which explores, astutely and entertainingly, not just baseball fiction but also nonfiction.

Paperback reprints are readily available of *The Natural* (New York: Farrar, Straus and Giroux, 2003, originally published in 1952), *The Universal Baseball Association, Inc., J. Henry Waugh Proprietor* (New York: Overlook, 2011, originally published in 1968), *The Great American Novel* (New York: Vintage, 1995, originally published in 1973), and *Shoeless Joe* (Boston: Mariner Books, 1999, originally published in 1982).

Chapter 5: *Ball Four*

Mitchell Nathanson's *Bouton: The Life of a Baseball Original* (Lincoln: University of Nebraska Press, 2020) is comprehensive and entertaining. Though written with Bouton's cooperation, the biography is, like its subject, proudly honest.

Ball Four: The Final Pitch (Nashville: Turner Publishing, 2014) includes not just *Ball Four* but also "Ball Five," "Ball Six," and "Ball Seven."

These updates were written ten, twenty, and thirty years after the original 1970 publication. For the more immediate reactions to the book's publication, see also Bouton's *I'm Glad You Didn't Take It Personally* (New York: Morrow, 1971).

Chapter 6: *The Boys of Summer*

The 2006 Harper Perennial paperback of *The Boys of Summer* includes a new epilogue and a new chapter about Pee Wee Reese written after his death. Other books by Kahn that this chapter draws on are *The Passionate People: What it Means to Be a Jew in America* (New York: William Morrow, 1968), *A Season in the Sun* (New York: Harper & Row, 1977), *Good Enough to Dream* (Garden City, New York: Doubleday, 1985), *The Era, 1947–1957: When the Yankees, the Giants, and the Dodgers Ruled the World* (New York: Ticknor & Fields, 1993), *Memories of Summer: When Baseball Was an Art, and Writing About It a Game* (New York: Hyperion, 1997), and *Into My Own: The Remarkable People and Events That Shaped a Life* (New York: St. Martin's, 2006).

There are too many good books about the Dodgers, including those discussed in this chapter, to list here. But some ought to be mentioned here because of their efforts to place the Dodgers in the context of their place and time. These include Jules Tygiel's *Baseball's Great Experiment: Jackie Robinson and His Legacy* (New York: Oxford University Press, 1983), Carl E. Prince's *Brooklyn's Dodgers: The Bums, the Borough, and the Best of Brooklyn* (New York: Oxford University Press, 1996), Tygiel's *Past Time: Baseball as History* (New York: Oxford University Press, 2000), Neil Sullivan's *The Dodgers Move West* (New York: Oxford University Press, 2003), Michael Shapiro's *The Last Good Season* (New York: Doubleday, 2003), Henry Fetter's *Taking on the Yankees: Winning and Losing in the Business of Baseball, 1903–2003* (New York: W.W. Norton, 2005), and David Krell's *"Our Bums": The Brooklyn Dodgers in History, Memory and Popular Culture* (Jefferson, North Carolina: McFarland & Company, 2015).

On Jews and baseball: Larry Ruttman's *America's Jews & America's Game: Voices of a Growing Legacy in Baseball* (Lincoln: University of Nebraska Press, 2013) has interviews with Jewish players, labor leaders, owners, executives, fans, and writers, including Kahn.

On whether O'Malley or Moses was more to blame for the Dodgers' departure: Fetter's *Taking on the Yankees* makes a strong case against

O'Malley. Sullivan's *The Dodgers Move West* offers a strong defense of O'Malley. Shapiro's *The Last Good Season* follows the 1956 goings-on both on and off the field and makes a strong case—in the spirit of Jane Jacobs' work—that neither O'Malley nor Moses appreciated what made cities work.

Chapter 7: *The Bill James Baseball Abstract*

Two useful books about James are *The Mind of Bill James* by Scott Gray (New York: Doubleday, 2006) and *How Bill James Changed Our View of Baseball: How a Complete Outsider Changed Baseball*, edited by Gregory F. Augustine Pierce (Skokie, Illinois: Acta, 2007). Alan Schwarz's *The Numbers Game: Baseball's Lifelong Fascination with Statistics* (New York: St. Martin's Press, 2004) is a comprehensive and entertaining history. Michael Lewis's *Moneyball: The Art of Winning an Unfair Game* (New York: Norton, 2003) ensured that Billy Beane would be remembered not as a failed prospect but as a baseball immortal. Ben Lindbergh and Travis Sawchik, in *The MVP Machine: How Baseball's New Noncomformists Are Using Data to Build Better Players* (New York: Basic Books, 2019), argue that the moneyball era is over and that winning teams, rather than drafting or trading for better players, are instead using new technologies to improve players' performances.

Benjamin Baumer, formerly a statistical analyst for the Mets, and Andrew Zimbalist, a professor of economics, teamed up for *The Sabermetric Revolution: Assessing the Growth of Analytics in Baseball* (Philadelphia: University of Pennsylvania Press, 2014), which argues convincingly that Lewis exaggerated the dichotomy between traditional and sabermetric approaches. The A's success in 2002, they noted, had less to do with the stats of Scott Hatteberg or Jeremy Giambi or David Justice than it did with the very traditional stats of shortstop Miguel Tejada and third baseman Eric Chavez, both of whom hit 34 homers that year, and of Barry Zito, Mark Mulder, and Tim Hudson, three of the top ten pitchers in the American League. Baumer and Zimbalist stress how factors other than James' writing, such as the increase in salaries after the advent of free agency and the growth of the Internet, led front offices to seek new ways to evaluate players. But if the authors debunk some stories about how sabermetrics evolved, they also reinforce how revolutionary it has been.

The self-published *Abstract*s are rare, but later versions of *The Bill James Baseball Abstract* (New York: Ballantine, 1982–1988) are fairly easy to find. So are many of James's other books, including *The Bill James Baseball Books* (New York: Villard, 1990–1992), *Whatever Happened to the Hall of Fame: Baseball, Cooperstown, and the Politics of Glory* (New York: Free Press, 1995), *The Bill James Historical Baseball Abstract* (New York: Villard, 1985), and *The New Bill James Historical Baseball Abstract* (New York: Free Press, 2001).

Chapter 8: Rotisserie League Baseball

Sam Walker's *Fantasyland: A Season on Baseball's Lunatic Fringe* (New York: Viking, 2006) entertainingly chronicles both Rotisserie's rise and Walker's own year managing a team. Jules Tygiel's *Past Time: Baseball as History* (New York: Oxford University Press, 2000) has an insightful chapter on fantasies of the 1980s, which included not just Rotisserie but camps where aging fans paid to play with their childhood heroes.

Rotisserie League Baseball, edited by Glen Waggoner, sometimes with Robert Sklar, was published by Bantam (New York, 1984–1993) and then by Little, Brown (Boston, 1994–1997). With a full awareness that nothing is more interesting to a Rotisserie player than his own team and nothing is less interesting to everyone else, I cannot resist including this excerpt about my own debut from the 1991 edition:

> There's nothing better than watching rookie owners humiliate themselves. "Rick Aguilera, $16." (Arm will fall off by June 1, we smirked.) "Carlton Fisk, $11." (This is the year he gets old, we pontificated.) "Lloyd Moseby, $9." (Ex–Blue Jay has-been, we snorted.) "Cecil Fielder, $19." (Ex–Blue Jay never-was, we hooted.) But John Rosen and Paul Aron, owners of the John Paul Popes, pretended they didn't hear us as they kept making mistake after mistake at the Tony's Italian Kitchen League auction draft. (What a pathetic team, we solemnly declared when it was all over.)
>
> "We" were the other owners in the league, the guys who spent the rest of the summer eating the Popes' dust. We figure it had something to do with the Papists being ex-altar boys and having an in with the Big Commish in the sky. (Funny, they don't look Catholic.) How else can you explain the fact that, rookie mistakes and all, the Popes led from wire to wire and coasted to a 16.5-point victory?

I suppose I should add that we never won again.

Chapter 9: Pete Rose: My Story and My Prison Without Bars

For Rose's defense: *Pete Rose: My Story* by Roger Kahn and Pete Rose (New York: Macmillan, 1989). For Rose's confession and excuses: *My Prison Without Bars* by Pete Rose with Rick Hill (Emmaus, Penn.: Rodale, 2004). For Rose's latest: *Play Hungry: The Making of a Baseball Player* by Pete Rose (New York: Penguin Press, 2019).

The best biographies of Rose are Michael Y. Sokolove's *Hustle: The Myth, Life, and Lies of Pete Rose* (New York: Fireside, 1990) and Kostya Kennedy's *Pete Rose: An American Dilemma* (New York: Sports Illustrated Books, 2014). Rose does not emerge from either smelling like a rose.

Giamatti's writings, including his statement to the press after the Rose deal, are collected in *A Great and Glorious Game* edited by Kenneth S. Robson (Chapel Hill, NC: Algonquin Books of Chapel Hill, 1998). You'll find evidence that his critics were right to say he was sometimes pretentious and that his admirers were right to say he loved the game.

Index

219

Index

Index

221

Index

Index

Index

Index

Index

Index

227

Index

Index